$12.50

THE FAR WEST AND THE ROCKIES
HISTORICAL SERIES
1820-1875

VOLUME IV

Rufus B. Sage in 1888

RUFUS B. SAGE
His Letters and Papers
1836-1847

with an annotated reprint of his

"Scenes in the Rocky Mountains
and in Oregon, California, New Mexico, Texas, and the Grand Prairies"

With an Introduction, Biographical Sketch and Notes by

LeRoy R. Hafen
Professor of History, Brigham Young University
and
Ann W. Hafen

In two volumes
Volume I

THE ARTHUR H. CLARK COMPANY
Glendale, California, U.S.A.
1956

To

JOHN EVANS

Outstanding Colorado Citizen

Former President, State Historical Society of Colorado

Contents

Illustrations

Introduction

Rufus B. Sage and his Book

When Rufus B. Sage at the age of nineteen left his Connecticut home in the summer of 1836, he was beginning ten years of great adventure. They would carry him over most of the American nation of his day, through the Western frontier territory, and across the border to Mexican soil. Not only was he to have unusual experiences; happily he was equipped by training and temperament to record those experiences and observations for the benefit of others.

The book that resulted from his major travels was exceptionally accurate and was full of valuable information. His letters that have survived, and that are printed for the first time in this volume, reveal an admirable character and contain graphic descriptions of persons, places, and events.

Rufus was born in Upper Middletown, now known as Cromwell, Connecticut, on March 17, 1817. He was youngest of the seven children of Deacon Rufus Sage and Jerusha Butler Sage.[1] Left fatherless at the age of nine, Rufus was early thrown largely upon his own resources, but by attendance at the common school and an academy he obtained the basics of an education. Upon this he built through his own efforts.

He was reared in a religious home, as his own letters

[1] His brothers and sisters, with their years of birth, were: Edmund, 1804; Jerusha, 1806; Martha, 1808; Elisha L., 1809; Frances, 1812; Benjamin, 1814. "Genealogical Record of the Descendants of David Sage, carefully prepared and revised by the author [Elisha L. Sage] from authentic records, Middletown, Conn., 1878."

and those of his mother amply testify. At fourteen he joined the Congregational Church. He signed the pledge-roll of the first temperance society in Connecticut and continued as a lifelong abstainer from spirituous drinks. He even refused tobacco, drank coffee seldom, and tea never. "The grand result is," as reported near the end of his years, "he has never been laid by from sickness for a single day during his whole life." [2]

He went to work at the newspaper office in Middletown and there learned the printer's trade. This skill was to provide him employment and give him important contacts and opportunities.

The travels and experiences of Rufus B. Sage from 1836 to 1841 are well described in his letters which we present below. His far western adventures, 1841-44, are recounted in detail in the volume we publish herewith. It seems advisable therefore merely to outline here the course of his travels for these periods.

When Rufus went alone to gaze on New York in the summer of 1836, he was filled with wonderment at the great city but he was not overawed. In fact he was soon, as he said, "as much at home as though I had always lived there." But in two months he had tired of the metropolis and was soon back home, making preparations for a farther journey. Now he was going out West, to the distant Ohio country, of which he had long dreamed. His sister Jerusha, who was married to a Presbyterian minister, lived at Marietta, and to this place Rufus would direct his course.

The remembered experiences of the journey he detailed in a series of letters written in the winter of 1838-39. By that time he had gained skill in writing

[2] *An Illustrated Popular Biography of Connecticut* (Hartford, 1891), pp. 107-108. The biographical sketch of Rufus B. Sage, giving the principal facts of his career, is reprinted as Appendix A. These data are supplemented by other information gleaned from Sage's own letters and from those written by relatives and friends and found in the Coe Collection of Yale University.

and was aspiring to authorship. The result was a graphic, readable account found in the letters published in this volume. On this journey he sailed down the Connecticut River, along the Sound to New York City, and up the Hudson to the vicinity of Albany. Then he took a six-day trip along the Erie Canal, part of the time riding the horse-drawn boat, part of the time walking the towpath. From Buffalo he tramped along the shore of Lake Erie to Ashtabula, Ohio, and then worked his way southward to Marietta.

Within a short time he was teaching school at sixteen dollars per month and board. One month of this and he was ready for something else. He worked as a compositor on the *Marietta Gazette;* then took a position as foreman with the newspaper at Parkersburg, now West Virginia. This paid him $364 per year, a wage he was proud to report.

In the early spring of 1838 Rufus and a partner launched a new venture. They bought a boat, loaded it with a cargo of ice for the southern market, and set sail down the Ohio. Their hopes for adventure and profit were high. At Fort Gibson, Mississippi, in late April he wrote home that he expected to clear $2000. But something miscarried, which he does not explain. Late in life he observed: "This transaction resulted in a money loss, but proved rich in experience and observation, for that which he then saw and heard in Louisiana and Mississippi transformed him into the future unrelenting foe of the slave institution" (*see* Appendix A).

While in Mississippi he took time to visit some ancient Indian mounds. He was intrigued by the ruins and wrote a description of them.[3]

By the first of August he was back in Marietta. Soon he had a newspaper position at Circleville, which is

[3] The manuscript article, found in the Sage papers at Yale University, is entitled: "Description of Remains of an Ancient Fortification at Sellerstown, eleven miles north of Natchez, Mississippi," by Rufus B. Sage.

midway between Columbus and Chillicothe, Ohio. Here he became active in the life of the community. He organized a debating society that held weekly meetings. "I find it a prolific source of improvement," he writes. "I have got so that I can speak in public quite well. Although I have not been here a great while, yet I am universally known about town; it is Mr. Sage, and Mr. Sage, even by persons not known by me from Adam. And, bye the bye, not boastingly, I am treated with much respect" (letter of July 11, 1839). He wrote a song which was sung on the Fourth of July and was published in the paper. Some of his writings were republished in other papers at this period.

Late in 1839 Sage moved to Columbus, Ohio, where he was a compositor on the *Ohio State Bulletin.* Here he improved his time by study at the state library and observed practical politics by attending the state legislative sessions.

The following year he engaged in the Whig political battle, first publishing a weekly campaign paper, and then a daily.[4] Writing to his mother on November 23, 1840, this young man of twenty-three could proudly report:

> I have been deeply and ardently engaged in the great political struggle which has just resulted in the redemption and salvation of our beloved country, and, I trust my exertions have contributed in no small degree to the consummation of that happy result. The friends of Harrison duly appreciate my endeavors, and Harrison himself is not ignorant or unmindful of them. I am personally acquainted with Gen. H. He was in this place last summer, at which time I was introduced to him by the Hon. Alfred Kelly. Upon hearing my name Gen. H. asked if I was the *Sage* that detected the author of the famous

[4] He was the principal editor of the *Harrisonian Straightout,* published at Columbus. Dale L. Morgan found a copy of the Columbus *Daily Political Tornado,* of October 28, 1840 (vol. 1, no. 19), with Sage listed as editor.—H. R. Wagner and C. L. Camp, *The Plains and the Rockies,* etc. (Columbus, Ohio, Long's College Book Company, 1953), p. 177.

> *forged Circular,* — and, on being informed of the fact, said he had *heard of me before.* The Gen. is a very clever sociable old man, — real good-hearted, honest, and talented fellow. I liked his appearance very much. My employment during the past summer, in a pecuniary point of view, has not been very profitable. However, when I have settled up my business, I am in hopes to have some *little* left. When Harrison takes his seat as President, I have good reason to believe that he will give some appointment under government, which will ensure me, if not a competency, at least, a living. Of this I am almost certain. I have arose in the world considerable of late, not withstanding my misfortunes.[5]

The untimely death of President Harrison or some other cause brought a change in Sage's plans and turned his face to the West instead of the East. A desire to explore the Oregon Territory had long stirred him. He induced a number of other young men in Columbus to join in planning an expedition into the far West.

"At starting, May 1, 1841," says his biographical sketch, "only five came to time, and only one besides himself reached Independence, Mo., at which point that one also left him. Undaunted by the gloomy outlook, after a delay of several weeks, Mr. Sage joined a party of Indian traders and pushed his onward way toward the setting sun."[6] His plan, as announced in a letter written before he set out, was to gather material and write a book about his observations and experiences.

Now began the three years of adventures in the Rocky Mountains and New Mexico that are recounted in the volume republished herewith. His travels, detailed therein, are summarized briefly here.

Leaving Independence, Missouri, on September 2, 1841, with the L. P. Lupton trading party, he traveled

[5] Letter No. 16, published below. *See also,* Appendix A, for an account of his aid to Harrison.

[6] *An Illustrated Popular Biography, op. cit.,* p. 108.

the Platte River route to Fort Platte at the mouth of the Laramie River. Two trips during the winter took him northeast to a trading location on the White River, of present northwest Nebraska. While awaiting the building of a boat to float the furs down the Platte, Sage made a hunting excursion up the North Platte to Devil's Gate, and then circled south over the Laramie Plains to return to Fort Platte.

On May 7, 1842, he began a difficult and unsuccessful attempt to boat furs down the Platte. Stranded in the thousand islands region of the lower river, Sage joined the detachment that tramped to Council Bluffs, on the Missouri River, and then floated down to Independence.

Finding his employer bankrupt and times hard at the settlements, Sage decided to return to the mountains as a "free trapper" and traveler. He journeyed over the Oregon Trail to the forks of the Platte River and then followed the South Fork to Fort Lupton in present Colorado. He continued south to the Pueblo on the Arkansas River and pushed on to Taos, New Mexico. Here he met Antoine Robidoux and rode with him to his fort on the Uinta River, eastern Utah of today.

In late October he joined a party and journeyed to Fort Hall, a British fur trade post on the Snake River in Idaho. A few days here were sufficient to give him a picture of Hudson's Bay Company operations.

Turning eastward again he traveled to and through the Colorado Rockies to reach the site of Denver. After spending midwinter in the Clear Creek Valley to the west, which later produced a wealth of gold, he rode down to Fort Lupton to obtain ammunition. Here in February, 1843, he met a former trapper, Charles Warfield, who was sporting a colonel's commission from Texas. He was recruiting men for an expedition against New Mexico. Sage enlisted.

The venture turned into a fiasco, but it carried Sage over much new territory, into a little fighting, and much hardship – all of which added notes for his intended book. After a victorious minor skirmish, his party was pursued by Mexicans who made away with the Texans' mounts. Rufus and his woe-begone companions footed it north to the Arkansas, where their filibustering party disbanded.

Sage returned to the Fort Lupton region and in the fall of 1843 he penetrated the mountains westward. He spent the winter hunting in the Estes Park area and in other sheltered valleys of the region. In the spring of 1844 he joined a company of traders who were returning to the States.

After traveling to Van Buren, Arkansas, Sage continued on to Ohio. Soon he was back in the newspaper game. His letters are silent or missing for this period, but his biographical sketch (in Appendix A) summarizes the story:

> In July, 1844, he returned to Columbia, O., and immediately issued a campaign weekly in support of Henry Clay for U.S. president, protesting with all earnestness against the annexation of Texas and the consequent extension of the slave power.[7] The result was a grand triumph in Ohio, which however, was neutralized in New York by the abolition vote, cast for Burney, thus giving the national election to James K. Polk, and setting in train the tremendous evils that followed. Mr. Sage next appeared in the editorial chair of the Chillicothe, O., *Gazette,* with which paper he severed his connection in 1845, and returned to visit his old home after an absence of ten years. In this quiet retreat he prepared his book of travels.

When the manuscript was nearly finished, Sage looked about for a publisher. His letter of October 15, 1845 (printed herein as number 23), gives his ideas and proposal. Following the unfavorable response of Paine & Burgess on October 21, Rufus Sage went to New York City. Whether he found temporary employ-

[7] He edited the *Ohio Coon Catcher* and the *Whig Battering-Ram.* Wagner and Camp, *op. cit.,* p. 177.

ment there, or devoted his time to setting the type for his book, is not revealed in extant papers. His being a compositor by profession would make him capable of doing the job himself. No satisfactory publication offers were made by January 12 (see his letter no. 24), and he concluded to postpone publication until spring.

An enquiry, written to his eldest brother, Edmund, brought a response on March 30 (Appendix E) advising acceptance of the "stereotype offer," as such an arrangement would permit publication of future editions, at small expense, and give Rufus control of the time and place of future issues.

On April 2 Rufus wrote to Carey & Hart, prominent publishers of Philadelphia,[8] indicating that the book, exclusive of the cost of the stereotype plates, should be produced for ten cents per copy. This publisher was interested, but responded on April 7 (Appendix F-1) asking for an explanation of Sage's figure and stating that their own calculations made the cost sixteen cents each for an edition of 1000.

Rufus wrote to his brother Edmund about financing the project. Edmund responded on April 20, offering to lend Rufus money to procure the stereotype plates. In the meantime, Rufus continued correspondence with Carey & Hart and on April 30 received from them an offer to publish his manuscript (Appendix F-2). Upon receipt of this news Rufus immediately apprised his brother of the proposition. Edmund responded on May 7 (Appendix E-4) with enthusiastic approval, offering to cancel his own proposal in favor of the proposition

[8] This publishing company was started by Mathew Carey in 1785. When he retired in 1821 his son Henry C. Carey and son-in-law, Isaac Lea, carried on the business. Abraham Hart was taken into the partnership in 1829, and the firm became Carey & Hart. Subsequently it became Lea and Febriger and is still doing business under that name. They specialize today in medical publications.

The Historical Society of Pennsylvania, at Philadelphia, has the greater part of the company's papers, except for the years 1822-49. The above information was kindly supplied on May 16, 1955, by R. N. Williams, 2nd, Director.

which gave promise of greater profits for the future.

A contract was made with A. P. Searing of New York to do the stereotyping of 300 pages for $337 (Appendix F-13). The matter of a map was discussed with Sage's publishers, who reported on May 22 (Appendix F-3) that to prepare and print 2000 maps would cost 7½ cents each, and that the price of the book would not warrant the additional expenditure.

The work went forward rapidly. The publishers received proofs from the stereotyper on May 29, liked the type and page size, and assured the author that "it will make a handsome book" (Appendix F-4).

Mr. Sage persisted in his efforts for a map. He contacted F. Mechelin, lithographer of New York, and submitted proposals to the publishers. On June 12 Carey & Hart agreed to pay $45 for 1000 copies of the "Map of Oregon" if "executed in a workmanlike manner" (Appendix F-6). Five days later the publishers sent Sage the map from "Fremont's Expedition" and agreed to pay five dollars extra to have the "map executed in a superior style." Apparently the map from Fremont's book was copied and was adapted by adding routes and certain locations to show Sage's travels. The map was not to be inserted in the paper-bound book, which sold for fifty cents; but was included in the cloth-bound volume, that sold for one dollar. The map was also sold separately.

The stereotype plates went to the publishers in July and the book was printed in August, 1846. In the meantime Sage had left New York City and returned home. On August 27 his publishers in Philadelphia sent 100 copies of the book in paper covers to Sage at Middletown, Connecticut. The copies in boards were not yet ready, but went forward shortly.

Rufus, as salesman, pushed his book with vigor. By September 8 he wrote to the publishers saying that the book was going well in Connecticut and that he expected the sales to reach 2000 copies for the year. The publishers reported on September 9 (Appendix F-12) that the first printing of 1500 copies in papers was exhausted, but that the second 1500 would be finished in a few days; also that the 500 "fine Edition," on calendar paper and bound in boards, had been printed. Reviews of the book had already appeared in the *New York Tribune* and the *New York Mirror.*

The publishers, in their letter of September 30, 1846 (Appendix F-13), give an account of costs and sales on the first 3500 copies of *Scenes in the Rocky Mountains,* by a New Englander. Sage received a royalty of 15% on the wholesale price. By being his own salesman he increased his profits considerably. To Rufus this was a matter of great importance; he wanted income enough to warrant an early marriage.

During the months spent in New York City, while arranging for publication of his book, Rufus had been concerned about his love affair with Marietta Miller, whom he had met after his return to Connecticut from the West. While we have none of his own or his sweetheart's letters, we learn something about Rufus' sentiments in the letter of a friend, written from New York on August 23, 1846:

> But has the meeting with your Dark-Brunette realized all the fond anticipations that you sometimes indulged in while in New York? Does her society fill the void in your heart and satisfy all the longing desires that the mind often feels when comparing the present with the past to imagine what the future will bring? if so, you are indeed happy! . . . I wish I were acquainted with your *dear, lovely, and charming* Brunette! I hope you love each other and that neither of you are the victims.[9]

Although Rufus' book sales in Connecticut were encouraging, his marriage was to be postponed for a full year while he tested his salesmanship in the Ohio

[9] Letter of J. A. Prince, found in the Rufus B. Sage letters, Coe Collection, Yale University.

country where he was well known. His brother Edmund took over the sales in New England.

By January 1, 1847, Rufus wrote to his mother from Somerset, Ohio, saying that his health and business prospects were "in a flattering condition. My books sell as well and even better than I had expected. In retailing them I can easily clear my $50 per month, cash in hand. I meet with success upon all sides, and hope soon to be in a condition to do something for you and for others. Enclosed you will find $5.00, which you will make use of as you see fit." He did not expect to return to Middletown until May. If Edmund had not sold his 500 maps in New England, Rufus said he would gladly take them off his hands. "I have just received 600 copies of books – my sales at retail average about 60 copies per week. I go from this place (Somerset) to Lancaster, and from there to Columbus, via Chillicothe and Circleville."

On March 15, 1847, the publishers wrote to Sage: "We accept your offer for 1000 Copies of your book at 50 per cent discount, provided the payment for the same is made at the time of ordering." (Appendix F-14).

The state of affairs between Rufus and Miss Miller during this period is revealed only through letters written by Edmund. On April 16, 1847, he writes thus to Rufus:

> We shall get tired of waiting for you to come home. Miss Miller in particular, if you put it off much longer. I am fixing up that short hill lot ready for you & it would be a Good Idea to get married as soon as Possible this summer so as to get seasoned well against next falls bleak and chilly blasts as I am afraid you will be too tender next winter that I shall not be able to get you out into the woods with me at all. Come on then I say and the sooner it is over the better & dont refuse a good offer when she sais she is ready in May or June tell her I am ready also & bring yourself to it & get tough so that you can do something next winter that will tell in future account.

Since Rufus was now thirty years old and his life pattern had been something of a migrant through the past ten years, Edmund seemed to feel a responsibility in pushing through his younger brother's marriage plans. In a letter of May 10 Edmund observed:

> Miss Miller is keeping school this Summer she soon expects to leave it however I believe suddenly along in June or July & come into our neighborhood ha ha. I suppose you are no stranger to her expectations & I think just as likely as not they agree with yours well that is all well enough & I shall be very happy to see you at my house.

Rufus appears to have returned to Connecticut in the summer,[10] but it was not until late fall that this announcement was made:[11]

> TO WHOM IT MAY CONCERN
>
> This may certify that notice of the intended marriage between Mr. Rufus B Sage and Miss Marietta M Miller Both of Middletown was given publicity before the congregation worshipping in the meeting house of the Second Baptist Church in Middletown on the first Lords day in November Inst, By
>
> JAMES HEPBURN Pastor of said chh
> Upper Middletown on 9th Nov 1847

They were married December 1, 1847. Rufus was thirty years old, his bride was twenty. They became the parents of five children – Winit Rufus, Theson Peter, Stedworth, Emeda, and Evalon.[12]

---

[10] Letter of Cousin George R. Woodruff to Rufus Sage, dated August 23, 1847. Coe Collection, Yale University.

[11] Found in the Sage papers, Coe Collection.

[12] From records in the Sage Family Bible, owned by a granddaughter, Mrs. Helen Sage Bernson, Cromwell, Connecticut, and inscriptions on the family monument in the local cemetery. These were inspected by the editors at Cromwell in the summer of 1953. The dates of birth and death of the Sage children are: Winit Rufus, March 1, 1855 – Nov. 20, 1935; Theson Peter, April 29, 1859 – October 5, 1885; Stedworth, August 15, 1864 – October 18, 1885; Emeda, July 4, 1867 – October 12, 1948; Evalon, November 16, 1870 – September 17, 1873.

Rufus Sage lived his last years as a farmer in the little Connecticut town where he was born. A biographical sketch, published when he was seventy-four years old, explains the adopted course of his life after years of traveling in the West.

> At this point (1846) came a change of long-cherished plans. An aged invalid mother required of him the care he could not find heart to deny. Yielding to her wishes, he married and set himself faithfully to solve the puzzling question so often discussed, "Will farming pay?" Mr. Sage says that it will. Satisfied with home comforts and busied with home interests, he has kept aloof from public office. . . He has been uniformly a studious and laborious man.[13]

He died at seventy-six on December 23, 1893; his wife followed him on March 22, 1900. A tall red sandstone shaft in the cemetery marks their graves. The old Rufus B. Sage house is still standing, a two-story building covered with shake shingles. Nearby is the house occupied by one of his granddaughters, Mrs. Helen Bernson, and her two children.

With Emeda, the last surviving daughter of Rufus B. Sage, the present editors had correspondence in 1939, concerning her father's books and papers. At that time she was unwilling to part with his letters. After her death, in October, 1948, the papers were acquired by Mr. W. R. Coe, prominent western Americana collector, and are now in the Coe Collection at Yale University. Access to the collection, and permission to publish letters and documents preserved therein, were generously given the editors by Yale University Library.

Sage's book on the West went through many printings during the first twenty years. The first edition included 3000 copies paper bound and without the

13 Reproduced as Appendix A in this volume.

map; 500 copies printed on calendar paper, bound in boards and with map inserted. In this edition the author was merely listed as "A New Englander." [14]

The "Second Edition Revised" was issued with the same title, except that Sage's name was inserted as author. It was published by Carey & Hart in 1847.[15]

In 1854 the book was re-issued, with the same title as in 1847, except that the publisher is "Henry Carey Baird (successor to E. L. Carey,) no. 7 Hart's Buildings, Sixth Street, above Chestnut." Eleven Woodcut illustrations were added. The next year it was printed as "Third Edition Revised," with G. D. Miller of Philadelphia as publisher.[16]

In 1857 it was published by Wentworth & Company in Boston. They simplified the title to *"Rocky Mountain Life; or, Startling Scenes and Perilous Adventures in the Far West, during an Expedition of Three Years.* By Rufus B. Sage." Twenty-five illustrations were included and the volume was bound with decorated and stamped cloth over boards. This edition was copyrighted by Wentworth & Company in 1857. A new one-page Preface replaced the two-page one of the first edition. The printing of the text was from the original plates, but the illustrations were counted in, thus altering the original pagination. No map was included.[17]

Editions are reported for the years 1858, 1859, and

[14] In Wagner and Camp, *op. cit.*, p. 178, the principal owners of first editions are listed. Dr. Nolie Mumey, of Denver, lent us his copy to do the checking for the present re-publication.

[15] The copy owned by Fred A. Rosenstock of Denver is in printed wrappers; the one in the Henry E. Huntington Library is bound in leather – a rebinding. The reverse of the title page is identical with the first edition, including "Printed by T. K. and P. G. Collins." No map is included.

[16] The title page was changed slightly to: *Wild Scenes in Kansas and Nebraska, the Rocky Mountains, Oregon, California, New Mexico, Texas, and the Grand Prairies: or Notes by the Way,* etc.

[17] The Denver Public Library copy of this edition carries on the title page, "Boston: Milton F. Hewes & Company, No. 77 Cornhill, 1857." But on the reverse, the copyright is in the name of Wentworth & Company.

1860.[18] Other undated cheap reprints were subsequently issued; one by Edward Canby, Dayton, Ohio, in "The Star Library." None of the numerous editions carried an index; all were printed from the original stereotype plates of 1846.

In later years Sage's book was nearly forgotten. Then reviving interest in Western Americana brought the volume to the fore. Serious students came to see what a valuable contribution Rufus Sage had made in accurately recording observations and experiences during his extensive travels in the West.

In the present work we publish first, the Rufus B. Sage letters; then reprint his book with annotations; and finally, in an Appendix, publish the more pertinent letters and papers related to Sage's life and writings.

The several printings of Sage's book invariably appeared without an index, but each contained an extended list of sub-headings on the "Contents" pages. In the old editions these sub-headings are repeated at the beginning of each chapter. Since this printing is provided with an index, the repetition of the chapter sub-headings is omitted. Except for this omission, only the pagination and running heads vary from the original printing of the work.

Through the generosity of Robert James Woods of Los Angeles, a copy of the paper bound, first edition was made available for reproduction of the original wrappers in this volume, and for the checking of other details of the original edition.

---

18 Listed in Wright Howes, *U.S.-iana,* etc., (New York: R. R. Bowker Company, 1954), p. 507. The Huntington Library copy of the 1858 edition is published by Wentworth & Company and has a title page similar to that used in 1857. At least one of the copies of the 1860 edition (in the State Historical Society of Colorado Library) carries the name of Thayer & Eldridge of Boston on the title page, but the copyright is the same as in 1857. Under Sage's name on the title page is this added line: "The Western Adventurer."

The Rufus B. Sage Letters

The letters of Rufus Sage are preserved in the Coe Collection of Yale University Library, by whose kind permission we publish them here. The letters cover the period from 1836 to 1847. They reveal clearly the background and environment of the young man, his attitudes, abilities, and aspirations. They portray him at nineteen, eager to see the world and test his talents. His rapid maturing is apparent. At age twenty-two in the new Ohio country, he has become an important newspaper man and has won a respected position in the community. In the presidential campaigns of 1840 and 1844 he edited and published vigorous political newspapers.

All of Rufus Sage's letters in the Coe Collection are reproduced herewith. That Collection also contains many letters written *to* him, rather than *by* him. The more important of these are printed in the Appendix to this volume. Others are summarized or referred to in the footnotes that accompany the Sage letters and to which they relate.

In the Sage Collection are a number of family letters, also. They include correspondence of Rufus B. Sage's grandfather, Elisha Sage, of his father, Deacon Rufus Sage, and of other members in the family relating to personal affairs and to life in Connecticut, 1789-1828. None of these are reprinted here. For a list of the Sage papers see Mary C. Withington, *A Catalogue of Manuscripts in the Collection of Western Americana founded by William Robertson Coe, Yale University Library* (New Haven, Yale University Press, 1952), pp. 236-37.

It seems advisable, in publication of the letters here, to keep annotations to the minimum necessary for a clear presentation of the story.

[LETTER NO. 1] BROOKLYN, SUNDAY, JUNE 19, 1836[1]

DEAR MOTHER I now find myself where I never before have been, in a truely beautiful place, alone, though surrounded by thousands and a stranger in a strange land. When I stepped into the steamer which was to convey me from dear Middletown (for I shall ever cherish a fond recollection of the place which gave me birth, at whatever distance I may be) my sensations were of the acutest kind but yet I was determined to brave it out, and so I did, smothering my feelings as much as possible. I had a fine passage down the Connecticut and a superb time on the Sound. O, it was a most enchanting sight to view the blue hills of the mainland on the left hand at the distance of many miles, tinged with the gold of the setting sun, and on the right, the green plains of the Island scarcely perceptable, the trees seemed to dance as we *sped* by them. The smooth waters of the calm ocean, speckled with the spread canvas of ships, and the sea gulls soaring in the air were delightful to behold. After tea I walked the deck to enjoy the scenery, it being rather cool I felt the need of my cloak as I thought I should before I left home, and I found it just the thing which I wanted. About nine o'clock we were called into the cabin to draw for berths and it was my good fortune to get one. So I retired to bed about ½ past 10, but not to sleep, for there was such a thundering racket. I could not sleep a wink all night, thus I lay in my narrow crib absorbed in reflection upon my own situation till near two o'clock in the morning when I arose and dressed myself. But what was my surprise upon looking for my shoes to find them gone! I fancied at once they were stolen! Yet I was determined not to let them go without some effort for their recovery, so I began to enquire of the hands concerning them and was directed to look for them in

[1] He had left home at Upper Middletown a few days before, probably on June 14.

such a place. I did, and found them with about 20 pairs besides, with shining visages neatly placed in order together. I then took and put them on and started to go upon deck when one of the waiters stepped up to me and said "a six pence sir." For what, said I. "Cleaning your shoes, sir." Returned "cuffe" I thought this kinder comical but rather than to get into any words I took out six cents and gave it to him for doing what I never asked. I then went upon deck and found we were passing with land on either side. In about half a mile's distance I discovered on my right hand there were woods as well as in upper Middletown. Soon upon looking south I saw the lighted streets of N.Y. in full view and as we drew nearer and began to pass them they were rendered as to appearance like so many dancing specteres. We gained and made fast to the wharf at the foot of Catherine Street market about 3 o'clock. And by the by if ever I saw a real forest of masts it was in the port of New York, vessels of all descriptions and from all nations were there huddled together as close as Ben will stow his oats in August. We waited till broad day before we landed. And then I had my trunk carried to the Steamboat office to leave till I knew where I was going, and what I was going about. New York is certainly a large city but somehow or other not the city I thought it was. It has many fine buildings but its splendor falls far below what I had anticipated. Instead of viewing it with wonder and astonishment as I expected that I being a raw Yankee should, I looked upon it far differently. I seemed as much at home as though I had always lived there. I went through the different streets as though they had been perfectly fermiliar to me. I called at 175 Water St. and enquired for Uncle George but found that he did not carry on business there now, nor did they know where he did, nor where he was to be found. I then went to see if I could find West, but he was not to be found at the office where he worked. So finding nobody I knew I thought I would go around and take a squint at the city, which I did. I have not time now to tell you all about it, and describe it minutely. You must therefore excuse me that till it is convenient for me to do it thuroughly. I met West in my excursion much to his surprise, as well as my own. He kindly offered to assist me to procure a bording place and to get into business then, but I told him I would go over the Brooklyn and find my Uncle first if I could, if I did not succeed should then thank him for his assistance. So I started for the ferry which I reached in a few moments, and crossed over to Brooklyn for that purpose. I enquired and enquired, but found nobody that knew a single syllible concerning him, and after a long search discovered no trace of him, and being very tired I gave up the chase. I then called at the office of the Brooklyn Daily Advertiser to see if I could get employment at the printing business. They were in want of no help but directed me to the Long Island Star office. I went there and succeeded in getting employment at 25 cts per 1000. My next start was to get a bording place. And I soon found one for 3 doll. 50 cts. per week, the cheapest I could procure. I then went back to N.Y. for my trunk and called on West and told him my success, and requested him to call over and see me, and recrossed and deposited my trunk at my boarding house in Short Metre. Being sleepy enough to repose on a hetchel. And tired enough to rest on the point of a lightening rod. But not withstanding my weariness and fateague, I went in the afternoon over most of the city. Brooklyn is a beautiful place but I must defer a description of it to some future time. Thus ended the day of my arrival here. Evening came on and I retired early to bed and had the sweetest night's rest I ever recollect of enjoying. When I rose the next morning I felt like a new creature and set down to the breakfast table with a keen appetite, I tell you.

But the cooking! O, the cooking! Good concience! What Yankee ever saw such cooking? It needs (I had almost said) a stomarch made of India Rubber to render it palitable. So much for the cookery. Now to go on, after breakfast I went to work at the office, No. 15 James St., where I had engaged the day previous and found myself very pleasantly situated. Much more so than I expected. My boarding place is No. 73 Poppolar street. It has been my fortune to fall into much better company than I did in Hartford. I cannot make it very proffitable to stay here, everything bears such an enormous price. I can pay my way it is true and save a little but yet I think I can make more in some place where I can live cheaper. You must not be surprised if I should leave this for some other place soon. Saturday afternoon as I was returning from dinner to work, I met Uncle George with his son going down to the ferry. He did not know me till I introduced myself. He resides No. 50 Delander Street, N. York. He said his family were well, that he had received my letter and was to have answered it that afternoon. I informed him what business I was in. And he seemed to be very much pleased. — But I have most filled out the sheet — so goodbye — Write soon, tell all about how you get along. This from your son,

RUFUS B. SAGE

To MRS. JERUSHA SAGE

[Envelope address]:
Mrs. Jerusha Sage Upper Middletown Conn.

[LETTER NO. 2] [1836, JULY 19]

DEAR MOTHER Having an opportunity to send as far as Middletown by a gentleman by the name of Hauxurst a particular friend of mine, one who boards at the same place with me, and a merchant of high respectibility, I thought that I could not in conscience let it pass without writing a line or two to you. Dear Mother, I am astonished. Why, it has really got to be fine times! Now here I have been in Brooklyn this five weeks and have not heard one word from Upper Middletown in the mean time.[2] You had ought to have heard from me at least twice in a week for I have sent papers as often as that, and a written word on the wrapper. I want to hear from home, do write as you can, or set some one else to write for you. Mr. Gear, Frances, Benjamin,[3] or some body. I dont much care who. I am well, and doing well, make money hand over fist, enjoy miself tollerable, and go to work at the old place. I board within a short distance of Uncle George, call on him once in a while. Come Mother, you must call down here and see me. I will pay your expenses, and treat you in the highest style. I am in a very agreeable family, Presbyterians by profession. Brooklyn is a fine place, not quite such a sink of polution as N.Y. But by the by, N.Y. is not near so bad a place as I thought for, yet it is bad enough. I shall probably continue in this place or in York till September, then I shall return home. But, dear Mother, there is one thing — I find, and how thankful I had ought to be too, that he who was the God of my fathers is still my God, and watches continually over my path, and has still preserved me in safety. Yes, Mother I have been kept in some measure from falling. And been enabled thus far to overcome the temptations by which I was surrounded. But I must stop —

P.S. — there was a fire yesterday, that is Sunday, by which four dwelling houses were burnt — do pray write soon

R B DeSage

Mrs. Jerusha Sage Upper Middletown, Conn.

[2] His mother had written him a letter on July 3, 1836 (reproduced in Appendix B), but it miscarried and was returned to the sender.

[3] Abial Gear was his brother-in-law, husband of his sister Frances. Benjamin was his brother.

[LETTER NO. 3] [BROOKLYN] TUESDAY JULY 25–1836
DEAR MOTHER You probably have by this time received a line from me dated the 19th of July, in which I stated that the letter was conveyed as far as Middletown by a gentleman by the name of Hauxurst. In that I was disappointed, for he, after receiving my bundle concluded not to go, and consequently dropped the package into the post office. To render it more compact I had done up with one wrapper a paper directed to you and one to Curtiss and directed them both to Curtiss, and in the one directed to you I enclosed a letter. Consequently I suppose there is a double postage to be paid on it. I am sorry it has so happened, but I cannot help it now. I wish you would pay the sum to Mr. Curtiss, and when I return home I will make it all right. O, dear me! Mother, I feel very much off the hooks at this time, I am now unwell and out of employ. I dont know, but I am affraid I am going to be sick. But as to employ, I expect to go to work in N. York in the course of a day or two, if well enough, at the corner of Nassau and Ann [?] streets. You must not be surprised if I should be at home before a great while. If there was good business for me to do there, I would not hesitate long. You will find me quite an altered person when you come to see me. But I have now to lament that I have been so lavish of my money. I have not yet laid up any thing. The fact is that though "experience is a dear school" it learns its pupils well. I shall hereafter look out for my pennies. I have been in a good school and improved by it, perhaps my improvement has amply compensated for my non-accumulation of property.— But what is the reason that I have not heard one word from home since I have been here? this is outrageous! I had almost made up my mind never to write home again — If I don't receive some word or other pretty soon, I am half resolved not to go home again as long as I live. — Such things

wont do — I can't stand it. It is unjust — it is unmerciful. Can it possibly be that I am forgotten? How is it that some of you don't write? "O tempores! O mores!" Such neglect! Am I cast off! And have I merited all this? — But it is not my intention to go on with such prate — In my last letter, I wrote for you to come down here — I now think that seeing things are as they are, you had better not till you receive word from me again as I am not decided what I shall do, or where I shall be in the course of a fortnight. Yesterday, I was in Newark, New Jersey, to day I am here in Brooklyn, to morrow in New York so you see that all these things must take off the chink by the wholesale. George Butler is going to Connecticut on Saturday. He will be the bearer of this letter. I have told his folks something about my circumstances which you can know by asking him — How changeable is this life, and my business especially, it is so fluctuating! Give a steady life I am sick of chance — But I believe I must be content till I have scraped together enough to buy a farm and then I am going to lead a farmer's life. That is the life for me — I wonder if Ben has got through his haying yet — If he will have anything for me to do if I should come home in the course of a month — let's see — that will fetch to the last of August — well, and if I stay at home a month or six weeks, that will fetch it to the time when I shall want to start for Ohio.[4] — Write and let me know — If B [Benjamin] has employment for me I'll come. I shall want to stay at home about that time, and I want to be busey in the meanwhile. I have a good many things to tell you of, that would interest, when I come home, what has fallen under my observation since my absence. I am not quite so green as when I went away. I can flurish now in true York style.— But, O, my head! it aches. I feel something as I did last

[4] His plans worked out about as projected here. It appears that he returned home in August and set out for Ohio in early October, 1836.

summer before I was taken sick — and as uneasy as a fish out of water — But I cannot afford to write so long a letter, after this style, 'twould spoil my market if the girls should see it — so I must stop, bidding you good by — Your affectionate son

RUFOIS B. DE SAGE

MRS. JERUSHIA SAGE

BROOKLYN — JULY 26, 1836[5]

P.S. You must write — it don't signify whatever may be the case — to the contrary — direct to Brooklyn —

R. B. SAGE

[LETTER NO. 4] [DECEMBER 11, 1836] MARIETTA[6]

DEAR MOTHER I beg a thousand pardons for my neglecting to write to you so long as I have. Although this is contrary to my principles, yet I was partly driven to it by necessity. And a part of that I may explain in the course of my letter. But enough of this — now for my story — When I last wrote you I was in Freedonia, York State.[7] I started from that place 28 Oct. and as I got cheated out of my ride across the Lake I was obliged to take the Pennsylvania Route, reached Ashtabulia 30th, went to see Mr. T. Smith's, found them living like pigs in the clover, the same identical old sixpences of the very same stamp. As to his circumstances, he has improved them much, by leaving Connecticut. His estate is now worth $1500, besides movable property to considerable amount. Tell Mrs. Dickinson I called on Mr. Colburn, found them well and much better off than at the East, he gets a good living, and some headway. He owns 5 acres of land, a house, and

[5] His mother's letter of July 24, 1836, is printed in Appendix B-2.

[6] Rufus had left Upper Middletown in early October. He went to New York City, up the Hudson, along the Erie Canal to Buffalo, along the shore line to Ashtabula, and then south to Marietta. A full and interesting account of the trip is given in Letters 12, 13, and 15.

[7] This letter is not in the Coe Collection. Fredonia is on the shore of Lake Erie, about midway between the cities of Buffalo and Erie.

keeps two cows, and works at his trade. I went to see Mr. Ira Brainerd, found them well and contented — getting along tollerable — But O,— I had almost forgotten to tell you Betsey Smith has got married and well too —*Nov. 1 I left for Marietta.* Cruised around well on my route, though; especially on the [Connecticut Western] Reserve. After making one stop of a few days at Ravenna, I reached Marietta *Nov. 18th,* found all our folks well, and Jerusha [8] as *big as a moose* and as *fat as an Opposum!* — I really believe this is the country to grow fat for Mrs. Gear [9] has thickened up, and I myself begin to incline that way.— But — pshaw! no more of this.— Now for something I did not tell you when I wrote last, I mean something Jerusha hinted in her letter in reference to my loosing my coat. While coming up on the York and Erie Canal I had it stolen from me, together with Mrs. Gear's letter, and several other articles, which were in it, during the night while I was asleep. It happened very fortunate that I lost no money with it. Just at night, that very day, I had a sum of money in my coat pocket, and had had it there for several days, which I removed and placed in my pantaloons. This I think, and I believe you will think so too, a very narrow escape. And thankful am I for it. Thus you see amid losses and crosses we always have something to be thankful for. This is *certain.* There is never anything so bad but what it can be worse. Mother Gear is in a terrible tue about her letter, she is afraid there was money in it, I wish you would take pains to enquire of Mr. Lewis to that effect and write me. I have been very fortunate as well as unfortunate. I have one consolation "that everything works for the best to those who love God." So it appears for me. I had been in this place but about two days before I had an application to teach school in the

[8] Jerusha Sage Gear, his eldest sister, living in Marietta, Ohio.
[9] Jerusha's mother-in-law.

Township of Warren, 5 miles from this place; which I accepted, and commenced school two weeks since. I have 16. dol. per month, and board, and might have had 20, if I had asked it.[10] I suppose you are anxious to know how I succeed — I have got along well thus far; and believe I shall continue to do the same. I am very pleasantly situated indeed and enjoy myself well as to health and mind. I keep in a splendid large brick school house situated on the bank of the beautiful Ohio, and can see the steamboats passing and repassing most any time if a mind to look.— Now for the beauties of Ohio.— It is now that language fails me to discribe. The most comprehensive words are but wind, and bear no weight at all upon the subject, words cannot represent nature, nor the pen paint its beauties. Genius is completely exhausted in the task and falls far below the undertaking. Imagination can only conceive, nor then arrive at reality. The very land is Poetry and the atmosphere is song. Old Connecticut! 'tis now that I forget thee! 'tis now that I substitute the far West in thy place. Say! who among thy inhabitants is poor! who have lack of this world's good! To him we would say the West is free and willing to receive the needy! who among you despises the West! who derides the idea of its fatness! Let him but once plow the ground, and but once sow his seed and then behold the harvest. Then, we presume, his derision will be changed to respect and his hatred to tender affection. Who is afraid of beasts of prey, or dreads the howling panther! Let him know there is no such thing nor beasts like them found here. Who dreads the bear! or is scared at the growling wild cat! Few are like them found here — But rare and seldom they — Who likes to hunt the deer and who to shoot the turkey? Do any wish for this? — To them we would say *Come*. Who searches after

[10] He tells more about his short term of one month as a teacher in Letter No. 15.

comfort, and who would gain enjoyment? — Who digs for golden ore, who seeks for hidden treasure? Yea — who would grasp at wealth and pick up gold as stone? Who would obey their interest and who their own best good? —

> To such we would say come
> No longer stay away
> If here you chance to roam
> Ther'll dawn a brighter day.

But ah! what is all this! My imagination has wrapt me almost into a trance. But is this fiction? — this truly is an enchanting country. If Ben [11] had come here 2 years ago, it would have been his makeing. Land was then cheap, now it is twice as much as it was then, perhaps as high nearly as at the east. The land near Ashtabula and on the Reserve is good very wet level and clayey. They raise great crops there but it is such land as I don't like. The southern and middle of the state is more broken and hilly, and I think more preferable. Wild land is from 8 to 12 dol. per acre. I think it would be best to go west; it is cheaper to the far West.

Ben, you hadn't better be in a hurry about comeing to this country. let me look around first and see what I can see.— But as to the country. I must candidly own it has far surpassed my sanguine expectations. But what have I here? — something from my beloved Brother Edmund [12] how kind he speaks — just hear him — thus he talks — "Rufus talks some of going to the West I believe, he is very fickle-minded. he has got the eighteen year old fever pretty bad, if he would go, and have to endure some severe hardships he would come back contented. I am afraid he won't do much any where he is so unsteady, he might do well if he only would." So he says — This is indeed a good recommendation

[11] A brother, three years older than Rufus.

[12] Rufus' eldest brother, born in 1804.

and were I at home I would present my grateful acknowledgements to him in person. I hope the eighteen year old fever will not carry me off; nor my unsteadyness destroy me. He seems to fear very much for me — such tender regard! I have some glimmering hope his fears will not be altogether realized — So much for commendation — now for something else — But — about writing home — it so happened that I could not write while on my journey, for various reasons, and since I have arrived here I have waited to see how I got along with my school before writing. Therefore I beg excuse. I have not room to tell you the fair prospects in this country for the enterprising, you must have patience to wait for that till my next letter — Benjamin had better make his calculations for the West — but let me look him out a good situation first. I know he would enjoy himself. It would just suit him. I wish he would write me. Jerusha sends her love to all. Mother Gear is well — enjoys herself well, sends her love to all, and would like to hear from home. Hiram [13] sends his love to Abial — is glad he is doing well and hopes he will do better.

With affectionate regards, hoping for your maternal prayers, I remain your ever loving son —

R. B. SAGE

P.S. Write soon

TO MRS. JERUSHA SAGE, NOV. 11,[14] 1836

[after the signature these lines are added]: Jerusha Gear and Mr. Gear talk of going to Ct. in the spring. The little one is a real cungerbug and pratler. Hiram has made vast improvement since he came here. He is about as good a preacher as I have come across. You

---

[13] Jerusha's husband, Hiram Gear.

[14] This date certainly is wrong. Rufus says in this letter that he reached Marietta November 18. In Letter No. 15 he says that the day after arrival at Marietta he had an invitation to teach school and that he began teaching the next week. He is writing this letter (No. 4) after he has been teaching two weeks, so the date is doubtless December 11, instead of November 11.

need not be concerned about me if I don't come home till next year. I can do very well here. Ohio seems much like home, but the soil is three times as good. It is quite thickly inhabited. You can scarce go a mile and a half any where without comeing to some house or clearing. The opinion some at the east have of the west is realy ludicrous, Edmund especially.

[written along the side of the letter]: Don't worry about me. I have cruised around well in this state. I have been since I left home more than 1500 miles. Traveling is very cheap, it cost me but about $15. I am but about 800 miles from you. R.B.S.

Tell Elisha [15] I have not forgot the mason trade.— This is the country for it.

[LETTER NO. 5] MARIETTA APRIL 16, 1837.

BELOVED MOTHER Notwithstanding it has been but a short time since I wrote you, I thought I could not, consistent with fillial regard, let this opportunity pass, without sending you a few lines.— But I am out of letter timber, therefore you must excuse my trash. It may be interesting, or it may not, just as it happens. Too! it is to ma, who understands me well. therefore, I need not be so much concerned.— The seventh of this month was the anniversary day of the arrival of Gen. Rufus Putnam, in this place, at the head of the Ohio company, to commence the settlement of the great Northwestern Terratory. This event happened in the year 1790 [1788], at which time this Eden of America, this goodly land, now so thickly inhabited, so extensively cultivated, so speckled with the mansions of industrious countrymen, and which forms so important a link in the chain of our national compact, was one vast unbroken wilderness, one trackless solitude, except, perchance, an Indian trail, or the rude wigwams

[15] Rufus' brother, born in 1809.

of the sons of the forest. Wild beasts were its inhabitants and beasts of prey its occupants. To render its gloom more dreadful, were heard, now the horrid cries of the panther, rendered doubly terrible by the shrill noise of an hundred echoes, now the snarling bear mingled in the general corus of the beasts of the woods. Then the red man ranged in triumph, lord of the forest. Then no white oppressor tormented him. No pale face was there to dispute his title or drive him from the land of his father's graves. Then the beautiful Ohio flowed majestically meandering towards the "great father of waters" with banks, on either side incumbent with the "buckeye" of the spring, the towering sycamore and graceful cypress. Then its silver waters were divided by no white man's bark, no oar spurned the curling wave save now and then the Indian's paddle — but now, how changed,— the wilderness has become a garden, the desert, a fruitful field, the rose now takes the place of the thorn, and the lilly that of the bramble. The spires of churches point heven-ward, where once the savages assembled to their powows and war-dances. Important cities have sprung up in a night & a day, and are growing, like Jonah's gourd. Now the river is alive with flats, rafts, and steamboats. Indeed, a mighty change has occurred! The Valley of the Ohio teems with inhabitants.— Four new states with an enterprising population of, from two to three million, already exist in this Terratory.— and another, grown past boyhood within a few days, threatens to demand admittance into our Union, of next Congress. These almost increditable things are wonders indeed.— This is a land of wonders.

There was a general turnout in this place to celebrate the 7th, which is as much thought of as the 4th of July at the East. They had what was called a "buckeye party" on the occasion, to which the most respectable citizens of the place, with myself, and the "bonny lasses" were invited. The tables were loaded with the choicest production of the land, and the richest viands. All were cheerful, gay and happy. The beauty of the place was there. And the day was pleasantly spent in social intercourse till pale evening gave the signal to retire to their several homes.— O, that this land, with its population, might increase in virtue, science and religion,— That it might become emphatically "the land of steady habits!" Then would it be, truly, mighty — a wonder and a praise in the earth.— but it is sadly the reverse.— with, (I am happy to say) some exceptions in these parts — Ignorance covers the inhabitants and gross darkness the people. the love of gain is predominant — licentiousness prevails — morals are low — communications corrupt — loose and vulgar — politeness violated — Religion scorned, despised, and scoffed — the Sabbath desecrated, profaned, broken, and trampled upon — Professors to piety looked upon with a suspicious eye. Society dead — politics debased — and Presbyterians uniformly called "blue skins." — Well ma, I believe I have run on rather too fast.— The people of the West are not so bad generally as above represented — it might prove true, in some places, but what would apply to some would not to all.— There are great diversities of characters here — some good and some bad — they are not so strictly moral as at the East — yet there is not so vast a difference as you might be led to suppose from what I have wrote.— I received a letter from Cousin Martha, Uncle Amos's daughter, a short time since. She writes, there has been a revival of religion in that place, and herself indulging a hope. The relations are all well. Nothing important other than good advice. I suppose the friends of religion in U.M. are now rejoicing in the glorious visitation of divine mercy.— O that they might be permitted to rejoice in the Lord alway, and to receive continually the smiles of his countenance! O that sinners everywhere might repent — and not only repent but do works meet for repentance.— and converts ne'er grow cold or forsake their first love.— But I must draw to a close — my sheet is nearly filled.— Wherever I am or in whatsoever station I am placed, I pray Heaven I may be enabled to discharge my duty faithfully both towards God and toward my fellow men. Then may I be permitted to close my life in peace, in hope of a glorious immortality beyond the grave.— Your affectionate Son — R. B. SAGE

[LETTER NO. 6]

Don't worry. MARIETTA MAY 22, 1837

DEAR SISTER,[16] — I have received so much neglect in letter ways of late, that I am almost prepared to give up the idea of *ever receiving one* from home.[17] There appears to be, I had like to have said, an unpardonable deficiency, on the part of eastern friends, in this particular. I would it were otherwise,— but, so it is, and I must bear it, how unpleasant so ever it may be. I have been to the Post Office several times of late with the anticipation of finding something for me and have as often been disappointed; till last evening, when I found a solitary newsbearer from Middletown, from which I learned of your arrival there, and received a *dunning* for a letter. However unjust the demand I haste to comply. I have nothing very much to write, unless some few incidents which have taken place since you left. The Hon. Daniel Webster arrived in this place on the 17th inst. with whom I had the pleasure of an interview. He is pretty much of a gentleman, of easy access,

---

[16] Mrs. Jerusha S. Gear, Rufus' sister, who had gone from Marietta, Ohio, to their old home in Connecticut for a visit.

[17] His mother wrote Rufus a letter on May 17, 1837 (printed in Appendix B-3. His sister, Mrs. Frances Gear, also wrote to him on the same date. This letter is in the Coe Collection, Yale University Library).

plain in his appearance, and quite sociable. His wife and daughter were as illy dressed as some of our kitchen girls about their work, and withall, what I call homely. Thus, plainness becomes the great. Sabbath before last I went to the *Baptist* meeting where there was Methodist preaching, by the Rev. J. Crawford; — pretty much of a brawler.— *Brother Dana,* preached last sabbath — better than *nobody.*— I saw a Mr. Poriggs (of Massachusetts) from Texas, a few days since, he represents it as *the finest country on which the sun ever shone.* He appeared to be a man of candor, and, as I think, his statements might be relied upon as *true.* The Baptist Convention is to meet in this place on Friday week.— I wonder what is to be done.— Mr. Sage, *"Maximus Pontifex et emperator Mundi,"* the cellebrated *"Astrologer,"* in compliment to my intellectual capacities, has changed my name from the heretofore simple Rufus B. Sage, and proclaimed me *Sir Rufus B. Sage,* Knight of St. Peter's "Key." Thus genius is *honored.* A subject of intense interest has been the conversation of the people of this place for a few weeks past. It was occasioned by the following circumstances: — a young lady of this vicinity (Eliza Allen by name) of interesting attainments, and high respectability, being a member of the Presbyterian Church, with character irreproachable, who had left home last summer, to reside with her aunt in Cincinnatti, who was at the head of a Millinery Establishment, where the young lady has since then been employed, it was her custom to attend a singing school, going just before sunset and returning in the evening, in company with her friends, she being under the watch of the church and the kind instruction of a loving aunt. A villain in the garb of a gentleman, who had two or three weeks before been at her aunt's, and drawn forth in an impertinent conversation some particulars respecting her family and place of residence, called again on the eve of the tragedy about to be related, and enquired for her, of her aunt, and was informed she was then at singing school. he then told her aunt an express had arrived from the young lady's father for her to come immediately home, as one of her brothers lay at the point of death, and as there was a steamboat ready for instant departure he begged of her not to be alarmed should she not return before going home. He then went in pursuit of the young lady, and having found her told her as above related to her aunt with this difference, that the express sent by her father was unwell at one of the city hotels — to him he was requested to conduct her immediately, that he might state to her the particulars. The young lady startled at this narration instantly went with her conductor, who after leading her thro' several sts., stopped at a house in which he told her was the express. She was then shown into a room and requested to sit down until the express who was in an adjoining apartment should be called. She [letter torn]. The villain then went out and as he did, shut the door and locked her in. Now for the first time she suspected treachery. Nor were her suspicions groundless. The inhuman wretch soon returned and offered her personal violence, which was often repeated. In this infernal den she was imprisoned for the space of a fortnight, (her food being brought her by a female friend) when one night (whether by accident or design) the door of her prison was left unlocked, and seizing the opportunity she escaped to her friends, and told *the horrid tale.*

O miserable world! how many monsters there are in the shape of men! — I have just received a letter from Benjamin which pleased me considerable, tell him I shall answer it soon.— The banks in this country have all stopped payment. Money is scarce — I see war advancing with broad and rapid strides from the plaines of Mexico.[18] — Our country has arrived at a critical crisis — Write immediately

RUFUS B. SAGE

MRS. JERUSHA S. GEAR U. MIDDLETOWN CONN.

I wish I could hear from home very soon [on the side of the letter]

[LETTER NO. 7] PARKERSBURG VA. NOV. 5, 1837
TO FRANCES GEAR,

Dear Sister: As you have several times requested me to write you, I now partly to gratify you, and partly as a matter of policy, commence the essay. But before I proceed I will explain myself, as to the policy of the thing, here you have it. I wrote mother some six weeks or two months since, and, by a letter from you to Jerusha, I learn that she has not yet received it; and considering the derangement of government conserns, I have reason to conclude it was intercepted, as in it I wrote an order on Benj. for the amount due me in mother's favor. It *poped* into my head that I could avoid a like recurrence, and smuggle the order to mother by addressing a letter to you. I have just written to Elisha and requested him to give the Postmasters a *blowing up,* for the above detention, and to see that mother hereafter gets her letters within a fortnight after date. I think this will bring affairs to about where they had ought to be. I hope soon to hear that B. & E. have made favorable moves towards a reconciliation of family parties. In the meanwhile I advise you not to be in quite so big a *tue* but use your best endeavors to effect peace — another thing — don't fear my judgment being got the better of by my brothers. I'll keep things straight with them, I understand how to steer full well, I know them well. I've been thro' the mill.

---

[18] The Texan Revolution of the preceding year was far from settled, and an uprising in New Mexico was to occur in the summer of 1837.

— You attend to Abial,[19] and see that you do nothing your self to agrivate present difficulties. Perhaps you think this an unnecessary hint, but I don't, there you see is the difference — Abial is a pretty clever sort of a chap after all, and mother had better followed my advice to rent the farm to him instead of Benj.— I told her, she never would get anything, in the time of it — but was only making trouble for herself — Thus I have proved a true prophet, as she will recollect.— If she had done as I advised, with regard to the farm, Benj. would have had to "clare de coup," which would have been the making of him. He had ought to have "met with the rubbers" as I did, then he would have learned what the world is made of.— But, as it is, I am afraid it will not go well with him "at all 'tall."— He never had ought to have got married — there was yours and mother's error in putting him up to it. I hope experience will prove a lesson to *you,* for mother is too old to learn. Dear Mother, I feel sorry for her, but let her look and see where her *mis-step* was made in the present *hobble.* Mother is somewhat of a *tuegacious* disposition, you know, and, I suppose Benj got a little fretted which is not altogether extraordinary. But — stop — there's Abial — I had ought to make him a few scratches, but I ha'n't room.— I thank him much for the few lines he wrote me, and hope he will favor me with some more the next opportunity — I made out to read them very well, so he need not be afraid on that score.— And again, I *must* write to mother — so if you look out, and are not in a hurry, I'll bid good speed,—

RUFUS B. SAGE.— You'll know who

[Lines added at bottom and along the margin of the letter]: If Elisha and Benj. expect me to go to Michigan at present, they will find themselves mistaken, for I shall not leave a $364 per year berth, to chase the wind.

[19] This apparently is Abial Gear, husband of Frances Sage Gear.

I have left Marietta for Parkersburg, Va. a $364 per year berth,— as foreman [20] good pay, &c. R.B.S.

MRS. FRANCES S. GEAR, UPPER MIDDLETOWN CONN.

[written on margin of first page]: You had better put a stop to the girls getting married or there wont be none left for me soon. R. B. SAGE

[LETTER NO. 8] Nov. 5, 1837

[RUFUS, from Parkersburg, Va., to his Mother. Written on bottom of letter to his sister, Frances Gear.]

DEAREST MOTHER, I have just been writing to Frances; you ask her and see if I ha'nt.— Well, I 'spose I must write you too or else there'll be an "old route."— You complained *bitterly* about my not writing before — I tell you I have wrote and put it in the post-office just one fortnight after the date of Jerusha's first letter home, and if you haint got it yet, it is thro' somebody's fault other than my own — I am sorry you didn't get it, for it contained a *"monstrous sight"* of good advice, together with an order as to Benj.'s note &c.— But, however, I here supply its place, and ask your acceptance of it as a small token of the respect of Rufus to his mother.— This is to certify that I have given to widow Jerusha Sage of Upper Middletown Conn. a certain note of hand, which I hold against Benj'n Sage of the aforesaid place, dated Dec. 18th A.D., 1834, for the sum of $22.50 cts, with interest.—

Said Jerusha Sage is hereby empowered to collect said note, and the interest lawfully accruing therefrom. — Witness my hand &c

PARKERSBURG, VA, NOV. 5, 1837 RUFUS B. SAGE

---

20 Sage was employed as foreman on the only newspaper in Parkersburg, present West Virginia. *See* biographical sketch, Appendix A. The fact that Rev. and Mrs. Hiram Gear, Rufus' brother-in-law and sister, had moved to Newark, Ohio (east of Columbus), may be the reason why Rufus moved to Parkersburg. In a letter of March 2, 1838, to Rufus, his sister Jerusha tells of the great religious revival going on in the Newark region (letter in the Coe Collection).

Jerusha would write you a few words so goodbye and may heaven grant you happiness and content— this from, your ever affectionate son

RUFUS B. SAGE

P.S. As Jerusha has concluded to defer writing till a few days, I improve the remainder of the sheet.— I think my letter to Elisha will cause some movements in the "Coon family."— I received one from him a while since, full of flattery and bright prospects.— But never mind that you rent the farm to Abial, for the present, at least till I come home and set things to rights. It would be a judicious move for Edmund will watch him that he keeps straight in the mean-while.— Tell Frances and A.— to write soon.— Tell her to pick me out a *good, nice, handsome, angel* ready for me; for I am going home to get a wife one of these days,— and mother, if you please, write as soon as you can, and don't be mad because I have talked so plain.—

R. B. SAGE

[LETTER NO. 9]

SAILING DOWN THE OHIO MARCH 18, 1838

DEAR MOTHER It has been longer than the accustomed interim since my last letter to you, for which apparent neglect, I must offer as an excuse my heretofore lacking of time and opportunity.— You will probably be surprised and somewhat at a loss to account for the date *et cetera* of this, but a few attendant explanations will I hope set all things to rights in regard to that matter. Know then that I, in company with a gentleman from Parkersburg, have purchased a vessel and laden the same with a cargo of Ice for the Southern market, each being equal partners in the profits or losses resulting therefrom. This, according to authentic information is the most profitable article transported from the North! if we meet with good success in the disposal thereof, we shall, at a moderate estimate, clear some $6 or 700 each. Our cargo was taken in at Parkersburg, the labor upon which, and incident expenses amounted to something like $125.— Thus you perceive I have an opportunity to ice a vast portion of the Union, gratifying my thirst for travelling, & adding (if smiled upon by a benificent Providence, who has ever watched over my path, protected me in my wanderings, and guided me by his own right hand, and heretofore prospered me, ignorant and young, inexperienced and unthinking, a stranger in a strange land) profit to pleasure. The country lying upon either side the Ohio is truly charming and delightful, exceedingly fertile and thickly populated. Indeed so much so that it far exceeds any idea I had previously entertained. The Towns and villiages, are numerous and beautiful, and many of great commercial importance. Cincinnati is, in my opinion, justly worthy of her title "Queen of the West."—While a multitude of other places, like Jonah's Gourd, the growth of a day and a night, are rapidly assuming the attitude of distinction for business, enterprise and wealth, and will, in all probability, soon take the lead of many eastern cities now their seigniors by hundreds of years.— But time and space induce a change of the subject. I was in Marietta on the 8th inst. found all well,— Hiram had just received a letter from Abial bearing word from you, & Francis.— I hope she will not be visited by a course of sickness.— Caution her to take care of her health, and tell Henry to be a good boy, and his father that he must trounce him whenever it is needed. I am happy to hear of so many revivals at the East, and pray that they may extend even to the West, for here I assure you they are needed. Here vice and irreligion are almost everywhere predominant and the followers of Jesus comparatively *few*.— I received a letter from Henry White three or four weeks since, and shall answer it the first opportunity. He seems to be in good spirits, and I hope he will do well. If any of our folks chance to see him soon, let him be informed where I am and what about. At the same time with the reception of Henry's letter, I received one from Cousin Martha Sage, of Fredonia, N.Y. in which was stated that she was to be united in *Hymen's silken bands,* to a young silversmith of the above place, in the course of a month.— All were well. — But I must draw to a close,— We are now within about 30 miles of Louisville Ky.— All is well, and be assured that I *shall try* to do as well as in me lies, wherever I am, or whatever my fortune here below. from your affectionate son

MRS. JERUSHA SAGE RUFUS B. SAGE

[LETTER NO. 10]

FORT GIBSON,[21] CLAIBORNE CO. MISS.
SATURDAY, APRIL 27th 1838

DEAR MOTHER: I arrived at this place a few days since and improve this first opportunity to write you. I should have written before but put it off on account of the attendant inconvenience. We intend retaking out our load at this place — in which case my share will stand me in $2,000 clear from all expenses.— This will detain us here 8 or 10 weeks — till the last of June. This I think we can do with perfect safety as to health. But I dread the idea of being so long in a Southern climate. It does not seem like home. Yet the country is pleasant and delightful in these parts and, in fact, truely charming. It is sufficiently broken to render it healthy, and for the South cool and celubrious. The landscape is amply diversified with hills and dales, brooks and rivers, to generate poetic aspirations and become a favorite retreat of the Muses. Oh, it is certainly enjoyment at the voluntary hints of inclination, to perambulate the woods, contemplate the beauties of nature, and indulge in the celestial flights of imagina-

[21] About twenty-five miles below Vicksburg.

tion, soaring aloft through the immense regions of etherial space, in rapturous delight to comingle with the shining multitudes which surround the Eternal throne, and hold sweet converse with nature's God. My heart swells with emotion — my soul bounds with delight, as I recall to mind those dulcet hours of pleasure which, when alone, retired from the noise and bustle of business, I have spent in the contemplation of nature, and in meditating upon the mighty works of him, whose existence is from Everlasting to Everlasting.— Yes, I love to be alone — I love to revolve the scenes I have passed through, when God by his Providence had favored me in every necessity. I aver it becomes a creature to be grateful, it surely becomes me.— But, O, the human heart — its hardness — its want of feeling! — I cannot feel the debt I owe — I cannot feel that burning flame of love which it becomes me to possess toward that being whose goodness has followed me all the days of my life — whose guardian kindness has protected me and guided me in all the way in which I have went — How can it be otherwise than that I should try to love and adore his goodness, and by trying I hope to love him more — that I ever may keep him before me as the great object of my affections. Although still ignorant of human nature, I have seen considerable of man and of different characters, I have contemplated him submerged in temporal pleasures and sensual voluptuousness — I have viewed him in the career of crime and watched his onward progress — I have studied into the sentiments and feelings of the profane swearer and person of low habits — I have meditated upon the steady increase of devotion, and analyzed the more frequent and growing libations of votairs to the shrine of Bachus,— I have considered the moralist in every corner and observed excess and searched into his feeling and motives,— self-love and self-interest bedim the brightest ray of the sun of morality.— I have volved, revolved, & re-revolved all these diversities in their diferent and important bearings, and find both by observation and experience that the path of virtue duty is the only road to the pleasure here and happiness hereafter.— Yes, I can retire to the woods as did (if I mistake not) Apollo of yore, view and contemplate the same vision that he saw. The story is this: — When young he was very anxious as to what course it became him to pursue in after life, with this subject in mind he one day retired to a grove and seated himself beneath a tree, where he fell into a trance. A personage of heavenly aspect stood by his side, and enquired what pressed so heavily on his mind.— He replied, the course of life wisdom would dictate me in future to pursue. Look to the left, replied the vision.— He looked and saw a path broad and pleasant to view — green and shady was the ground — the wayside was bedecked with flowers of the most beautiful and diverse collors — in it immense crowds were passing on and all seemed gay and happy.— At the entrance stood a female form of bewitching beauty, urging and enticing listeners to travel her path. She said her name was Pleasure and her road the way of happiness. Seeest thou this, asked the vision.— Yes, this surely must be the road of pleasure and happiness — I will enquire for you of the old man yonder as to that before you look further. He has travelled this road for many years & can answer from experience.— Say, traveller, tell us your experience in travelling this path.— Why, I started in it believing it the road of happiness, and everything seemed to invite on to enjoyment.— The glorious form of Happiness was before me, and the appearance already within my grasp,— but to the weary the green grass becomes as thorns, and those beautiful flowers exhale an envenomed perfume which causes a sickening atmosphere. Yet look, the form of happiness is nearer and brighter than before. I will pursue and hope ere long to attain the summit of my wishes, good bye.— then with eager haste he joined the throng in the pursuit.— But want of room prohibits the remainder, which I promise in my next.

Requesting you to write, that I may receive a letter upon my arrival at Marietta I remain as ever yours

RUFUS B. SAGE

MRS. JERUSHA SAGE

[LETTER NO. 11] MARIETTA AUG. 21, 1838

DEAR MOTHER I returned to Marietta from my trip South, three weeks since. I should have written before; but not being in a writing humor, I have sent papers as a substitute for letters. I did not hear one word from home or from Marietta during the five months that I was absent and as you may well suppose had become extremely solicitous to hear. About a fortnight before my return Jerusha caused to be transmitted to Cincinnati, a letter from you, to me, but upon calling at the P.O. there was none for me, thus it was missed. I have been informed as to the contents.— I have been somewhat unfortunate in a pecuniary point of view, and shall consequently transfer my intention of returning East, for some time yet.[22] I shall continue working at my trade till then,— Let Abial manage the farm and keep things together at home as well as he can.— Postpone the idea of selling the farm for the present. I like the western country very well, but perhaps you might not.— I am glad Benj'n has gone West, he may do well yet. Wages are good here.— By the by in my last letter to you written while in Mississippi, I commenced a story and promised the remainder in my next.— It has been so long since, I have almost forgotten were abouts

[22] What happened to spoil the bright financial prospects alluded to in his previous letter is not revealed. In the biographical sketch, reprinted in Appendix A, it is merely reported that the venture with the boat of ice "resulted in a money loss."

I left off, but guessing at the place I will resume and scribble the remainder in brief.— Look yet again, said the vision.— he looked, and behold the crowd still rushed on in the way of pleasure with blind precipitancy, regardless of all but the phantom of their pursuit, till at last a tremendous precipice intercepting the path, and unable to stop their course, over it they plunged headlong and were swallowed up in the Gulf of Oblivion which fearfully yawned beneath.—"What thinkest thou of their end?"— Truely the end of pleasure is real pain,—"View now the opposite course, this is the path of Virtue!" Again he looked. The road at first appeared rough and rugged, difficult & uninviting; obsticles appeared numerous, & discouragements many: — but advancing onward, the road grew smoother, the difficulties began to lessen, while contentment & inward satisfaction beamed from the Countenance of the way-faring — Their destination was for the temple of happiness which was situated upon a hill at the end of the way — Their enjoyment increased as they progressed onward, till at length, having ascended the hill, they reclined in the bowers of bliss. "Hast thou beheld this asked the vision.— Yea, truly,— I am convinced that the path of Virtue is the only way to true Pleasure and Happiness.— The falling of a tree then disturbed his repose & forthwith the vision disappeared,— Appolo resolved henceforth to pursue the path of virtue. — But the story being now finished, a change of subject is necessary to fill out my letter.— I was offered $75 per month to work at my trade while at the South, working a while in Louisville, Ky. I got $10 per week, — should have stayed there longer, but pay was not so ready as might have been. Aunt Sophira & Uncle Woodruff are to move to this place next month according as they wrote to Jerusha,— they are well.— Jerusha is at present somewhat unwell, I hope she will soon be better, other than that, we are all well here. I don't know how long I shall continue in this place. But wherever I may be, it shall be my endeavor to do the best I can. I wish I could hear from the youngsters in U.M. — Please write as soon as this is received, meanwhile believe me as ever your affectionate son

RUFUS B. SAGE

P.S. My health continues to be good, never better.

P.S. again.— I re-open my letter to announce the important intelligence that Jerusha has presented her husband with another responsibility in the shape of a *little darter*.— All doing well. R. B. SAGE

[LETTER NO. 12]

CIRCLEVILLE[23] PICKAWAY CO. SEPT 12. 1838

DEAR MOTHER, BROTHERS, SISTERS, GRAND-MOTHERS, UNCLES, AUNTS — COUSINS, FRIENDS AND EVERYBODY THAT EVER SAW ME: —

GREETINGS: — Two long years having now nearly elapsed since I bid adieu the scenes of my childhood and early days and started lonely and sorrowful on my long journey to the distant west, to which I had long previous resolved to go, and thinking you would be interested in the perusal of a brief account of my adventures since then in detail, I concluded to inscribe to you this my first general Epistle.— The memory of home, however humble, wherever situated, produces sensations of pleasure sweet and abiding, never to be eradicated. It calls into existence a thousand recollections of the past, of scenes of different character, pleasing and instructing to reflect upon. There is a charm in the very name; —"Home, sweet home, there is no place like home."— a man of feeling can seldom leave home but with regret. The man who loves his home is worthy of respect, for it,— 'tis the worthless and degenerate, in

[23] About twenty miles south of Columbus, Ohio. Here Rufus worked on the newspaper and became a prominent person in the community.

most cases, who care nothing of, or hate the reminiscense of home, who the furtherest from it, are the better pleased,— Not so with me,— while thought and feeling retained, thy remembrance, dear home, ever shall remain. It was with the greatest reluctance as I took the parting view that I turned my face to leave both it and my native land. Painful indeed was the struggle with my feelings, which recollection revives in all its freshness. A subsequent recurrence to that time gave birth to the following lines: —

Oh land of the Pilgrims! my own native land,
And verdant Connecticut, thou,
Engrav'd on my memory, ever shalt stand
Beloved and remembered as now

Thou home of my childhood and my blooming years
Where joys and where sorrows befell,
How could I restrain my fast flowing tears
As I sorrowing bid thee farewell.

Upon thy grassy banks, sweet river, I stray'd,
While I mus'd in the bland zyphur's breath,
To hear the sweet music thy silver waves play'd
Then to me seemed the knel-tone of death.

Sad feelings usurp'd dominion o'er me,
From the depths of my bosom I sigh'd
As I mus'd and revolv'd the self-form'd decree,
Thee to leave and the land of my pride.

Unthinking I spoke, (and the echos return'd
Repeating each word as I said
While the wind whistled long, and the willows they moan'd
As they gracefully wav'd o'er my head.)

"Native land! dearly loved! — How can I depart,
Far hence, so far distant from view
And leave thee, alas! thus dear to my heart,
So sadly to bid thee adieu?

Ah, yes, I must leave thee, beloved, I must,
  Fate calls me to leave my dear home;
By her stearn decree from thy side I am thrust,
  A stranger and lonely to roam.

Fate must be obeyed, tho' ignorant I
  Of what may befall me below,
Yet I trust to his care who ruleth the sky,
  Then why should I linger to go?

Say, river, sweet minstrel, why mournfully thus!
  And why should thy waters thus mourn?
Why, pray thee, these shrill notes so deathlike rehearse
  As if I should never return?—

And ye pretty willows, why weeping are ye,
  As if for the loss of a friend
Fate willing, again these groves I shall see,
  And you from the sun's heat defend!

Relations, and friends, so dear and so kind,
  And country remembered are you,
As I go from my home, and leave you behind
  Reluctant, I bid you adieu.

Well to commence my narrative:—All the things I took with me, on leaving, I stowed into a valiece, and all my money into a wallet, amounting only to $22.50 cts to bear the expenses of a journey of 1300 miles. Mournfully, I traced my way to Middletown, and embarked on board steamboat for New York, where I arrived the next morning after leaving. Here I made several calls, and then proceeded to the foot of Cortlandt st., where I took the steamer Swift-sure for Albany.— I did not feel in the humor to enjoy much the new scenes presented to my view, but however, I formed the idea that the Hudson was truly a most majestic stream, which, although I have since seen many larger, is not yet fully eradicated.— I was in no ways disposed to gain acquaintence on board, and therefore spent most of my time brooding over my own thoughts, thus loosing a favorable opportunity for the study of men and manners. The fact was, I knew so much I had forgotten how to improve,— were this not the case it would have been otherwise, for travelling is a fine school.— I arrived in Albany, the second day from New York,— Albany is too well known to need a description here, so I pass.— Leaving immediately, I took the tow path of the Erie Canal, and proceeded 24 miles on foot, when it getting late and I, being tired, stoped to await the arrival of a boat: one soon coming, I jumped on board to enjoy the pleasures of canal travelling.— On entering the cabin, I found the only passengers to consist of myself, an elderly lady, and her daughter,— at first I was rather bashful, as is always the case when in presence of the ladies, but soon getting into conversation I became acquainted and time passed off very pleasantly. The young lady was a beautiful girl of 18, interesting and intelligent; — the mother gave out several hints that she would not be unwilling to see her daughter settled in life by marriage, and I had vanity enough to suppose that she would not object to such an arrangement being brought about through me: — she was very urgent that I should take up my residence in Cannajoharrie, where she lived. The young lady herself would be sure I should call if I ever should come near that place, asserting it would be her pleasure to see me. — I like to chat with a pretty girl, 'tis then time seems as not.— How sweetly pass the hours,— a day is as a moment quickly gone! — Twas thus two days sped by. It was near one o'clock on the morning of the third that we reached Cannajoharrie, where, after accompanying them to their residence, I took leave of mother and daughter. That day to me was lonesome, long & dreary were the hours and joyously they lingered on; my feelings were those of melancholly. Confinement on a canal boat, is no ways agreeable to a naturally roving, restless, disposition fond of novelty. There is too much sameness, which makes time without company doubly tedious. Thus passed that day. Toward night, however, by recruiting our number amounted to four with myself, — but I was alone in the gentlemen's cabin. Late in the evening, as our boat was laying by at Syracruse, being very sleepy, I pulled off my coat and folding it up deposited it on a stool beside my berth; then throwing myself upon my cot was quickly transported into the region of sweet unconsciousness. Phoebus had rose resplendent o'er the eastern hills, ere drowsy Morpheus left my frame, and bustle bade me rise; — I then arose, and looking for my coat — 'twas gone, no trace of it remained, and search to find it proved no good. What should I do? A coat I sure must have.— A clothing store was near by, so I went and purchased a substitute for $13.50 cts, which reduced my purse to 2 dols. 75 cts. — Want stood grinning at me, friends, at a distance, and work not near; — but as it happened my passage to Rochester had been previously paid, so I went on with the boat. I strove to banish my bad feelings by conversation and in a measure succeeded. Chit-chat was the introduction to the relation of stories, and listening smoothed the rough current of wearisome hours, Chit-chat is the organ of information, it always brings forward something new or something interesting. An incident was here related which I transcribe. I have it from a person acquainted with the individuals concerned who declared it strictly true: — It was as follows: — A young lady had received for some time the addresses of one of the opposite sex and a mutual regard for each other had ripened into a matrimonial engagement. This state of affairs upon being disclosed to her parents met with their decided disapprobation; they utterly opposed anything of the kind. they forbid her lover from ever again coming near their house, and our heroine from speaking to him more. This arrangement seemed to have the desired effect. The young man had left that part of the state for a place to them unknown. But the daughter was sorrowful and dejected, and was frequently heard to say: "I'll be revenged for this!" This continued for an interval of some two or three weeks, when one morning early she was nowhere to be found. Search for her proved vain. And for two long years not one sylable could be learned as to her fate, or what had become of her, although inquiry followed inquiry and search followed search — long and continued. Her parents had given up the hope of ever seeing her again, and were almost distracted on her account.— They reproached themselves that by their opposition they had been the occasion of all this: — remembering her threats, they feared she had put an end to her own existence.Bitter and keen were their relentings for their harshness.— but still her fate continued involved in mystery. Her story, as afterwards made known was this: she had formed her plan of revenge, and had made the necessary preparations for effecting it unknown to any but herself. She cut her hair short and taking the clothes of one of her brothers, who was absent, she dressed herself in the costume of a young lad and started off for the canal which she reached at Utica; here she hired herself out to the captain of a boat as a driver of the horses, & for the term of one year. No one suspected her sex, so completely had she altered her appearance and changed her voice. During this time she frequently saw her father passing in his steamboat, and making inquiries for her.— The next year she engaged for the same length of time, nor was her sex known till near the close of it. One stormy night after taking her turn at driving the horses, another came to take her place, and, as she dismounted he caught hold of her in a playful manner, and in the act tore open her vest, leaving her bosom exposed, unbeknown to her.— In this condition she went into the cabin. In a joking way one present spoke: —"Well, I declare, you must be a girl!"— Upon this, overwhelmed with — [?] and thinking the secret known; she acknowledged herself as such, and told the whole story, about leaving her parents.— As it happened, an individual was acquainted with her father, and had heard of the singular manner in which she left.— They arrived in the neighborhood where her father lived, in the morning; and this person went and informed him of the singular discovery of his long lost daughter. Upon this information he came and took her home, and soon the scurfy canal driver was transformed into a beautiful young lady. And was received by her parents as one risen from the dead. Shortly before, her former lover had returned, and now renewed his visits. In the course of two months she became the happy bride of him of her choice, being satisfied with the ample vengeance she had taken.— Thus we whiled away the time. We had one passenger on board who was a sailor; he amused us much with his oddities and long sea-stories. He was a real jovial son of the ocean, and withal a man of good sense.— Joking, chating, with the ladies, or talking politics, or any thing to pass away time on a canal boat, is acceptable.— On the morning of the third day from Syracruise we were obliged to stop on account of the canal having broke away a few miles ahead. This would detain us some two or three days before we could proceed. I concluded to start on foot, and received a part of my money paid for my passage back again, which increased my stock 1$. With this I took my valliece and departed. I reached Rochester that night, it being a much shorter route by road than by canal. Rochester is a flourishing city, beautifully situated on the Gennisee River, and is a place of great business. Its main street, for stir and bustle, much resembles Broadway, New York City.

The Gennisee Falls afford conveniences for mills and numerous manufacturing establishments; they are considered as quite a curiosity. It was here that the famous Sam Patch, after leaping down the falls of Niagara, and performing various other wonderful feats, made his last and fatal spring, and ended his exploits with his life. Rochester has a population of some 20,000.— The next day I took the Buffalo Road for the latter place, passing through several towns, the names of Churchville, and Batavia are the only ones my memory has retained.— Batavia may be called a truly handsome place. It is laid out on an even plain in a regular manner. On the west side it [is] washed by a small river, the name of which I have forgotten. This place was rendered famous, in 1836 as the theatre of warlike preparations and enactments, occasioned by the extortions of those at the head of the land offices instituted by what is called the "Holland Purchase." The animosity of the people was directed towards them, and a rising for demolishing all these offices was the consequence, first to commence in this place. Their object would have been effected had the building not been guarded by cannon previously mounted for its defense. A great excitement still existed in these parts.— Nothing occurred further, worthy of notice till I arrived at Buffalo. This place, situated at head of the Lake navigation, is of great commercial importance, and is too well known to need description. My intention. Leaving this place, nothing occurred further, worthy of note, till I arrived in the neighborhood of Buffalo; about two miles past from which is a Swiss Settlement. This people have many peculiarities. It was curious to me to see the women hobbling about in their wooden shoes, driving a team, or at work in the field. In one field I saw six old women digging potatoes, and three girls behind them picking them up,— the way they made the potatoes rattle was worth seeing.— not a man near. In another field was a woman digging, and her daughter, a beautiful girl of sixteen or eighteen, picking them up, and a man leaning on the fence talking with her.— This was too much for me; addressing him I exclaimed —"Why not take hold, my good fellow and help them!"—"O, they are doing well enough!" was his careless reply.

(Continued in my next.)[24]

I am at present in Circleville, Pickaway Co. Ohio. My prospects are very fair.— The people are kind, and I enjoy myself much,— I am boarding with a minister of the United Brethren Church, the Rev. Wm. Rhinehart.— The Presbyterian minister of this place, Rev. F. Putnam I esteem much.— The Lord is my protector, I am willing to trust to him at all times, knowing that he will do all things well,—(This is Nov. 29th,) I have now been here nearly 12 weeks.— In two weeks from this I have engaged to work as foreman in the Office of the Scioto Watchman, a weekly paper printed in this place,— $360, good wages — If I am not disappointed, this will be a snug berth for me.— The editor is a rich old farmer, said to be worth from $30, to 50,000 dols.— I have not received one word from home since last winter, while in Parkersburg, Va.— You may well suppose I am anxious to hear.— Two weeks since, I got a letter from Jerusha,— all well, and one from Henry White.— In a couple of years, if the Lord is willing, I shall be at home.— Meanwhile, may He, from whom nothing is hid, preserve our lives, and keep us safe from the evil which is in the world, with consciences void of offence both towards God and towards man, (Thus far the Lord hath led me on.)

Yours, with fond esteem

RUFUS B. SAGE

Jerusha Sage, et caetra

[24] The story is continued in Letter No. 13.

[LETTER NO. 13] CIRCLEVILLE APRIL 25th, 1839

DEAR MOTHER, BROTHERS, SISTERS,
RELATIONS, & FRIENDS: —

One long year has elapsed, and I have but, a few weeks since, received one letter from home, during that time. Although it has so happened, you are not to be blamed, (or, at least, Mother,) for as I have learned, several were written to me, if I did not receive them; thus I am in duty bound to exonerate you from the charge of wilful negligence, which I had several times been tempted to make.— I am verily happy to hear that things are getting along so well at home; but likewise proportionably sorrowful that my dear mother is not in the enjoyment of good health. The arrangement she has made with her property, meets with my approbation.— As for myself, I am, by the mercy of God, healthy, happy, & contented. I may continue in this place some length of time. My wages are $7 per week. — I received a letter from Jerusha, a short time since, —they are well. In accordance with her request, as well as at the suggestions of my own feelings, I shall in my next letter (providence permitting) in five or six weeks from this time, remit to my mother, a mite in the pecuniary line; meanwhile I hope to receive an answer to this, containing all the news in and about the place of my nativity: — concerning the girls and boys, young folks and old folks, in detail.— In compliance with a request to that effect, I am induced to continue the narration commenced in my last, to which I have given the Sir-name of

ADVENTURES IN THE WEST

Buffalo is handsomely situated at the out-let of Lake Erie, and is the principal emporium of North-western commerce. Though occupying a low, level, and, in some parts, swampy site, it is, notwithstanding, in a very flourishing condition. The lowness of its situation subjects it to occasional inundating from the Lake, particularly during strong westernly winds, of several days continuance; sometimes accompanying immense loss of property. The Eastern part of the city, being more elevated, is an exception from these last remarks.

In the last war between Great Britain, and the United States, the then village of Buffalo was the scene of various military operations; at which time it was burnt to the ground by the former power in connection with the Indians, but it has rapidly recovered, and now almost incredibly outstrips any thing that can be offered in comparison with what it once was; its population being near 25,000. Buffalo possesses an air peculiarly foreign: — proceed to the Lake, the theatre of business, stir, and bustle, and there you will hear as many different languages spoken and see almost as many diverse people, as ancient Rome could boast of within her walls, while she was the metropolis of the known world. There your ears are saluted with the Indian gibberish, the various dialects of the German, French, Italian, Spanish, Welch, Scotch, Irish, and English languages; and you will perceive in striking contrast the manners and customs of those different nations. This place bids fair to become one of the greatest and most important cities of the north.

Being unable to obtain employment at this place I left early the next morning on foot and took the Lake road for Westfield, at which place an Uncle and Aunt of mine resided,— a distance of 60 miles from Buffalo. Previous to this, however, I had purchased a cake of gingerbread for my breakfast, which had reduced my small stock of money to the trifling sum of 37½ cts, to defray the expenses of the long journey before me. I had not proceeded more than half a mile on my way, eating my gingerbread as I went along, till I fell in company with a young man who was in a somewhat similiar condition with myself; having served on the canal the past season, as a driver, he had been cheated out of all his wages by his employer, who had ran away; he was on his way to his parents, who resided about thirty miles distant; his funds had become exhausted, nor had he wherewith to procure even a morning's repast; so I gave him one half of my own, thankful that it was in my power to bestow so small a favor upon a needy fellow creature.

We continued together for some miles before taking leave of each other, and mutually resolved and promised that to however straightened circumstances fortune might reduce us, we would ever conduct ourselves in an honest and upright manner; and then, with many good wishes for each other's good, we parted.

I pursued my way, musing upon the various contingencies to which mankind are subject in their chequered course thro' life; one is elevated by fortune's favors, another is brought low by her frowns. Sometimes a seeming misfortune is productive of the greatest advancement of one's interest; while on the other hand, apparent good fortune may be the occasion of its greatest detriment. On this account it is always best to cherish a due mediocrity of temperament in regard to either the one or the other.— There is sweet consolation in the belief, which it becomes each one to cherish, that, if we endeavor to do our duty, all things will ultimately work together for our good; therefore, the maxim of our Savior to one, in such case, is beautifully applicable, "Care not for the morrow; but let the morrow take care for the things of itself; sufficient unto the day is the evil thereof." I for one am willing to take the world as it comes.

The portion of country bordering on Lake Erie is level and clayey, and the scenery from the lake shore is beautiful. In a clear placid day, hundreds of vessels and steamboats of various sizes are to be seen; their merry canvass spread and fluttering in the breeze, while foaming surges gaily dance, and onward press their sudden steps, and lash the sounding shore with nature's melody. I defy any sensible man to traverse the shores of this inland sea without feeling something of the spirit of poetry. Things as they are here possesses too many beauties not to attract some attention, not to enliven the imagination in some degree.

I was three days on my route when I reached a place called Freedonia, where, by accident, I learned that an uncle, on my father's side, resided there, whom I accordingly visited, and spent a couple of days with him. Here I found several cousins, of whose existence I had before received no intimation. They were all well, and apparently glad to see one of their relatives from the "land of steady habits." At this town I obtained employment at the office of the Fredonia Censor, where I continued for a week or ten days.

During this time I boarded with a lady by the name of Moore; at which place I found fellow boarders of various religions, professions, and principles, from the atheist down to the humble follower of Jesus. There was a young man by the name of Sherman, and apparently quite an intelligent person, who had, according to his own words adopted the belief that this life is all that pertains to man, that death is an eternal sleep, that the human race is but circumstantially superior to the brute creation, that there is no God, that the Bible is the fabrication of man, that Jesus Christ was as much of an imposter as Mahomet. He even attempted to sustain his baseless theory by reason and argument, and in order to prove that the bible was false, he pretended to point its inconsistencies, stating that its system of morality was unequal and unjust, and its requisitions absurd and rediculous: for instances, he referred to the passage where it says "If any man take away thy coat, let him take thy cloak also." What, he asked, is the justice or equity in this, if a man steal your coat, to chase after the thief and give him your cloak? or what is the use, if a man asks you to go a mile, to go with him two? or what sense in the act, if a man strike thee on the one cheek, to turn to him the other? He then endeavored to point out its inconsistencies and contradictions, and argued that the testimony of no person on any case in a court of jurisprudence, would be received as truth, that was contradictory in itself: he then asks, why should the bible be received as authentic, when different portions are so at varience with each other?—These various objections I tried to answer as well as I could, and, as I think, succceded in that endeavor.—Here I became acquainted with a young man by the name of Stork; he seemed to be a man of good principles, and being endowed with no small mental capacities, he was quite an agreeable person. He disclosed to me a small item of his history, somewhat in the following manner: he was born of poor parents, and all the knowledge he was master of, he obtained by his own exertions. By the death of both father and mother, when he was quite young, he had been thrown upon his own responsibilities, and was compelled to steer his course lonely and unprotected thro' this cold and unfriendly world. Experiencing at one time smiles of fortune, and at another time her frowns, he became inured to her sportive frivolity, without being affected by either. The golden rule was director of his conduct, and the bible the man of his council. Honesty swayed his intercourse with man, and integrity dictated the words of his mouth.—For two or three years previous to this coming detail he had served in the capacity of a school teacher. The last quarter he had taught in the village of Leadi, N.Y., where he was introduced, one evening, at his boarding house, to a young woman, on whom he afterwards called, several times, at her father's house. It so happened that a fellow by the name of Smith was paying his addresses to her. Possessed of no sound principles, and influenced by no sense of honor, he was base enough to attempt and reckless enough to accomplish her seduction, and then, to cap the climax of his vile conduct, he left her, whom he had so cruelly treated, in prospect of her soon becoming a mother, and crossed into Canada to avoid the consequences.— Thus circumstanced, at the instigation of her parents, our heroine was induced to swear Mr. Stork the father of her child. This, as you may well suppose, took friend Stork with the greatest surprise; but as he possessed no means of proving to the contrary, the court pronounced him guilty, and sentenced him to marry the girl, or pay the amount adjudged, to the support of the child.— He refused to do either; and declared that, "rather than submit to this sentence, I will be imprisoned! I will see my body rot and crumble away,— by piece-meals! — while I amuse myself by watching the ants as they bear off even the last fragments of my corporial frame, thro' the key-hole of the door of my gloomy dungeon! and hear the insects sing their requiems to my ashes! before I will conform to it!" Accordingly he was thrust into jail, where he remained in confinement one year. Meanwhile by means of his friends he procured Gibson's *System of Surveying,* and by dint of intense application became master of the art. Upon his release, he began its practice which is his present employment. I asked him what had become of the unfortunate girl who had occasioned him so much trouble. He said he had recently seen her, in Buffalo, as he was passing thro the street of a certain quarter, upon business, standing in the door of a house of ill fame; and, said he, "I pitied her condition, as I hurried past in silence."— I sighed in reply, and involuntarily exclaimed "alas! how often doth the heartless and unfeeling conduct of man, prove the ruin, temporal and eternal, of innocent and virtuous females, and plunge them into the vortex of degredation and misery!"— I re-visited my uncle's on Sunday, and also attended a meeting of the "Christians." They differ from the Unitarians only in respect to baptism,— immersion they believe the only true mode of administering that ordinance.— The next day I got one of my cousins, Martha S.— to mend a rent in my pantaloons, which had been received by a fall upon the ground,— My pantaloons had been made tight, with straps, which were buckled around my foot, and by a sudden fall upon my hands and knees, and there being nothing to yield, of course they were torn half in two across the knee joint.— While they were in process of mending, several jokes were passed in reference to the peculiarities of the fashions and the inconveniences resulting therefrom.— Among other things, a story of this sort was related by cousin Martha, one evening she was invited and did attend an apple-pareing *bee,* where was collected a number of young gentlemen and ladies, who as is customary on such occasions, spent the time more in sport and amusement, than in attention to business. Here they lingered till a late hour of the night; and in the interim a young chap who was related to the woman of the house, being inordinately full of life and fun; in performing an *astonishing* feat of agility, by jumping over a chair, as he thought, to the surprise and admiration of those present, he met with a sad disaster in the bursting of his pantaloons, at a part, which he would rather preferred to have remained entire.— As he intended to accompany some one of the ladies home, he was not thus to be thwarted in his designs, not withstanding the reiterated peals of laughter, joined in by all, at his expense. He, accordingly, went and deposed himself in bed, and sent his pants down to the ladies, with a request that they should be mended. This was what none were willing to refuse to comply with, although no one was over anxious for the job. The result was they were mended, and he had the pleasure of escorting his lady to her residence.— So you see a person should not give up for trifles! — (Answer this immediately, for I am over anxious to hear from home, yours affectionately,

RUFUS B. SAGE

[LETTER NO. 14] CIRCLEVILLE JULY 11th 1839

DEAR MOTHER: — By the reception of your last, I am placed under the pleasing obligation of answering it, which I gladly embrace this opportunity to discharge. I should have performed this long before, had not the multiplicity of other cares and duties prevented. Even at the present instant my time is so stinted that I cannot continue the narrative I proposed to write, and must, therefore, necessarily postpone the same till my next. My health, has been remarkably good ever since my return from the South, and, indeed ever since my arrival in the West.— I hope, by the blessing of him, in whose hands are the dispensations of life and health, that this inestimable boon may be continued to me till my return to my native land. I feel that I have much, very much, to be thankful for; and that I never can discharge the debt of gratitude incurred to the great Father of all.— You wrote me that you were in no particular want of money for yourself, and proposed that I should advance $200.00 to meet the mortgage on the place.— This proposition, it is not impossible but that I may comply with; — still let not this derange any calculations you may have previously formed. Life is uncertain, and subjected to many changes and vicissitudes; consequently all things temporal are shrouded in uncertainty.— We can place no sure dependence upon any thing.— I hope that in the course of a year or so, that I shall be able to visit home in much better circumstances than when I left. But still I like Ohio well.— I am doing very well here at present, and enjoy myself much better than could be expected.— Thro' my exertions, principally, there has been a Society established in this place, called *La Sociēte des Dēbats,* or the Society of Debates, which is now in a very flourishing condition. We hold our meetings once a week and have sometimes very interesting and animating discussions.— I find it a prolific source of improvement.— I have got so that I can speak in public quite well.— Although I have not been here a great while, yet I am universally known about town; it is Mr. Sage, & Mr. Sage! even by persons not known by me from Adam. And, by the bye, not boastingly, I am treated with much respect.— The season, thus far, has been quite healthy, and favorable to the growth of the various crops. Wheat will yield an abundant harvest.— Corn and potatoes are in a very flourishing condition, and should we have rain soon, the farmers will be richly repaid for all their toils.— We had a very fine time here on July 4th, I wrote a song which was sung on the occasion, which I send you published in this day's paper.[25] You see, I have got to be quite an author, and some of my writings are being re-published, as you perceive by the *Religious Telescope,* which I likewise send you.— I wish you would send me papers occasionally, and write soon,— I shall shortly write you a long letter in continuation of my narrative.— If you are in need of some small pecuniary favors, let me know and I will endeavor to supply you.— I heard from Jerusha some short time since, she is well, and complains of your not writing to her.— But I must close, So wishing you the enjoyment of life, health, prosperity, and every needed blessing, and praying of a kind Providence to protect us all, I remain

Your affectionate son, RUFUS B. SAGE

MRS. JERUSHA SAGE

[25] This is reproduced as Appendix C.

[LETTER NO. 15] MARIETTA, NOV. 8th, 1839

DEAR MOTHER, etc: When I last wrote you, I promised a continuation, in my next text, of my "adventures in the west," hoping in the interim to receive a letter from home. But in this, I have been disappointed. No letter has made its appearance, and no intelligence from you has been received, by me, save a single newspaper, on whose margin were traced the words *"all well."* This was no small gratification, for even a paper from Old Connecticut, is a rich treat.—As it is now some 2 or 3 months, since my last, and knowing that you are anxious to hear from me,— having at the present time a little leasure, my love of home and esteem for relations and friends, constrain me catch up the epistolary pen, and communicate, upon paper, with those, between whom and me, many intervening miles mark the separation line. I left Circleville for this place (Marietta) last week, and shall leave here, if nothing prevents, for Columbus in about 3 weeks.— All are well here.— Little Jerusha has got to be quite a girl.— My wages for this winter will be $10.00 per week.— You inquired in your last when I thought of returning.— In reply, I cannot tell. Probably in a year and a half, (if Providence permits).— As for raising $200.00 to pay up the mortgage on the place, I will not promise,— yet it may be that I will.— My health has been uniformly good, since I have been in this country.— You must excuse my not adding further, while I resume my narrative where I left off.—

Nothing further occured worthy of note while there. The next day I returned to Fredonia, and in a few days left that place to resume my journey westward, having replenished my purse with $5 or $6, as the result of my labor. Taking the Lake road for Ashtabula, I travelled on foot a day or two, when meeting a man going along the same road with a wagon & team, I bargained for a passage to my place of destination. Thither we arrived in the course of two days. Passing through the northern extremity of Pennsylvania, on the way, we had occasion to stop at a house to purchase oats for our horses; — on entering I found an old woman and three daughters; they inquired where I was from. I replied "from Connecticut." "From Connecticut! — are you from Connecticut! — Do tell, what part!" "Middletown, Middlesex Co." "Oh dear, it has been this 12 years since I've seen the old county of Windham, and very near as long since I've seen any body from there.— Oh, I do wish I could see it once more before I die." "It would undoubtedly be a great satisfaction to you." "Yes, it would really; and only those in like circumstances can know and feel how much of a satisfaction it would be.— I love the name of Connecticut, and any one from there seems to me like a brother or a sister!" — In Ashtabula I found some acquaintances, with whom I spent a day or so. Leaving that place, I proceeded on foot, and passing thro' Warren, arrived at Ravenna, in the course of three days. There I procured employment for a day or two, and then continuing my journey, reached Akron,[26] on the Ohio canal, and proceeded down the toe-path on foot. By this time my funds became nearly exhausted and I was reduced to the necessity of contenting myself with but one meal per day. Continuing on in search of employ, my purse was at length entirely exhausted by the time I reached Massilon,[27] hungry and fatigued. Not succeeding in getting work there, I went to a baker's and asked for a few cakes, telling him my destitute situation, and offered him some of my clothes in exchange, which he refused, but gave as much I would take, of his eatables. I renewed my journey, and while my cakes lasted, fared

[26] Sage had followed the Lake Erie shore line from Fredonia, through Erie, Pennsylvania, to Ashtabula, about ten miles west of the Ohio state line. Here he turned due south some forty miles to Warren, and then westward to Akron.

[27] About twenty miles south of Akron.

very well. The next day, my supply being consumed, I began to feel the demands of appetite quite pressing, & about noon, I called at a tavern, and informing the landlord of my circumstances, offered my gloves for a dinner. These he rejected, but said he would give me a dinner. Hunger compelled me to accept of his bounty. Passing on, the day following, hunger induced me to call at a private house to ask for a bit of bread. I there repeated my story, and after answering all the various quizzing interrogatories, into particulars, of the landlady, and receiving no satisfaction from their kindness, it being now enervated, [?] thanking her for her generosity, I departed. I then formed a resolution, that thereafter, I would submit to almost any inconvenience or deprivation that nature could endure, rather than subject myself to the mortification of asking for a thing, the bestowal of which might be considered a gift. I have, by nature, an independence that scorns to receive, aught from another, as a gift, for which it is out of my present power or future intentions to make return. Such being my disposition, my feelings on this occasion may be easily imagined to have been none of the most pleasing kind. A person, possessed of an undue portion of stubborn independence in a time of want, might easily be led to commit some desperate act, in violation of the laws both of God and man,— led by the cold indifference and uncharitableness of those among whom he may chance to fall. Too proud to make known his wants, which to him seems but another term for begging, when other resources are cut off, he often commits theft as the only alternative, although previously he may have been strictly honest. Such being the fact, and as one sin is the parent of many, we need not wonder at the frequent commission of crime in a mixed community where selfishness and illiberality are predominant. Indulging in some severe reflections upon the treatment I had just received, I continued my journey, determined to tax my appetite and forebearance to the utmost. All that day and the next till about 10 o'clock in the morning, I kept my resolution, by which time I had reached the town of Coshocton, where were two printing offices. There was no employment to be procured at either; but on stating my need and requesting the loan of $2 or $3, a printer advanced $2 for me; and, on learning that I had had no breakfast that morning, kindly invited me to breakfast at his house, which I accordingly did. I left soon after to renew my journey, for Marietta, now within 80 miles distance. On my route I fell in company with an old man with whom I travelled a couple of days. He was a firm believer in witchcraft, enchantment, &c, and related many curious stories to confirm his belief; some of which I will relate.

"Wonst I had a rifle that were bewitched, and I couldn't hit nothin' with it, if only a short piece off; I were always a fust rate marksman and could kill a deer or turkey 60 rods distant, as easy as not, and never miss; so I knew it were no fault of mine, nor of the rifle, for I had used it long enough before to know that. I knew it were certainly bewitched, not ony cause of that, but cause a fellow had got mad with me about a month before that, who I always thought to be a he-witch, and he'd done it. One day I went out a huntin' and come upon a deer; it were but 10 yards distant when I fired, and I didn't hit him, altho' my rifle were loaded with two balls. It served me just so twist arterwards, which provoked me most outrageously; but I wouldn't break the spell, yet, though I knew how. In going home I went by that fellow's house, and he ax'd me, how I'd made out a hunting. I told him no how at all. He larf'd. I told him he knew well enough how I'd made out, and if he kept that spell on my rifle the devil would have him for game to-morrow, for he had enchanted it. Well, the next day I tuck my gun, a coal and an axe & went out into the woods; I picked out a hickory tree,— hewed off the bark smooth on one side, then took the coal and draw'd his picter on the hew'd place and made a heart just where it ought to have been; then I tuck my axe and split a place in the centre of the heart and drove into it an oak wedge; I loaded my gun with two balls and fired at the wedge and hit it right in the centre, fair. Well, that day I killed two deer and my rifle always did well enough after that. That are fellow who bewitched it was pleaguy kearful to take off the spell before I had a chance to break it, for he knew well enough what would have been the consequence if he hadn't.— I've seen a good many rifles, in my day who were bewitched, in the same way.— I always know how to manage them. But, taint every one can do it; 'tis ony the fust born, of a family, that has the power to break charms in any way. There is a good many different ways to do that. I knew a fellow wonst, whose gun was charmed, that put into it a silver button for a ball, and made the picter of the one he thought had charmed it, upon an old brown board, and shot it through the middle. The witch, who was an old woman, were shot thro' the heart, by ony firing at it, and killed immediately.— I don't know how tis so many folks come to be witches and wizzards. But I've hearn tell that the Old Harry went around with a paper, and would offer to give such folks as he thought he could get, certain powers that others hadn't, if they'd agree to be his, and write down their names on the paper. Indeed, wonst of a stormy night in the winter when the wind blow'd dreadfully, and were awful cold too, just about at 9 o'clock, I were setten by the fire, and a great tall man, dress'd in black, with a pretty ugly face too, I tell you, come into my house and ax'd me if I wouldn't put my name onto something he held out to me. I tuck 't and look at it; it were just like a black piece of leather, and was chuck full of names. I seed among them the names of some I knowed. I allow'd what it were. So I told him he couldn't cotch me in that trap, for I worn't the coon for him, and he might go to the devil with trash! He grin'd and turn'd round, and went off. When he turn'd to go, I tho't I seed a rousin long tail to him, and I smell'd brimstone, but I warn't cartain. I rally believe it were the Old Harry *himself;* and if I'd put my name on that are thing he wanted me to I would have been a wizzard."

In the course of four days I arrived in Marietta, about 7 o'clock in the evening, where I found my sister and her family all well, and much surprised at seeing me. You will readily conclude that I was no little pleased at having reached the termination of my journey, after encountering so many trials and troubles by the way. But my anxiety now was to find employ for the winter, which was relieved by an application, the next day, to teach a school in the township of Warren, 5 miles below Marietta, which I accepted. The other articles of agreement were soon arranged, and I commenced teaching the week after. The building in which I taught, served the double purpose of school house and church. It was a choice place for ideas to expand and shoot forth, as there were plenty of holes in the fabric, that the tender faculty might not be too much compressed, or the lungs suffer for want of fresh air. A chimney was erected at one end of the building, with a huge fire-place, in which might be placed a half cord of wood without much trouble; but the greatest inconvenience connected with a fire built in it, on a cold day was, that as fast as one could warm himself on one side, he would nearly freeze on the other; and it was very harrassing to me to hear the continued yelp of "please to let me go to the fire," from a dozzen voices at once, all day long. As all of the children could not be permitted to be at the fire constantly, on account of room, complaint was made to the parents, that the teacher would keep them away from the fire till they nearly froze. The almost unanimous conclusion of the sympathizing parents was that I was too hard-hearted to have the management of children; the precious little creatures — they were not going to send them to school to freeze to death. At length, many solicited the directors, that the school should be discontinued, and such an arrangement was effected, after one month's duration. I returned to Marietta much depressed in spirits, and nearly determined never again to act in the capacity of teacher of a common school.

We received a paper from Abial two or three days since. We are all well. Jerusha will write in the course of 4 or 5 weeks. I shall leave for Columbia, the 27th inst. where you will direct your next letter.— Write immediately.

Your affectionate son
RUFUS B. SAGE

[LETTER NO. 16] COLUMBUS O. NOV. 23, 1840

DEAR MOTHER: It has been a long time since I have written to you. My excuse for this apparent negligence and remissness on my part is the extreme hurry I have been in ever since the first of May. As a substitute for letters I have sent you my papers regularly, both weekly and daily, supposing that they would afford you an equal gratification at far less expense. My health during the past summer has been remarkably good, for which I cannot be too thankful to the great Dispenser of life and its attendant comforts and blessings. My career for the past six months is well known to you. I have been deeply and ardently engaged in the great political struggle which has just resulted in the redemption and salvation of our beloved country, and, I trust my exertions have contributed in no small degree to the consummation of that happy result. The friends of Harrison duly appreciate my endeavors, and Harrison himself is not ignorant or unmindful of them. I am personally acquainted with Gen. H. He was in this place last summer, at which time I was introduced to him by the Hon. Alfred Kelly. Upon hearing my name Gen. H. asked if I was the *Sage* that detected the author of the famous *"forged Circular."* [28] and, on being informed of the fact, said he had *heard of me before.* The Gen. is a very clever sociable old man,— real good-hearted, honest, and talented fellow. I liked his appearance very much. My employment during the past summer, in a pecuniary point of view, has not been very profitable. However, when I have settled up my business, I am in hopes to have some *"little"* left.

When Harrison takes his seat as President, I have good reason to believe that he will give some appointment under government, which will ensure me, if not a competency, at least, a living. Of this I am almost certain. I have arose in the world considerable of late,[29] notwithstanding my misfortunes.

I often think of you, dear mother,— of home; how my heart longs to be there! This wish I shall most probably gratify,— possibly next spring,— if my life is spared. I have almost fully determined upon that.

Mother, I have not received a letter from you for near a year.— Why don't you write? I had one from Frances three or four months ago. About the middle of August, I saw Wm. Wiltshire Riley, who passed through this place on his way to Selina, Ohio. He said he had seen you. I have not heard from our folks in Marietta, for some weeks, by letter. However, they are well. I assure you I am extremely anxious to hear from home. Tell Frances to write. Tell me all about

---

[28] The nature of this is explained below, in Appendix A. Mr. Sage was first employed on the *Ohio State Bulletin.* Later he edited and published a campaign paper, first a weekly, then a daily.

[29] He is now twenty-three years old.

affairs there. I expect to spend the winter in this place. Hoping to see you in the spring, and imploring the giver of all things, that he would grant you health and comfort, I remain your affectionate Son

RUFUS B. SAGE

TO MRS. JERUSHA SAGE

[LETTER NO. 17]

INDEPENDENCE, JACKSON CO. MISSOURI
SUNDAY, MAY 30th, 1841

MY VERY DEAR MOTHER Little did I think while penning my last letter to you, that my next would date from this place; yet so it is. 'Tis to myself even strange. The fact of the business is, I have, for a long time had a wish to explore the Territory of Oregon. While in Columbus a number of my acquaintances with myself, decided upon a visit to that region, and shortly after started for St. Louis, expecting to join the American Fur Company and proceed with them. We arrived in St. Louis too late, for the Company had left; and now we are waiting in this place the departure of an independent Company which is to leave here about the 20th of July, with whom we are to go.[30] The journey is a safe one; no danger is to be apprehended from the Indians. We are to get from $20 to $25 per month — every thing found. My design is to collect materials for a *book,* which I intend publishing upon my return.[31] How long I shall be gone I know not, possibly two years. I shall be able to communicate meanwhile, with my friends once in six months. Immediately upon my return, should Providence permit it, I will hie to the land of my fathers,— to the friends I left behind me. I anticipate that the intended expedition will add to my

[30] The trading company was headed by Lancaster P. Lupton, as explained later in the annotations to Sage's book.

[31] The fact that he made the trip with the avowed purpose of reporting his experiences and observations in a book, explains his keeping of notes and the resultant accuracy of his writing.

health, as it has that effect upon all those engaged in the Fur Trade. Thus having explained my conduct and intentions, permit to ask the reason why I have not received a letter from home for nearly a year? Am I altogether forgotten by those I hold dearest, and whom distance renders more dear? Can it be so? and yet it so seems. What have I done to merit such neglect? This is now, if I remember right, the *fourth* letter I have written home since I have received a line from any of them! It grieves me to think of it. I cannot forget my dear mother — my brothers, and sister, and friends, and though I am not permitted to hear from them, I can pray for their health and prosperity,— spiritual and temporal.

Abial would do very well in this part, by working at his trade. Good blacksmiths get from $30 to $40 per month and are sure of employ. Goods & Groceries are nearly double the price they bring in Old Connecticut. Land is from $10 to $15 per acre, partly improved. Produce fetches a reasonable price. It can be raised in immense quantities, with scarce any labor. The soil is the richest and most productive of any I ever set my eyes upon. The climate is remarkably healthy, no fever and ague and very little sickness of any kind. This place is about 12 miles from the Indian Territory. We have a host of Indians about us, but they are very friendly — I like them. Two or three weeks since, I took an excursion into their country and came back much delighted. They are civilized and many of them very wealthy — owning large & well cultivated farms. Their country could not be better in quality of soil. Their pararie lands are like a perfect paradise, covered with a virdure unknown to the east, and wild flowers — Oh, some of the most beautiful I ever beheld,— you have none such in your Atlantic flower-gardens. A pararie scene is perfectly enchanting.

The times in this state are very hard at present. The

people in this neighborhood seem clever, but there is too much loosness of morals to suit me. Religion receives but little attention here. "Oh Lord revive thy work!" Let not these thy creatures so transcendently blessed with heaven's choisest temporal gifts, live as unmindful of their Creator and as thankless as the brutes that perish!

As for myself, I love to be thankful and have enough to be thankful for. I have good health, am clothed and fed and what of temporal things would I covet more! Oh God, give us all a contented mind and a thankful heart.

But I must close my disconnected epistle. Should you receive this two weeks from its date, you must answer it immediately, as I shall be able to receive it before leaving. If not, 'twill be no use to answer it under 8 months, as I cannot get your reply. God, who has hitherto guarded me, will still continue to protect – in him is my trust, and may he watch over and protect us all, and grant that we may yet meet again on earth, before our final meeting around his throne above. Your Son

RUFUS B. SAGE

MRS. J. SAGE

Give my best respects to all enquiring friends. [Written on margin of letter.]

[LETTER NO. 18] INDEPENDENCE, MO. AUG. 21, 1841

BELOVED MOTHER: Distance but strengthens in me the cords of filial affection which bind to my heart the memory of her who taught me first to know and feel a mother's love. How often is she the sole theme of my thoughts! — How do I long to see her and experience the rich pleasure her presence was wont to impart to me in my childhood hours! But cruel fortune, at least for the present, has denied me that enjoyment. As intimated to you in my last, I leave in three or four

THE HOME OF RUFUS B. SAGE
Cromwell, Connecticut, 1953

RUFUS B. SAGE FAMILY MONUMENT
Cemetery at Cromwell, Connecticut, 1953
Standing, Mrs. Helen S. Bernson, granddaughter of Sage

days for the Rocky Mountains, where I expect to winter. If my life & health is spared I shall return in June next, when you may hope to hear from me again. I may then, if nothing prevents, visit the scenes of my childhood and grasp the hands of those whom the ties of sociality and consanguinity have rendered dear.

Give yourself no uneasiness about me. That great and good Being who has from my childhood watched over and guarded me in all my wanderings, will still protect me, in the Rocky Mountains as well as otherwheres. His presence will prove as cheering and his arm as powerful among the dangers which will there surround me, as among thousands of earthly friends. In Him I trust — and trusting fear not.

I am paid for the adventure, and think it will prove beneficial to me, in more ways than one. I may visit Oregon before coming back — possibly not. If I return east next spring, it will be for the purpose of visiting Washington — I have a thing or too in my head that I need not name.

My health is good. I have received one letter from Jerusha since I have been in this place. They are all well. It is now nearly a year since I got a letter from you! What's the reason? Why didn't you make Francis or Abial write? You know I would like to hear from them. I shall write you again the first opportunity. Write me a letter so that it will reach this place about the last of May next that I can get it immediately upon my return.

Excuse my brevity — time will not permit me to write you a long letter now. I leave on Monday — day after tomorrow.

May heaven bless and save us all —
Crown our days with happiness,
And bring us to our graves
In peace.

Your affectionate Son, RUFUS B. SAGE

[LETTER NO. 19]

INDEPENDENCE, MO. JULY 20th, 1842.

DEAR MOTHER: I have just arrived in this town from my trip to the Rocky Mountains, much improved in health and increased in flesh.[32] Thanks to the goodness of God, truly become me, who has preserved me safe from all the dangers and hardships through which I have been called to pass! I spent the winter in the Mountains on the headwaters of the Platt River, and as pleasantly as could be expected in a place so remote from civilized society and its enjoyments. The greatest occasion of uneasiness and discontent to me was being deprived the privileges of the Sabbath and Sanctuary. How often have I uttered the heart-felt exclamation of the pious David: "How amiable are thy tabernacles, O Lord of hosts! — My soul longeth, yea even fainteth for the Courts of the Lord; — my heart and my flesh cry out for the living God! A day in thy courts is better than a thousand! I had rather be a door-keeper in the house of my God than to dwell in the tents of wickedness." I never properly estimated those privileges till I had become deprived of them; and having been thus deprived, I can never cease to love and value them while Providence prolongs my unprofitable existence.

The whites in that country are worse than the Indians. The latter are friendly and well disposed, and in several things furnish examples worthy of the imitation of those who lay a higher claim to civilization. In hospitality they excell all others. Upon going into their lodges, you are invited to eat, the first thing. They will even give to a stranger the last mouthfull they have for their families, and if objections are made on that account they will reply "Our wives and children can do without eating a long while — *eat, eat!*" When they invite you to partake of their hospitalities, they invari-

[32] The detailed account of this first trip to the mountains is recorded in Sage's book, reprinted herewith.

ably set before you the very best they have, and the heartier you eat the better are they pleased. And this is all gratuitous. When told that in the country of the whites it was the custom to pay for eating, they expressed great astonishment at such gross meanness. With exceptions in some particulars their behavior while at home is such as would well befit a strictly moral community; — (that is, when not under the influence of liquor). The chastity of the Sioux women, as far as my observation extended, surpasses that of their fairer sisters. Indeed, it is seldom you see a prostitute among them. Since I left the States, I have been among the following nations — Shawnees, Delawares, Kickapoos, Iowas, Sacs, Pottowotomies, Mohaws, Osages, Otows, Pawnees, Shians and Sioux, by all of whom I have been treated with great friendliness. Indeed, there is no danger to be feared from any of the above tribes, if a person keeps on his guard. I have collected the materials for a work upon that country, which, when time permits, I shall write out. I have collected specimens of *gold* and *mineral coal* which can be procured in that neighborhood in almost any quantity. It is a country rich in minerals. The climate is most delightful — soil fertile — but scarcity of timber will prevent the country this side of the Mountains from ever being very thickly populated by the whites. The case is quite the reverse in Oregon. Our only subsistence during the past winter was buffalo meat, which, by the by, is the *best meat I ever tasted.*— I have many interesting things to write, but space will not permit. My intention has been to return home this summer, but the times are so hard and money so scarce, that I am afraid I shall have to defer it, much against my will. Possibly I may return to the Mountains and spend the ensuing winter there.— I don't know. If I do, upon my return next spring, if Providence smiles upon me, I shall bring with me from $500, to 800,00, & return home immediately to visit those I hold dearest on earth, my mother and brothers & sisters. I am pained at not having heard a word from home for nearly two years. I expected [to] have found letters for me immediately upon my arrival at this place,— but disappointment clouds my brow and sinks my spirits low. *Do please to write me as soon as you get this.* I can get the letter if you write immediately. I am so anxious to hear. Tell Francis to write. I will write to her in a few days when you may expect to hear what I design to do. Tell Elisha, Abial, Benj. & Edmund to write or send me papers. Give my love to all, and God bless and prosper them all; and if the great disposer of human events should so will it that we never meet again on earth, thanks to His mercy we may yet hope to meet around his throne in the heavens, where the wicked cease from troubling and the weary are at rest — where all sorrow & sighing shall be done and parting shall not be known. In a few days I shall write again. I shall forward you papers.

Again I pray, God bless you all — God preserve you all. Your affectionate son,

RUFUS B. SAGE

(TO MRS. J. SAGE)

[Address on envelope]:
Mrs. Jerusha Sage Upper Middletown, Conn.
(care of Elisha Sage)

[LETTER NO. 20] WESTPORT, AUG. 10th, 1842

DEAR MOTHER: I start this morning for the Mountains. Contrary to my expectations, I am so hurried that I have only time to write you these few words. I am well — Shall possibly be back to Independence in Dec. next. Dangers beset my path it is true, but my trust is in God.

Write.— I can get your letters. Good bye

RUFUS B. SAGE

[LETTER NO. 21] COLUMBUS, O. AUG. 17th 1844

DEAR MOTHER: Blame me not, that I have neglected to write you before this. There has been such constant and pressing demand for every spare moment of my time that it has been a thing almost impossible for me to discharge the duty which affection so earnestly enjoins upon me. It has now been 16 days since I arrived in this city,[33] and you must have seen by the papers I have sent you, that I am surrounded with all the bustle and hurry of business.[34] I heard on the day of my arrival, by a gentleman of Marietta, whom I happened to meet, of the death of Jerusha's husband. I wrote to her immediately, and received an answer by return mail.[35] She was well; and imparted to me the gratifying intelligence that my dear mother was yet in the land of the living. She was in want, and I sent her a small present relief. May God protect her & her fatherless children. She complained of receiving little consolation or encouragement from her other brothers. Shame on them. They might at least whisper a word

[33] Sage's book of mountain adventures ends with his arrival at Van Buren, Arkansas, on July 4, 1844. He must have made his way almost immediately to Columbus to have arrived there on August first.

[34] He quickly entered into politics, issuing a campaign weekly in support of the Whig candidate, Henry Clay, "protesting [as his biographical sketch records] with all earnestness against the annexation of Texas and the consequent extension of the slave power. The result was a grand triumph in Ohio, which, however, was neutralized in New York by the abolition vote, cast for Burney, thus giving the national election to James K. Polk, . . ."

[35] His sister's letter of August 8, 1844, is in the Coe Collection. It reveals her love for her brother, her abiding religious faith, and gives some news from Connecticut.

The Collection also contains Jerusha's letter of August 17, 1844. From it one learns that Rufus had intended to visit his sister at Marietta in the early winter but had disappointed her. "It would rejoice my heart exceedingly," she writes, "to see you as actively engaged in the cause of God as you have been the past summer in political cause. I do think you would lay up more treasures in heaven. . . I should like to know how you are off for clothes. Have you plenty of shirts, collars, and stockings. If not let me know and I will try to make some and have them ready for you in the spring." She was teaching a school for colored children and some money had been raised to pay her, since her husband's death.

of comfort to her disconsolate ear,— it would cost nothing.

It seems like old times again to hear from you. It has been now, nearly 4 years since my ears were blessed with such news. I have been away beyond the Rocky Mountains, and in New Mexico and Northwestern Texas. Since I left the United States I have spent most of the time in travelling. I suppose I must have travelled during the last 3 years, 15 or 16,000 miles. God has blessed me with improved health, and has returned me safe from all dangers.

I cannot write fully, my circumstances, for I have not time. Excuse me therefore. Suffise it to say my present prospects are more favorable than they have been for a long time.

If He from whom all blessings flow, grant me his favor, I will endeavor to return home within a year. I intended to have done this long since, but how truly it is, we know not what a day may bring forth.

Changes! Oh, dear! I am almost afraid to receive a letter from home. Write me, however, and let me know the worst.— Disguise nothing.— Tell me all the news. Tell them all to write me. Give my respects to all — brothers, sisters, cousins, friends. Do write as soon as you get this.

And may God take care of you and us all, and preserve us for a heavenly home. Your Son

RUFUS B. SAGE[36]

MRS. JERUSHA SAGE

[LETTER NO. 22] COLUMBUS OHIO. DEC 18, 1844

DEAR MOTHER: I ask pardon for not answering your letter sooner. This the hurry of business prevented, contrary to my inclination. A thrill of joy ran over me, when it came to hand, and, upon opening it, I recog-

[36] Upon receipt of this letter his aging mother wrote the reply printed in Appendix B-4.

nized the well known hand-writing of her who next to my God is uppermost in my thoughts,— a thing my eyes have not rested upon for a period of some four years. You cannot imagine how anxiously I longed to hear from home, but scarcely knew whether I was writing to the living or dead, and when your answer came to hand, I trembled, and hesitated to break the seal, for fear of unwelcome news. The agony of suspense was quickly over on hearing that you were well. It was then I thanked my God that your life and health, with my own, had been precious in his sight. And it is my prayer that it may so continue till we meet again. When I left home I had confidently intended on returning within a year or two at fartherest. But nearly eight long years have elapsed since that time, and I am no nearer than at first. I have received several letters from Elisha's daughter,[37] (and, by the by, I feel proud that she is my neice,) in the last of which she expressed the confident hope that I should spend the ensuing Thanksgiving with my friends in old Connecticut. I know not what induced her to hope so, for I have not calculated on returning till next spring, which, God willing, I shall certainly do.

I am completely sick of this world, and more especially of the people that are in it. I have become almost a misanthrope, though cherishing, as I deem, the purest sentiments of universal benevolence. How inconsistent! I am a friend to every one in need, no matter how deserving or undeserving he may be,— for my heart yearns over the miseries and misfortunes of poor humanity! but I claim no living soul as my friend, and have long since come to the conclusion that there is no such thing in existence as friendship devoid of selfishness.

---

[37] Elizabeth, twelve-year-old daughter of Rufus' brother Elisha. These letters are filled with such revealing specifics that we reproduce them in Appendix D.

I have often thought that could I obtain a partner of life's joys and sorrows, and with her hie to some sweet valley in the mountains hundreds of miles from any human being, I there might spend the remainder of my days in happiness. But there are two things I have fully resolved upon,— to take the world just as it comes, and to get married just as soon as I am able to support a wife.

It seems from my niece's account, that all the old maids have got married off.— things are so changed that I fear I shall find myself a stranger in my own home. Yet of all the world that is the only place I do love.— I love everything that belongs to it — and if I ever do marry, I think it will be there. Upon this, I feel like Isaac. But, I have written a parcel of nonsense! Excuse me. Tell Frances to write. Tell Elisha's Maria I received her letter and shall answer it soon. Tell Edmund's Elizabeth I am happy to see that she has improved so well. I should like to have her write. Give my love to all my nieces and nephews, and tell them to be good girls and boys and learn as fast as they can.

Hoping to hear from you *soon* I subscribe myself yours

RUFUS B. SAGE[38]

J. SAGE

[LETTER NO. 23]

UPPER MIDDLETOWN, CT., OCT. 25 [15], 1845

MESSRS. PAINE & BURGESS [62 John St., New York]

DEAR SIRS: At the suggestion of a gentleman of your City, I address you this relative to a matter of business now in hand. Having devoted an interval of three years

---

[38] According to the biographical sketch reprinted in Appendix A, "Mr. Sage next appeared in the editorial chair of the Chillicothe, O., Gazette, with which paper he severed his connection in 1845, and returned to visit his old home after an absence of ten [nine] years. In this quiet retreat he prepared his book of travels."

to travel in the Rocky Mountains and countries adjacent, (viz: from the fall of '41 to the summer of '44,) I have nearly completed a work, with the following for its title: "Scenes in the Rocky Mountains, Oregon, California, New Mexico, Northwestern Texas and Grand Prairies; coupled with Sketches of Adventure during an Excursion of three years, and a General Description of those Countries, their Geography, Geology, Resources, Curiosities, Favorable Localities, Present Condition and Different Nations inhabiting them: Arranged from Personal Observation and Authentic Data obtained in the interim." The work will be ready for the press in about three weeks. It will contain some 400 or 450 pages octavo.— 1,200 ems long primer per page.

As its title indicates, it goes "into the full merits" of the different subjects treated upon, which are severally disposed of in a concise and comprehensive manner. My journal of travel carefully excluded all prolixity, but gives a full description of the various countries passed over, their geological character, mineral resources, indigenous production, climate, health, favorable localities for settlements, inducements for emigration, feasible routes from the U.S., together with a minute description of both Oregon and California,— their mountains, rivers, lakes, harbors, means of intercommunication, commercial and agricultural advantages, settlements,— their situation, etc.,— improvements, missionary stations, population both white and native, and, in fact, everything connected with them interesting to the public mind. In addition to this I give a plenary account of the various Indian tribes encountered in my peregrinations,— their local situations, territories, numbers, characters, habits, peculiarities, and present conditions. My sketch of adventures abounds with thrilling details so arranged in the general order of the work as to render it interesting to the public at large. In writing it I have scrupulously avoided that dryness and insipidity common to most travellers, and, while my acting motto has been to express myself in as few words as possible, I am flattered in the belief of not failing to elicit the deep interest and attention of the public mind, and securing for it a ready perusal and speedy sale. I say this not without due deliberation, having heretofore had no little experience in matters of public taste connected with the public press. But what will immeasureably enhance the value and importance of my proposed work is the vast amount of *new material* of which it is composed, such as has never, as yet, been treated upon by any other author,— and such as cannot fail to *"make talk."*

There is no doubt in my mind that a work of this kind is loudly called for at the present time, and I have every confidence of its being a profitable undertaking. The premises would warrant my saying much more in its favor, but space forbids; however, I may safely assert one thing in conclusion,— an examination of it will prove its real merits to exceed the faint outlines presented in the above. My reason for speaking thus unreservedly in reference to this matter, is to afford you some idea of the ground upon which the following positions are based, and in deciding upon them I shall expect you to do it with the distinct *proviso* of its being as represented:— if the suggestions meet your mind:

1st What will you give for the copy-right, granting certain reservations for the present or a future edition — or for it without reserve? — state your most favorable terms.

2d Your conditions for publishing the work on shares. — for one third, or one half, or what?

3d Your charge for publishing an edition of 10,000 copies, bound in the common form? — a rough estimate of course.

In your answer to these, should other proposals occur to you, please state them, bearing in mind, however, that those based upon the 1st and 2d of the foregoing would be more favorably entertained. Please state, also, how soon the work might be issued from your press. Address your reply to Rufus B. Sage, Upper Middletown, Ct., at an early date if possible, as I am anxious to decide in reference to this matter.

Respectfully your obt. serv't.

RUFUS B. SAGE.

P.S. Should it prove incompatible with your existing engagements to accede to the above propositions, you will confer a favor by enclosing this letter with your reply. R.B.S.[39]

[LETTER NO. 24] NEW YORK, JAN. 12th 1846

DEAR MOTHER: I write to relieve your anxiety on my account, as well as to appologize for not having previously so done. I arrived in this city early on the Friday morning succeeding my departure from home,— am now boarding at no. 28 Cliff St. (price $ per week,)— Am quite pleasantly situated — in business and doing tolerably well; — in fact, my present prospects may be regarded as good. I should have written to you some time since, but deferred it in order to state something definite with regard to myself, such as would probably prove satisfactory to all inquiring relatives.

---

39 The following reply to this letter was received:

62 John St New York Oct 21, 1845

MR. RUFUS B. SAGE

DEAR SIR Your esteemed favor of the 15th came duly to hand.– We have as much on hand as we can attend to till the 1 Jany, & cannot consistently do any thing for you at present. Should your MSS. remain unpublished till that time we might make you some sort of a proposition.

Respectfully your obdt servant

We return your letter as requested. PAINE & BURGESS

Mr. Sage soon went to New York and began negotiations with other possible publishers.

I have concluded to postpone my publication for the present, fully convinced that I can do better than to accept any offers yet made,— in this there has been no lack; but I am determined to go for *profit* and not for glory, consequently you are not to look for the *grand experiment* till next spring. I suppose some of my over inquisitive (pretended) friends will regard this conclusion as indicative of defeated plans and purposes, — yet they need not give themselves uneasiness on my account,— I presume to know my own business best, and shall so act. Enclosed you will find two dollars for your especial benefit to be expended as you see fit — for *tea,* shoes, wood-cutting, or any thing else. I shall send you more soon, providence permitting. Tell Frances my debt to her shall be cancelled ere long, but first of all I must remit to Edmund the $16 which will soon be due from me to Benham, and get him to settle the account. Edmund has not a few good streaks about him — notwithstanding all that the tongue of jealousy may have uttered. As intended, I called on Miss Miller, and found that the kindly efforts of M. T. Merwin, Esq., had failed of their designed effect,— in future, he might as well keep *mum,* as also my *very good friend* Mrs. Noble,— if she was guilty of the part, in a dirty, low-bred transaction. I suppose her to have been. I can and do forgive, but shall never forget the double-distilled, quintessence of meanness evinced by a meddlesome clique on the occasion referred to.[40]

It will be my purpose to disencumber your homestead from all debts in the course of the present year, which I confidently hope and expect to do, God willing, — I may then come home and take care of you, as is

[40] As indicated here, and also in the letter to Rufus from his brother Edmund, dated Feb. 28, 1846 (Appendix E), some persons had spread slanders about Rufus and had attempted to alienate Marietta Miller, the girl he was courting.

doubtless my duty. Meanwhile, let Elisha do the best he can with the farm.

Well, we have now entered upon a new year, and I am fully resolved, for my own part, to enter upon a new life. Ten years I have spent in studying others, and have yet *myself* to learn. In view of this, I feel to exclaim, "Oh, God, show me my *whole self,* and teach me what I am and what is my destiny!" Our Heavenly Father has been very kind unto me, and, why should I not evince my gratitude in a life devoted to His service? Oh, let me establish a character with Him, and then all assaults upon reputation will prove as clouds before the sun — the clouds may for a while obscure and bedim, but, as the former is perpetual and the latter transitory, who will pretend that a short obscuration can annihilate the bright effulgence of its future glory? Oh, God, teach me to live above the world while I live in it!

I have not sent *that letter* to the fellow who requested me "to consider him as my friend." Sometimes I am tempted to do so.

My health is good,— much better than when I was at home,— I shall probably visit you as soon as my book comes out,— how soon that will be, I cannot speak positively, but confidently expect it will not be a very great while.— I wrote to Jerusha last week, giving her some advice which in due time will reach you. — Tell Charles Butler I have not as yet made any disposal of his poetry, but will endeavor to do so as soon as a suitable occasion is offered. He will need a great deal of careful practice to become a proficient *popular* poet, tho' he need not be discouraged on that account. This from your son

RUFUS B. SAGE

MRS. J. SAGE

[LETTER NO. 25] SOMMERSET, O. JAN. 1st, 1847[41]

DEAR MOTHER I should have written to you before, but I supposed you had learned of my whereabouts and whatabouts per letters of cousin Jane Woodruff, as thro' the medium of her correspondence I have been duly advised of your wellfare since I last saw you. But though I have so long remained silent, rest assured you are not forgotten by an absent son. I suppose you will be more interested to learn about my health and business prospects than of anything besides; and, through the blessing of an ever-kind Providence, I have the happiness to inform you that both are in a flattering condition. My books sell as well and even better than I had expected. In retailing them I can easily clear my $50 per month cash in hand. I meet with success upon all sides, and hope soon to be in a condition to do something for you and for others. Enclosed you will find $5.00, which you will make use of as you see fit. If you have no very urgent need for it all, please give a part of it to Frances on my account. I hardly expect to return to Middletown before May, and Abial can, if he chooses, remain at least for the next year, at the old place. God willing, on my return, I will discharge the encumbrances of your estate, and put affairs in a rather more pleasant condition so far as concerns yourself. As to the farm, give yourself no uneasiness,— I will give directions relative to it, per letter, provided I do not return sufficiently soon to attend to it personally.

I suppose Edmund has got sick of book-peddling by this time. Ah, ha, ha! I can beat him at it, with half an effort. According to his orders, I had 500 maps struck while in N.Y., and forwarded them to his address,— leaving bill for him to discharge, which I hope he has

[41] Since the preceding letter was written, Sage had completed arrangements for publication of his book and the volume had been issued in 1846. An account of these developments has been given in the Introduction.

done. If I had had said maps with me, I might have sold them all, long before this; and if he has not already disposed of them, I will take them off his hands, and pay all charges. I can make a handsome speck upon them. I have just received 600 cops. of books — my sales at retail average about 60 cops. per week. I go from this place (Sommerset) to Lancaster, and from there to Columbus, via Chillicothe and Circleville. A note from you will reach me at Columbus.— My regards to all our friends, and show this letter to Edmund. My wish is that he provide for your present comfort, and I will be responsible for whatever reasonable charges he may make for same.

With Great haste and much affection, Your Son,

RUFUS B. SAGE

MRS. J. SAGE

P.S. Jerusha and other friends at Marietta were all well when I left — Dec. 22d. A few days since I forwarded to her a sum of money sufficient to meet her wants for some time. She sees a great deal of trouble, but her friends are very kind to her.

R. B. SAGE[42]

---

[42] This is the end of the series of Rufus B. Sage letters in the Coe Collection. A personal search with Mrs. Helen S. Bernson in August, 1953, in the attic of the old Rufus B. Sage house at Cromwell failed to reveal any additional letters.

Scenes in the Rocky Mountains

Rufus B. Sage

[In this volume: the Preface and Chapters I to XVI]

PRICE FIFTY CENTS.

SCENES IN THE

ROCKY MOUNTAINS,

OREGON, CALIFORNIA, NEW MEXICO, TEXAS AND GRAND PRAIRIES:

OR,

NOTES BY THE WAY DURING

AN EXCURSION OF THREE YEARS:

WITH A DESCRIPTION OF

THE COUNTRIES PASSED THROUGH.

BY A NEW ENGLANDER.

PRICE FIFTY CENTS.

PHILADELPHIA:
CAREY & HART, 126 CHESNUT STREET.

For Sale by G. B. Zieber & Co., Philadelphia; W. H. Graham, New York; Redding & Co. and Halliburton & Co., Boston; Wm. Taylor & Co. and N. Hickman, Baltimore; Drinker & Morris and Nash & Woodhouse, Richmond, Va.; J. W. Cook, Pittsburg; G. W. Noble, Louisville, Ky.; C. Marshall, Lexington, Ky.; Robinson & Jones, Cincinnati; J. C. Morgan, J. B. Steel and B. M. Norman, New Orleans, and M. Boullemet, Mobile.

1846.

CAREY AND HART'S LIBRARY OF HUMOROUS AMERICAN WORKS, WITH ILLUSTRATIONS BY DARLEY.

Vol. I.—Price 50 Cents.
THEATRICAL APPRENTICESHIP
AND
ANECDOTAL RECOLLECTIONS OF SOL. SMITH, ESQ.,
COMEDIAN, LAWYER, &c.,&c.
WITH EIGHT ORIGINAL DESIGNS.

Vol. II.—Price 50 Cents.
PICKINGS
FROM THE PORTFOLIO OF THE REPORTER
OF THE
NEW ORLEANS "PICAYUNE."
WITH 8 HUMOROUS DESIGNS.

Vol. III.—Price 50 Cents.
MY SHOOTING-BOX.
BY FRANK FORESTER.

Vol. IV.—Price 50 Cents.
AUNT PATTY'S SCRAP-BAG.
BY CAROLINE LEE HENTZ,
AUTHOR OF THE "MOB CAP," &c.
WITH DESIGNS BY DARLEY.

Vol. V.—Price 50 Cents.
A QUARTER RACE IN KENTUCKY,
AND OTHER STORIES.
BY W. T. PORTER, ESQ.,
EDITOR OF THE "BIG BEAR OF ARKANSAS," &c. &c.

Vol. VI.—Price 50 Cents.
MODERN CHIVALRY,
OR THE ADVENTURES OF
CAPT. FARRAGO & TEAGUE O'REGAN.
WITH TEN ILLUSTRATIONS BY DARLEY.

FACSIMILE OF THE FRONT AND BACK WRAPPERS OF THE ORIGINAL EDITION, 1846

From the copy in the collection of Robert James Woods, Los Angeles

SCENES

IN THE

ROCKY MOUNTAINS,

AND IN

OREGON, CALIFORNIA, NEW MEXICO, TEXAS, AND THE GRAND PRAIRIES;

OR

NOTES BY THE WAY,

DURING AN EXCURSION OF THREE YEARS,

WITH A

DESCRIPTION OF THE COUNTRIES PASSED THROUGH,

INCLUDING THEIR

GEOGRAPHY, GEOLOGY, RESOURCES, PRESENT CONDITION, AND THE DIFFERENT NATIONS INHABITING THEM.

BY A NEW ENGLANDER.

PHILADELPHIA:
PUBLISHED BY CAREY & HART.
1846.

Printed by T. K. & P. G. Collins

PREFACE

The growing interest entertained by the American public in reference to the subjects mainly treated upon in the volume now before the reader, is deemed a sufficient apology for its appearance. The late act of our National Legislature in the annexation of Texas, bringing with it, as it does, a very considerable portion of the Province of Santa Fe, together with the existing hostilities between our own and the Republic of New Mexico, preparing the way for a no distant acquisition of the Californias, not to mention the recent agitation of the American claim to the *whole* of Oregon, as yet scarcely subsided, has directed the attention of most minds more than usually towards the affairs and conditions of the Great West — particularly that section of it contiguous to the Rocky Mountains. But although our newspapers teem with professed descriptions of those countries embraced within its limits, and are redundant with animadversions upon their admitted importance – while the ambitious politician prates of them learnedly, and quotes by the day from fugitive paragraphs of doubtful verity, gleaned here and there as chance may favor him – a palpable ignorance is evinced throughout in regard to a vast store of interesting particulars.

To fill up in some measure this wide vacuum of general information, is the author's object in his present undertaking. With this view he has endeavored to present a full and comprehensive picture of the real condition of regions so attractive as are the above, and in so doing he is conscious of having erred in no important particular. Whatever is affirmed, may be relied upon as matter of fact; while details of a questionable nature may be inferred from the guarded language in which they are expressed. So far as his personal knowledge is concerned, he has spoken without reserve; but information based upon second-hand authority, is given as such.

The catalogue of facts relative to the manner in which the fur trade is conducted, and the enormities chargeable upon the individuals engaged in it, may be objected to as unnecessarily minute; but, regarded, as it should be, as one of the explanatory causes of Indian degradation, it will hardly fail to secure a ready acquiescence from the reader. Justice to the "red man" demands only a rehearsal of the simple truth, that condemnation may be awarded to the doubly guilty.

The narrative of the Texan expedition sent against New Mexico in the spring of 1843,with its mishaps, and conflicts with the Mexicans and Indians, added to a statement of its surrender to the U.S. Dragoons, and the causes which led to its final dispersion, will doubtless claim attention, as being the only account of it hitherto published.

In his notes of travel it has been the author's endeavor to avoid prolixity; and, while his acting motto has been to say as much as possible in a few words, he has not withheld full descriptions of the various scenes and countries that met his view during his lengthy excursion. He is well aware that his style is partially deficient in the ease and gracefulness peculiar to some writers; but here he would offer no apology – it is *his own,* and for it he neither asks the favor of critics nor expects their lenity.

Fully persuaded that a work of this kind will prove acceptable at the present time, the author would fain believe the public in general are more regardful of its intrinsic merits than of the garb in which it appears, and with these observations he is content to abide the result.

New-York, July, 1846

CONTENTS

Chapter I

Chapter II

Chapter III

Chapter IV

Chapter V

Chapter VI

Chapter VII

Chapter VIII

Chapter IX

Chapter X

Chapter XI

Chapter XII

Chapter XIII

Chapter XIV

Chapter XV

Chapter XVI

SCENES

IN

THE ROCKY MOUNTAINS, ETC.

CHAPTER I

MY purpose in visiting the Rocky Mountains, and countries adjacent, having hitherto proved a fruitful source of inquiry to the many persons I meet, when aware of my having devoted three years to travel in those remote regions, and I am so plied with almost numberless other questions, I know of no better way to dispose of them satisfactorily, than by doing what I had thought of at the outset, to wit: writing a book.[1]

But, says one, more books have been already written upon subjects of a kindred nature, than will ever find readers.[2] True, indeed; yet I must venture one more; and this much I promise at the start: it shall be different, in most respects, from all that have preceded it; and if I fail to produce an agreeable variety of adventures, interwoven with a large fund of valuable information, then I shall not have accomplished my purpose.

Yet, 'why did I go?—what was my object?' Let

[1] In his letter of May 30, 1841, written at Independence, Missouri (Letter No. 17), Sage announced that he planned to write a book about his contemplated trip. In reprinting the book obvious typographical errors have been corrected. Sage's footnotes are identified by his name in brackets.

[2] Among the books published during the preceding decade, which were related to the same general territory, the following notable ones were doubtless seen by Sage: Washington Irving's *Astoria* (1836) and his *Bonneville* (1837), Samuel Parker's *Journal of an Exploring Tour* (1838), Zenas Leonard's *Narrative* (1839), C. A. Murray's *Travels in North America* (1839), T. J. Farnham's *Travels* (1841), Joseph Williams' *Tour* (1843), Josiah Gregg's *Commerce of the Prairies* (1844), Lee and Frost's *Ten Years in Oregon* (1844), and J. C. Fremont's *Report* (1845). Also, he probably saw in the newspapers the Western adventure series by W. A. Ferris (1843-44), and that of Matt Field (1843-44).

me explain: Dame Nature bestowed upon me lavishly that innate curiosity, and fondness for things strange and new, of which every one is more or less possessed. Phrenologists would declare my organ of Inquisitiveness to be largely developed; and, certain it is, I have a great liking to tread upon unfrequented ground, and mingle among scenes at once novel and romantic. Love of adventure, then, was the greater prompter, while an enfeebled state of health sensibly admonished me to seek in other parts that invigorating air and climate denied by the diseased atmosphere of a populous country.[3] I also wished to acquaint myself with the geography of those comparatively unexplored regions, — their geological character, curiosities, resources, and natural advantages, together with their real condition, present inhabitants, inducements to emigrants, and most favorable localities for settlements, to enable me to speak from personal knowledge upon subjects so interesting to the public mind, at the present time, as are the above. Here, then, were objects every way worthy of attention, and vested with an importance that would render my excursion not a mere idle jaunt for the gratification of selfish curiosity. This much by way of prelude,— now to the task in hand.

While yet undecided as to the most advisable mode of prosecuting my intended enterprise, on learning that a party of adventurers were rendezvoused at Westport, Mo.,[4] preparatory to their long and arduous journey to the new-formed settlements of the Columbia river, I hastened to that place, where I arrived in the month

[3] Trips into the far West were rather generally recognized as a means of promoting health, and various travelers testified to the benefits they had experienced. Especially were persons suffering with tuberculosis encouraged to try a journey beyond the frontier.

[4] For an account of the emigrant party and of the trip of the group that went to California, *see* John Bidwell, *A Journey to California,* etc. (San Francisco, John Henry Nash, Printer, 1937). Joseph Williams' record, published in vol. III of the present *Far West and the Rockies Series,* gives an account of that section of the emigrant company that trekked to Oregon.

of May, 1841, with the design of becoming one of their number. In this, however, I was doomed to disappointment by being too late. A few weeks subsequent marked the return of several fur companies, from their annual excursions to the Indian tribes inhabiting the regions adjacent to the head-waters of the Platte and Arkansas rivers, whose outward trips are performed in the fall months. Impatient at delay and despairing of a more eligible opportunity, for at least some time to come, I made prompt arrangements with one of them, to accompany it, *en route,* as far as the Rocky Mountains, intending to proceed thereafter as circumstances or inclination might suggest. This plan of travelling was adhered to, notwithstanding the detention of some three months, which retarded its prosecution.

I would here beg indulgence of the reader to a seeming digression. The peculiar locality of the places to whose vicinity he is now introduced, owing to the deep interest cherished in the public mind relative to the Oregon country, will doubtless call for more than a mere passing notice: I allude to the towns of Independence and Westport. Situated as they are, at the utmost verge of civilization, and upon the direct route to Oregon and regions adjacent, they must retain and command, as the great starting points for emigrants and traders, that importance already assumed by general consent. Their facilities of access from all parts of the Union, both by land and water, are nowhere exceeded. The proud Missouri rolls its turbid waves within six miles of either place, opening the highway of steam communication, while numberless prime roads that converge from every direction, point to them as their common focus.[5] Thus, the staid New Englander may

[5] The Santa Fé Trail and its "Commerce of the Prairies" were largely responsible for the founding and rise of both towns. Independence, after the town site of Franklin was washed into the Missouri River, became the principal early starting point of the Trail. Kansas City and its present suburb of Westport, later succeeded to the role of outfitting depot.

View on Missouri River opposite Fort Leavenworth.

exchange his native hills for the frontier prairies in the short interval of two weeks; and in half that time the citizens of the sunny South may reach the appointed rendezvous; and, nearer by, the hardy emigrant may commence his long overland journey, from his own door, fully supplied with all the necessaries for its successful termination.

Independence is the seat of justice for Jackson county, Mo., about four hundred miles west by north of St. Louis[6] and contains a population of nearly two thousand. Westport is a small town in the same county, near the mouth of the Kansas river,— three miles from the Indian territory, and thirty below the U.S. Dragoon station at Fort Leavenworth. The regular routes to Santa Fe and Oregon date their commencement at these places. The country in this vicinity is beginning to be generally settled by thrifty farmers, from whom all the articles necessary for travellers and traders, may be procured upon reasonable terms.

Starting from either of the above points, a short ride bears the adventurer across the state line, and affords him the opportunity of taking his initiatory lessons amid the realities of prairie life. Here, most of the trading and emigrant companies remain encamped for several weeks, to recruit their animals and complete the needful arrangements, prior to undertaking the toilsome and dangerous journey before them.

The scenery of this neighborhood is truly delightful. It seems indeed like one of Nature's favored spots, where Flora presides in all her regal splendor, and with the fragrance of wild flowers, perfumes the breath of spring and lades the summer breeze with willing incense; — now, sporting beside her fountains and revelling in her dales,— then, smiling from her hilltops, or luxurating beneath her groves.

[6] The present highway is 245 miles. The route on the twisting Missouri River was of course much longer.

I shall never forget the pleasing sensations produced by my first visit to the border-prairies. It was in the month of June, soon after my arrival at Westport. The day was clear and beautiful. A gentle shower the preceding night had purified the atmosphere, and the laughing flowerets, newly invigorated from the nectarine draught, seemed to vie with each other in the exhalation of their sweetest odors. The blushing strawberry, scarce yet divested of its rich burden of fruit, kissed my every step. The buttercup, tulip, pink, violet, and daisy, with a variety of other beauties, unknown to the choicest collections of civilized life, on every side captivated the eye and delighted the fancy.

The ground was clothed with luxuriant herbage. The grass, where left uncropped by grazing herds of cattle and horses, had attained a surprising growth. The landscape brought within the scope of vision a most magnificent prospect. The groves, clad in their gayest foliage and nodding to the wind, ever and anon, crowned the gentle acclivities or reared their heads from the valleys, as if planted by the hand of art to point the wayfarer to Elysian retreats. The gushing fountains, softly breathing their untaught melody, before and on either hand, at short intervals, greeted the ear and tempted the taste. The lark, linnet, and martin, uniting with other feathered songsters, poured forth their sweetest strains in one grand concert, and made the air vocal with their warblings; and the brown-plumed grouse, witless of the approach of man, till dangerously near, would here and there emerge well-nigh from under foot, and whiz through the air with almost lightning speed, leaving me half frightened at her unlooked for presence and sudden exit. Hither and yon, truant bands of horses and cattle, from the less inviting pastures of the settlements, were seen in the distance, cropping the choice herbage before them, or gambolling in all the pride of native freedom.

King of the Shawnees.

Amid such scenes I delight to wander, and often, at this late day, will my thoughts return, unbidden, to converse with them anew. There is a charm in the loneliness — an enchantment in the solitude — a witching variety in the sameness, that must ever impress the traveller, when, for the first time, he enters within the confines of the great western prairies.

One thing further and I will have done with this digression. Connected with the foregoing, it may not be deemed amiss to say something in relation to the Indian tribes inhabiting the territory adjacent to this common camping-place. The nearest native settlement is some twelve miles distant, and belongs to the Shawnees. This nation numbers in all fourteen or fifteen hundred men, women and children. Their immediate neighbors are the Delawares and Wyandotts,— the former claiming a population of eleven hundred, and the latter, three or four hundred. Many connected with these tribes outstrip the nearer whites, in point of civilization and refinement,— excelling them both in honesty and morality, and all that elevates and ennobles the human character. Their wild habits have become in a great measure subdued by the restraining influences of christianity, and they themselves transformed into industrious cultivators of the soil,— occupying neat mansions with smiling fields around them.

Nor are they altogether neglectful of the means of education. The mission schools are generally well attended by ready pupils, in no respect less backward than the more favored ones of other lands.[7] It is not rare even, considering the smallness of their number,

[7] The Shawnee Mission is most famous. Begun by Reverend Thomas Johnson in 1830, it became a notable institution of the frontier. For its history *see* Martha B. Caldwell, *Annals of Shawnee Methodist Mission and Indian Manual Labor School* (Topeka, Kansas State Historical Society, 1939). The Kansas State Historical Society, which supplied us with a copy of this 120-page volume, now administers the remaining mission buildings, one of which is an interesting museum.

Shawnee Maiden.

to meet among them with persons of liberal education and accomplishments. Their mode of dress assimilates that of the whites, though, as yet, fashion has made comparatively but small inroads. The unsophisticated eye would find prolific source for amusement in the uncouth appearance of their females on public occasions. Perchance a gay Indian maiden comes flaunting past, with a huge fur-hat awkwardly placed upon her head,—embanded by broad strips of figured tin, instead of ribbons,—and ears distended with large flattened rings of silver, reaching to her shoulders; and here another, solely habited in a long wollen under-dress, obtrudes to view, and skips along in all the pride and pomposity of a regular city belle! Such are sights by no means uncommon.

These tribes have a regular civil government of their own, and all laws instituted for the general welfare are duly respected. They are also becoming more temperate in their habits, fully convinced that ardent spirits have hitherto proved the greatest enemy to the red man. The churches of various christian denominations, established among them, are in a flourishing condition, and include with their members many whose lives of exemplary piety adorn their professions.

Taken as a whole, the several Indian tribes, occupying this beautiful and fertile section of country, are living witnesses to the softening and benign influences of enlightened christian effort, and furnish indubitable evidence of the susceptibility of the Aborigine for civilization and improvement.

CHAPTER II.

AFTER many vexatious delays and disappointments, the time was at length fixed for our departure, and leaving Independence on the 2d of September, I proceeded to join the encampment without the state line. It was nearly night before I reached my destination, and the camp-fires were already lighted, in front of which the officiating cook was busily engaged in preparing the evening repast. To the windward were the dusky forms of ten or fifteen men,— some standing, others sitting *a la Turk,* and others half-reclining or quietly extended at full length upon the ground,— watching the operative of the culinary department with great seeming interest.

Enchairing myself upon a small log, I began to survey the surrounding objects. In the back ground stood four large Connestoga waggons,[8] with ample canvass tops, and one dearborn, all tastefully drawn up in crescent form. To the right a small pyramid-shaped tent, with its snow-white covering, disclosed itself to the eye, and presented an air of comfort. To the left the caravan animals, securely picketed, at regular distances of some fifteen yards apart, occupied an area of several acres. Close at hand a crystal streamlet traced its course, murmuring adown the valley; and still beyond, a lovely grove waved its branches in the breeze, and contributed its willing mite to enliven and beautify the scene. The camp-fires in front, formed a kind of gateway to a small

[8] The famous wagon took its name from Conestoga, Pennsylvania, place of manufacture. See *The Conestoga Six-Horse Bell Teams of Eastern Pennsylvania,* Published by John Omwake for Private Distribution (Cincinnati, 1930) [no author listed].

enclosure, shut in as above described. Here were congregated the company, or at least, that portion of it yet arrived. Some had already spread their easily adjusted couches upon the ground, in readiness for the coming night, and seemed only awaiting supper to forget their cares and troubles in the sweet embrace of sleep.

Every thing presented such an air of primitive simplicity not altogether estranged to comfort, I began to think it nowise marvellous that this mode of life should afford such strong attractions to those inured to it.

Supper disposed of, the area within camp soon became tenanted by the devotees of slumber,— some snoring away most melodiously, and others conversing in an animated tone, now jovial, now grave, and at intervals, causing the night-air to resound with merry peals of laughter. At length the sleep-god began to assert his wonted supremacy, and silence in some measure reigned throughout camp.

The bed of a mountaineer is an article neither complex in its nature nor difficult in its adjustment. A single buffalo robe folded double and spread upon the ground, with a rock, or knoll, or some like substitue for a pillow, furnishes the sole base-work upon which the sleeper reclines, and, enveloped in an additional blanket or robe, contentedly enjoys his rest. Wishing to initiate myself to the new mode of life before me, I was not slow to imitate the example of the promiscuous throng, and the lapse of a few moments found me in a fair way to pass quite pleasantly my first night's repose in the open air.

With the first gray of morning I arose refreshed and invigorated, nor even suffered the slightest ill effect from my unusual exposure to a humid and unwholesome night-air. The whole camp, soon after, began to disclose a scene of cheerfulness and animation. The cattle and horses, unloosed from their fastenings, and accompanied by keepers, were again permitted to roam at large, and in a short time were most industriously engaged in administering to the calls of appetite.

After breakfast I improved the opportunity to look about and scan more closely the appearance of my *compagnons de voyage*. This opened to view a new field for the study of men and manners.

A mountain company generally comprises some quaint specimens of human nature, and, perhaps, few more so than the one to which I here introduce the reader. To particularize would exceed my limits, nor could I do full justice to the subject in hand by dealing in generalities; — however, I yield to the latter. There are many crude originals mixed with the prime ingredients of these companies. A genuine mountaineer is a problem hard to solve. He seems a kind of *sui genus,* an oddity, both in dress, language, and appearance, from the rest of mankind. Associated with nature in her most simple forms by habit and manner of life, he gradually learns to despise the restraints of civilization, and assimilates himself to the rude and unpolished character of the scenes with which he is most conversant. Frank and open in his manners and generous in his disposition, he is, at the same time, cautious and reserved. In his frankness he will allow no one to acquire an undue advantage of him, though in his generosity, he will oftentimes expend the last cent to assist a fellow in need. Implacable in his hatred, he is also steadfast in his friendship, and knows no sacrifice too great for the benefit of those he esteems. Free as the pure air he breathes, and proudly conscious of his own independence, he will neither tyrannize over others, nor submit to be trampled upon,— and is always prepared to meet the perils he may chance to encounter, with an undaunted front. Inured to hardship and deprivation, his wants are few, and he is the last to repine at the misfortunes which so often befall him. Patience becomes as it were interwoven with his very nature, and he submits to the greatest disasters without a murmur. His powers of endurance, from frequent exercise, attain a strength and capacity almost incredible,—such as are altogether unknown to the more delicately nurtured. His is a trade, to become master of which requires a long and faithful apprenticeship. Of this none seems more conscious than himself, and woe to the *"greenhorn"* who too prematurely assumes to be "journeyman." His ideas, his arguments, his illustrations, all partake of the unpolished simplicity of his associations; though abounding often in the most vivid imagery, pointed inferences, and luminous expositions, they need a key to make them intelligible to the novice.

His dress and appearance are equally singular. His skin, from constant exposure, assumes a hue almost as dark as that of the Aborigine, and his features and physical structure attain a rough and hardy cast. His hair, through inattention, becomes long, coarse, and bushy, and loosely dangles upon his shoulders. His head is surmounted by a low crowned wool-hat, or a rude substitute of his own manufacture. His clothes are of buckskin, gaily fringed at the seams with strings of the same material, cut and made in a fashion peculiar to himself and associates. The deer and buffalo furnish him the required covering for his feet, which he fabricates at the impulse of want. His waist is encircled with a belt of leather, holding encased his butcher-knife and pistols — while from his neck is suspended a bullet-pouch securely fastened to the belt in front, and beneath the right arm hangs a powder-horn transversely from his shoulder, behind which, upon the strap attached to it, are affixed his bullet-mould, ball-screw, wiper, awl, &c. With a gun-stick made of some hard wood, and a good rifle placed in his hands, carrying from thirty to thirty-five balls to the pound, the reader will have before him a correct likeness of a genuine mountaineer, when fully equipped.

This costume prevails not only in the mountains proper, but also in the less settled portions of Oregon and California. The mountaineer is his own manufacturer, tailor, shoemaker, and butcher; and, fully accoutred and supplied with ammunition in a good game country, he can always feed and clothe himself, and enjoy all the comforts his situation affords. No wonder, then, his proud spirit, expanding with the intuitive knowledge of noble independence, becomes devotedly attached to those regions and habits that permit him to stalk forth, a sovereign amid nature's loveliest works.[9]

Our company, however, were not all mountaineers; some were only "entered apprentices," and others mere *"greenhorns"*— taking every thing into consideration, perhaps, it was quite as agreeably composed as circumstances would well admit of. In glancing over the crowd, I remarked several countenances sinister and malign, but consented to suspend judgment till the character of each should be proven by his conduct. Hence, in the succeeding pages, I shall only speak of characters as I have occasion to speak of men. As a whole, the party before me presented a choice collection of local varieties,— here was the native of France, of Canada, of England, of Hudson Bay, of Connecticut, of Pennsylvania, of New York, of Kentucky, of Illinois, of Missouri, and of the Rocky Mountains, all congregated to act in unison for a specified purpose. It might well require the pencil of Hogarth to picture such a motley group.

[9] Although not so famous or talented a writer upon the Western mountaineers as was George F. Ruxton, Sage does precede the young Englishman in writing and publishing a good description of the Mountain Man of the West. Ruxton's books, *Adventures in Mexico and the Rocky Mountains* and his *Life in the Far West* were first published in 1847 and 1848 respectively. The latest editions, edited by L. R. Hafen, were published in 1950 and 1951. Irving's pen pictures, however, in his *Bonneville,* had preceded Sage's portrayal.

Our company had not as yet attained its full numerical strength; a small division of it was some distance in advance, another behind, and at least two days would be necessary to complete the arrangements prior to leaving. The idea of spending two days in camp, notwithstanding the beauty of its location, was by no means agreeable; but as the case was beyond remedy, I quietly submitted, and managed to while away the tedious interval as best I could.

A brief acquaintance with our commandant, found him a man of small stature and gentlemanly deportment, though savoring somewhat of arrogance and self-sufficiency,— faults, by the way, not uncommon in little men. He had been engaged in the Indian trade for several years past, and had seen many "ups and downs" in former life. Graduating from West Point in his younger days, he soon after received the commission of Lieutenant of Dragoons, in the U.S. Army, and served in that capacity for some six or eight years, on the frontier and at Forts Gibson and Leavenworth. Possessed of the confidence of his men, his subsequent resignation was the occasion of much regret with those he had been accustomed to command. The private soldier loved him for his generous frankness and readiness to overlook minor offenses, even upon the first show of penitence.

Such unbounded popularity at length excited the jealousy of his brother officers, and gave birth to a combination against him, which nothing could appease short of his removal from the army. Aware of his ardent temperament and strong party notions as a politician, and equally violent upon the opposite side, they managed to inveigle him into a discussion of the measures and plans of the then administration of national affairs. Arguing in the excitement of feeling, he made use of an unguarded expression, denouncing the Chief Magistrate. This was immediately noted down, and charges were promptly preferred against him, for *"abuse of a superior officer!"* The whole affair was then referred to a Court Martial, composed exclusively of political opponents. The evidence was so strong he had little to expect from their hands, and consequently threw up his commission, to avert the disgrace of being *cashiered,* since which he has been engaged in his present business.

He appeared to be a man of general information, and well versed in science and literature. Indeed, I felt highly gratified in making an acquaintance so far congenial to my own taste.[10]

An accession of two waggons and four men having completed our number, the morning of September 4th was ushered in with the din of preparations for an immediate start. The lading of the waggons was then severally overhauled and more compactly adjusted, and our arms were deposited with other freight until such time as circumstances should call for them. All was hurry and confusion, and oftimes the sharp tone of angry dispute arose above the jargon of the tumultuous throng.

---

[10] Sage nowhere names this leader of the trading party. But we are able to identify him from the description and information here given, as Lieutenant Lancaster P. Lupton. Perhaps one of the reasons why he does not name the commandant is because, as mentioned later, he is hauling several barrels of prohibited whiskey out to his trading posts for barter with the trappers and Indians.

Lupton was born in New York state in 1807. He entered the U.S. Military Academy in 1825 and graduated four years later. In 1833 he was appointed a lieutenant in the newly created First Dragoons and in 1835 commanded Company A while accompanying Colonel Henry Dodge and the Dragoons to the Rocky Mountains. He resigned from the army in March, 1836, came west, and built his fort on the South Platte. He joined the gold rush to California in 1849. Later he settled in northern California and died near Arcata on August 2, 1885. – L. R. Hafen, "Old Fort Lupton and its Builders," in the *Colorado Magazine,* VI, 220-26.

At length the word was given to advance, and in an instant the whole caravan was in motion; those disconnected with the waggons, mounted upon horseback, led the van, followed by the teams and their attendants in Indian file, as the loose cattle and horses brought up the rear. The scene to me portrayed a novelty quite amusing. I began to think a more comical-looking set could scarcely be found any where; but the events of the day soon convinced me of my mistake.

Travelling leisurely along for some six or eight miles, strange objects were seen in the distance, which, on nearer approach, proved a company of Mexican traders, on their way to Independence for an equipment of goods.[11] As they filed past us, I had full scope for the exercise of my risibilities.

If a mountaineer and a mountain company are laughable objects, a Mexican and a Mexican company are triply so. The first thing that excites attention upon meeting one of this mongrel race, is his ludicrous apology for pantaloons. This is generally made of deer or buffalo skin, similar to our present fashion, except the legs, which are left unsewed from the thigh downwards; a loose pair of cotton drawers,

[11] This was doubtless the company reported from Independence on Sept. 21, by a correspondent whose letter was published in the *Daily Missouri Republican* of September 28, 1841, as follows: "The company from Santa Fé arrived some time since, as doubtless you have heard ere this. Only one or two of the old traders have returned; the majority of the party being composed of those who freighted out goods in the Spring. Some Spaniards accompanied them for the purpose of taking out merchandise the coming year; they brought along with them 70,000 or 80,000 dollars, and a quantity of valuable furs. The trip has been the most expeditious one ever performed." It may be the same Mexican company on their return, that is reported in the *Missouri Republican* of October 21, 1841; as quoted from the *Missourian* of the 9th: "A large caravan, consisting of thirty wagons and about three hundred and fifty mules, left our town a short time ago, en route to Santa Fé.—The expedition is superintended by Seignoirs Armeho, Charvois and Monsieur D. Gordis. They take with them seventy-two tons of goods. Our town is now comparatively quiet, and the traders who occasionally cheered the dull monotony of our village, have generally left, either for Santa Fé, Chihuahua, or the Rocky Mountains."

Wagon Train.

cut and made in like manner, and worn beneath, imparts to his every movements a most grotesque appearance, leaving at each step of the wearer his denuded leg, with that of his pantaloons on one side, and drawers on the other, fluttering in the breeze! The next thing that meets the gaze, is his black, slouching, broad-brimmed hat, *(sombrero)* though little darker than the features it obscures, and far less so than the coarse, jet-colored hair that protrudes from beneath it, and falls confusedly upon his shoulders. Next, if the weather tolerates the habit, a coarse parti-colored blanket *(charape)* [serape] envelopes the body, from his shoulders downwards, fixed to its place by an aperture in the centre through which the head is thrust, and securely girted at pleasure by a waist-band of leather. His arms, if arms he has, consist of a rude bow and arrows slung to his back, or an old fusee, not unfrequently without flint, lock, or ammunition; but doubly armed, and proudly, too, is he who can carry a good rifle with powder and lead — even if he *be* ignorant of their use.

Thus appearing, these creatures, some mounted upon mules, with heavy spurs attached to their heels, (bearing gaffs an inch and a half in length, jingling in response to the rolling motions of the wearer,) ensconced in bungling Spanish saddles, (finished with such ample leather skirts as almost hid the diminutive animal that bore them, and large wooden stirrups, some three inches broad,) were riding at their ease; while others, half naked, were trudging along on foot, driving their teams, or following the erratic mules of the caravan, to heap upon them the ready maledictions of their prolific vocabulary. Passing on, we were accosted:

"Como lo pasa, cabelleros?"

The salutation was returned by a simple nod.

"Habla la lengua Espanola, senors?"

A shake of the head was the only response.

"Es esta el camino de Independenca?"

No reply.

"Carraho! Que quantos jornadas tenemos en la camino de Independenca?"

Still no one answered.

"Scha! Maldijo tualmas! Los Americanos esta dijabelo!"

By this time the crowd had passed and left us no longer annoyed by its presence. The conclusion irresistibly forced itself upon my mind, "if these are true specimens of Mexicans, it is no wonder they incite both the pity and contempt of the rest of the world." Subsequent intercourse with them, however, has served to convince me that first impressions, in this case, instead of exceeding the reality, fell far short of the true mark!

Continuing our course, we saw large numbers of prairie-hens, and succeeded in killing several. These birds assimilate the English grouse in appearance, and are a dusky-brown color,— with short tails, and narrow-peaked wings,— and little less in size than the domestic fowl. Their flesh is tender and of superior flavor. When alarmed, they start with a cackling noise, and whiz through the air not unlike the partridge. They are very numerous on the frontier prairies, and extend to the Rocky Mountains, Oregon, California and New Mexico.

About sundown we reached a small creek known as Elm Grove,[12] and encamped for the night, with every indication of an approaching storm. Strict orders were accordingly given for securing the animals, and the process of "picketing" was speedily under way. This consisted in driving small stakes ("pickets") firmly into the ground, at proper distances apart, to which the animals were severally tied by strong cords,— a plan that should find nightly practice among all travel-

[12] Elm Grove, also called Round Grove, was located about forty miles beyond Independence. *See* vol. III of this *Series*, p. 28.

lers of the grand prairies, to prevent those losses which, despite the utmost precaution, will not unfrequently occur.

Timber proved quite scarce in this vicinity, and it was with great difficulty we procured sufficient for cooking purposes. The men now began to prepare for the coming storm. Some disposed of themselves in, and others under, the waggons, making barricades to the windward; others erected shantees, by means of slender sticks, planted in parallel rows five or six feet apart, and interwoven at the tops, so as to form an arch of suitable height, over which was spread a roofage of robes or blankets,— while others, snugly ensconced beneath the ready pitched tent, bade defiance to wind and weather.

Being one of those selecting a place under the waggons, I retired at an early hour to snooze away the night; and despite the anticipations of an unpleasant time, I soon lost myself in a sweet slumber, utterly unconscious of every thing around me. In thoughts I wandered back to the home of my childhood, to converse with friends whose names and features fond memory has chained to my heart, while imagination roamed with delight amid those scenes endeared to me by earliest and most cherished recollections. But all the sweet pencillings of fancy were at once spoiled by the uncivil intrusion of a full torrent of water, that came pouring from the hill-side and forced its impetuous way into the valley below,— deluging me from head to foot in its descent. My condition, as the reader may well suppose, was far from being enviable. However, resolved to make the best of a bad thing, after wringing the water from my drenched bedding, I selected another spot and again adjusted myself to pass the dreary interval till morning; this I succeeded in doing,— how or in what manner, it is unnecessary to say. Sleep was utterly out of the question, and I am quite sure I never hailed the welcome morn with greater delight than on this occasion.

Others of the company fared almost as bad as myself, and there was scarcely a dry bed in camp. But the little concern evinced by the mountaineers for their mishap, surprised me most. They crawled from their beds, reeking with wet, as good humoredly as though their nocturnal bath had in no wise disturbed their equanimity, or impaired their comfort.

The morning proved so disagreeable two of our party, who were accompanying us for the purpose of adventure, concluding this a kind of adventure they were unwilling to meet, wisely resolved to take the back track, and accordingly left for home. Towards night the rain ceased, and, the clouds having dispersed, we were again *en route*. Travelling on till late, we encamped in the open prairie, and early the next morning resumed our course. Having reached a small creek, about 10 o'clock, we halted for breakfast, where another Santa Fe company came up. This proved a party of Americans, with some six or eight waggons and a large number of horses and mules, on their homeward journey. They had also in their possession an elk nearly full grown, two black-tailed deer,[13] an antelope and a white-tailed fawn.

Through them we received intelligence of a battle recently fought between the Pawnee and Arapaho Indians, at the lower Cimarone Springs, south of the Arkansas. The former had been defeated with great slaughter,— losing their horses and seventy-two of their bravest warriors, to increase the trophies and enliven the scalp-dances of their enemies. This action occurred directly upon the Santa Fe trail, and the dead yet bestrewed the prairie, as our informants passed, half

[13] The black-tailed deer are larger than the common deer, and are found only in the snow-mountains. For a description of them the reader is referred to subsequent pages. [Sage]

devoured by wolves, and filling the air with noisome stench as they wasted beneath the influence of a scorching sun.

An approving murmur ran through the crowd while listening to the recital, and all united to denounce the Pawnees as a dangerous and villanous set, and wished for their utter extermination.

CHAPTER III.

CONTINUING our course, we bore to the right, and struck the northern or Platte trail,[14] and, after travelling eight or ten miles, made camp upon a small creek skirted with heavy timber, called Black Jack. An early start the next morning brought us to the Wakarousha, a considerable tributary of the Kansas, where a junction was formed with our advance party. The territory lying upon this stream as far south as Council Grove, (a noted place on the Mexican trail, 144 miles west from Independence,) belongs to the Pottowatomies. These Indians are very wealthy and are partially civilized,— the most of them being tillers of the ground. Their dwellings are of very simple construction,— large strips of bark firmly tied to a frame-work of poles with small apertures to admit light, furnishing the exterior, while the interior is finished by the suspension of two or three blankets between the apartments, as partitions, and erecting a few scaffolds for bedsteads. The fire-place in warm weather is out of doors, but in the winter it occupies the centre of the building, from which the smoke — unaided by jamb or chimney — is left to find its way through an opening in the roof. Some, however, are beginning to improve in their style of architecture, and now and then we find a tolerably spacious and comfortable house among them.

[14] Later called the Oregon Trail. To this point they had followed the Santa Fé Trail. Their route ahead is to be approximately that of the Bartleson-Bidwell party that had gone out in the preceding spring. With that former party had traveled Reverend Joseph Williams. *See* his narrative reproduced in the preceding volume of this *Series,* for an account of the trip and the route.

The Catholics have several missionaries with this tribe,[15] and are using great exertions, if not to ameliorate their condition, at least, to proselyte them to their own peculiar faith. The missionaries of other christian denominations are also devoting themselves for their benefit, and not unfrequently with gratifying success.

The remainder of the day was occupied in crossing the creek — a task by no means easy,— its banks being so precipitous we were compelled to lower our waggons by means of ropes. In so doing it required the utmost caution to prevent them from oversetting or becoming broken in the abrupt descent.

The night following was passed upon the opposite bank. After travelling some twelve miles the next day, we encamped a short distance to the right of the trail, at a place known as the Springs. Scarcely had we halted when two footmen appeared from an opposite direction — one of them leading a horse — whom a nearer advance proved to be a white man and an Indian. The former was immediately recognized by our *engages* as an old acquaintance, by the name of Brown,[16] who had been their recent *compagnon de voyage* from the mountains. His story was soon told. A few days subsequent to his arrival in the States, a difficulty had occurred between him and another person, who received

[15] The Potawatomi Mission, established by the Jesuits on Sugar Creek, near present Centerville, Kansas, on March 10, 1839, is doubtless the one referred to, according to Nyle M. Miller, Secretary of the Kansas State Historical Society. For an account of the removal of the Potawatomies to this place and of the Catholic missionary work among these Indians, *see* G. J. Garraghan, *The Jesuits of the Middle United States* (New York, America Press, 1938), II, pp. 175-235.

[16] We are unable to positively identify this man. He may be the Baptiste Brown of Brown's Hole on Green River and who later was on the jury at Taos that tried the murderers of Governor Charles Bent in 1847. He could be John Brown who was on the upper Arkansas and the Greenhorn in 1846 and before, who married Jim Beckwourth's wife and later lived with her at San Bernardino, California. *See* J. S. Loveland (ed.), *Mediumistic Experiences of John Brown, the Medium of the Rockies* (3d ed., San Francisco, 1892).

a severe wound from a knife by the hand of Brown during the affray, when the latter was necessitated to consult his own safety by a hurried flight. He accordingly bade farewell both to enemies and law, and left for the Indian country — travelling most of the way by night. Two weeks afterwards he arrived in the Kansas nation, and remained with the Indian now accompanying him, to await our return.

Having listened to his story, I began to survey his strange companion. He was a village chief of the Kansas (Caw) tribe, and the first of his race I had ever seen so nearly dressed in his native costume. In person he was tall and stout-built,— with broad shoulders and chest, brawny arms and legs, and features evincing the uncontaminated blood of the Aborigine. His hair was closely shaved to the scalp, with the exception of a narrow tuft centerwise from forehead to crown, so trimmed it stood on end like the bristles of a warring hog; then his whole head and face were so lavishly bedaubed with vermilion, our experienced city belles would doubtless have considered it an unpardonable waste of that *useful material!*

A string of bears'-claws, tastefully arranged, encircled his neck, while ample folds of brass wire above the wrists and elbows furnished his armillary, and from his ears hung rude ornaments,— some of silver, others of brass or iron — cruelly distending the flexible members that bore them. A dirty white blanket drawn closely around the shoulders enveloped the body, which, with a breech-cloth and leggins, formed his sole covering. A bow and arrows, slung to his back by a strap passing over the left shoulder and under the right arm, were his only weapons. A belt, begirting the waist, sustained his tobacco-pouch and butcher-knife, and completed his attire and armament.

Thus habited appeared before us the Caw chief, holding in one hand the lead-rope of his horse, and in

THE CAW CHIEF

the other the wing of a wild turkey, with a long-stemmed pipe, carved from a hard red stone, handsomely wrought and finely polished. Taken altogether, he presented an amusing spectacle — a real curiosity.

Having shaken hands with the company and turned his horse to graze, in a few moments his pipe was subjected to its destined use, and, as the inhaled fumes merrily curved from his mouth and nostrils, he ever and anon presented it for the indulgence of the bystanders. His knowledge of English was limited to the simple monosyllable "good," which he took occasion to pronounce at intervals as he thought proper.

Sept. 8th. Continuing on, we encamped towards night at a small creek within six miles of the crossing of the Kansas river. Here a bevy of our chief's villagers, rigged in their rude fashion, came flocking up, apparently to gratify their curiosity in gazing at us, but really in expectation of some trifling presents, or in quest of a favorable opportunity for indulging their inate propensities for theft. However, they found little encouragement, as the vigilance of our guards more than equalled the cunning of our visitors. During their stay we were frequently solicited for donations of tobacco and ammunition, (as they expressed it,) in payment for passing through their country. This was individually demanded with all the assurance of government revenue officers, or the keepers of regular toll-bridges, strongly reminding one of the petty nations upon the borders of Canaan that required tribute of the Israelites passing through them to possess the land of their forefathers.

Sept. 9th. Early in the forenoon we came to the Kansas, and were employed till nearly night in effecting a ford.[17] This proved rather difficult, as the water was deep and the bottom sandy; — the course, bearing directly across, till near midway of the river, follows

[17] For a discussion of crossings of the Kansas River and of maps of the Oregon Trail (which Sage is following) *see* volume III of this *Series*, p. 216.

the current for six or eight hundred yards, and then turns abruptly to the opposite shore. The Kansas, at the crossing, was not far from six hundred yards wide, with steep banks of clay and sand. The fording accomplished, we travelled some six miles, and encamped for the night. Our visitors yet honored us with their presence; some, under pretence of trading horses; others, of bartering for tobacco, whiskey, coffee, and ammunition; but most of them for the real purpose of begging and stealing.

The Caw Indians are a branch of the Osage tribe — speaking the same language, and identified by the same manners and customs. They number a population of sixteen hundred, and claim all the territory west of the Delaware, Shawnee, and Pottowatomie line, to the head waters of the Kansas. Their main village is on the left bank of the river, a few miles above the crossing. Their houses are built Pawnee fashion, being coniform and covered with a thick coat of dirt, presenting a hole at the apex to emit the smoke, and another at the side to serve the double purpose of a door and window. The whole building describes a complete circle, in whose centre is placed the hearth-fire, and at the circumference the couches of its inmates. Its floor is the bare ground, and its ceiling the grass, brush, and poles which uphold the superincumbent earth forming the roof and sides.

The Caws are generally a lazy and slovenly people, raising but little corn, and scarcely any vegetables. For a living they depend mostly upon the chase. Their regular hunts are in the summer, fall, and winter, at which time they all leave for the buffalo range, and return laden with a full supply of choice provisions. The robes and skins thus obtained, furnish their clothing and articles for traffic.

As yet, civilization has made but small advances among them. Some, however, are tolerably well educated, and a Protestant mission established with them, is beginning its slow but successful operations for their good,[18] — while two or three families of half-breeds, near by, occupy neat houses, and have splendid farms and improvements, thus affording a wholesome contrast to the poverty and misery of their rude neighbors.

The distance from Independence to this place, by the mountain trail, is some eighty miles, over a beautiful and fertile country, which I shall hereafter take occasion to notice more fully. Before leaving, we were further increased by the accession of two Canadian *voyageurs* — French of course. Our force now numbered some twenty-four — one sufficiently formidable for all the dangers of the route.

Sept. 10th. Resuming our way, we proceeded till late at night, still attended by our Indian friends; (not the originals, but a "few more of the same sort," who *kindly* supplied their places,— seeking to levy fresh drafts upon patience and generosity.) These were more importunate for liquor than any preceding them — though, in fact, the whole nation is nowise remiss in their devotion to King Alcohol. One fellow, in particular, exhausted all his ingenuity to obtain the wherewith to *"wet his whistle."* He was a shrivel-faced old man, and occasioned much sport, from his supplications in broken English, which ran pretty much as follows:

"Big man, me. Chief,— Black Warrior. Me, American soldier! Love Americans, heap. Big man, me! Love whiskey, heap. White man good. Whiskey good. Love whiskey, me,— drink heap whiskey. No give me whis-

[18] On September 16, 1830, the Missouri Conference of the Methodist Episcopal Church at St. Louis appointed Reverend William Johnson as a missionary to the Caw, or Kansas, Indians, and his brother Thomas to the Potawatomies. Joseph Williams – *see* volume III in this *Series,* p. 216 – traveled with William Johnson toward his mission in May, 1841. Rev. Johnson died on April 10, 1842.— Caldwell, *Annals of Shawnee Methodist Mission, op cit.,* p. 44.

key drink? Me, Chief. Me, American. Me, Black Warrior. Heap big man, me! Love Americans. Take him hand, shake. White man good. Whiskey good. Me love whiskey! Love him heap! No give Black Warrior whiskey? No? — one leetle drink? Whiskey good. Me love him. Make Black Warrior strong. Big man, me,— Chief. American soldier. Me love American. Shake him hand. Fight him, bad Indian, no love white man. Kill him. White man good. Me love white man. Whiskey good. Me love whiskey. No give Black Warrior whiskey,— one leetle drink? Me, Chief. Big man, me." Etc.

In this strain the old fellow continued so long as he found listeners, but without success, although, as I afterwards learned, two waggons were freighted with the noxious article; [19] none of it was suffered to find its way down the throats of our thirsty guests.

Pursuing a westerly course, nearly parallel with the Kansas, for three successive days, we passed the 14th encamped at Big Vermilion, for the purpose of procuring a quantity of hickory for gun-sticks and bow-timber. Hickory is unknown to the Rocky Mountains, and this being the last place on the route affording it, each of our company took care to provide himself with an extra gun-stick. Small pieces, suitable for bows, find market among the mountain Indians, ranging at the price of a robe each, while gun-sticks command one dollar apiece, from the hunters and trappers.

We were also careful to provide an extra quantity of ox-bows, axle-trees, &c., as a resource in case of accidents or breakage. These are articles with which every caravan should be furnished on a journey across the grand prairies.[20]

---

[19] Such liquor was prohibited by the United States Government for trade with the Indians. Hence the care with which it was concealed.

[20] Similar precautions were regularly taken by travelers at Council Grove on the Santa Fé Trail.

In this vicinity a species of shrub, which I had before noticed in various places, (designated as "red-root" by our voyageurs,) became quite abundant. The red-root is highly esteemed as a substitute for *tea,* and my own experience attests its superiority of flavor to any article of that kind imported from China. In appearance it is very similar to the tea of commerce, and it affords at all times a most excellent beverage. It is found only upon the prairies between the frontiers and Big Blue, and in some portions of the Rocky Mountains.

Leaving Big Vermilion, we travelled rapidly the two days subsequent, and arrived at the North Fork of Blue,[21] — a large and deep stream, tributary to the Kansas. We were here detained till the 24th — the creek being impassable on account of high water.

However, the beauty of the place and variety of its landscape scenery, served in a great measure to alleviate the weariness of delay. The country was most agreeably interspersed with hills, uplands, and dales — amply watered and variegated with woods and prairies, attired in all the gaudy loveliness of wild-flowers. The busy bee, afraid of the cruel persecutions of man, had here sought a secure retreat to pursue, unmolested, her melliferous employ, and fill the dark chambers of her oaken palaces year by year with honeyed stores. The air was almost vocal with the music of her wings, and the flowerets were enlivened by the gentle touches of her embrace. The odor of honey filled the breeze, which, wafting the mingled melody of birds and insects with the incense of flowers, o'er the smiling prairie till lost in space, seemed more like the breath of Eden than the exhalations of earth.

As might be supposed, we were not slow in levying upon the delicious stores, which the industrious insects, claiming this as their dominion, had laid away for themselves. During our stay no less than four bee-trees

[21] Commonly called the Big Blue.

were levelled, and every pan, kettle, pail, keg, or empty dish in the whole camp was filled to overflowing, and every stomach to repletion, with honey of almost crystalline transparency. The great abundance of deer, turkey, and other game in the vicinity, also contributed their share of amusement, and enlivened the interval of detention.

At length, by a partial subsidence of the water, we were enabled to effect a crossing and renew our journey. Pursuing a course W.N.W., on the 27th we met a small party of whites on their return from the mountains, and, yielding to the temptation presented by a luxuriant and well-wooded valley, with a pretty streamlet, the two parties made common camp. Our new acquaintances were taking a large drove of horses, and several domesticated buffalo, with them to the States. Their horses had been mostly obtained from Upper California, the year previous, by a band of mountaineers, under the lead of one Thompson.[22] This band, numbering twenty-two in all, had made a descent upon the Mexican *ranchos* and captured between two and three thousand head of horses and mules. A corps of some sixty Mexican cavalry pursued and attacked them, but were defeated and pursued in turn, with the loss of several mules and their entire camp equipage: after which the adventurers were permitted to regain their mountain homes, without further molestation; but, in passing the cheerless desert, between the Sierra Nevada and Colorado, the heat, dust, and thirst were so intolerably oppressive, that full one half of their animals died. The remainder, however, were brought to rendezvous, and variously disposed of, to suit the wants and wishes of their captors.

---

[22] Philip Thompson. For an account of the horse-stealing expedition *see* vol. I of this *Series,* pp. 236-43. A biographical sketch of Thompson is given in L. R. Hafen, "Fort Davy Crockett, its Fur Men and Visitors," in the *Colorado Magazine*, XXIX, pp. 20-23.

The buffalo, in possession of our wayfaring friends, had been caught while calves, and reared by domestic cows. They appeared as tame and easily managed as other cattle. One of them, a two-year-old heifer, was rather vicious in its habits, having been spoiled, while a calf, by the too great familiarity of its keeper. After listening to a full exposition of its bad qualities, our commandant offered to bet he could handle, or even ride, the unruly beast at pleasure.

"Can you?" said the owner. "Do it, and my best horse is yours!"

"I take all such offers!" returned the commandant. "A horse could not be easier earned!" he continued, stepping towards the ill-tutored animal. "Come, boss! — Poor boss! — bossy, bossy!" addressing the buffalo, which commenced advancing,— at first slowly, then, with a sudden bound, ran full tilt against the admirer, leaving him prostrate upon the ground, as it turned away, dancing and throwing its heels exultingly at the exploit.

"Bless my stars!" he exclaimed, on recovering himself; "I'd no idea 'twould serve me so!"

"Ha, ha, ha!" retorted the owner. "You seem to pick upon a strange place for a snooze! What in the world were you doing before that skittish beast?"

The roar of laughter which followed, told how well the joke was relished by the crowd.

Reports from the mountains brought intelligence of recent difficulties between the whites and Sioux,— the latter having murdered several trappers. A battle had also been fought in the Snake country, in which the Sioux were defeated with a loss of twenty killed and wounded,— the whites suffered in the loss of their leader (Frapp) and four others.[23] Another affair had

[23] *See* L. R. Hafen, "Fraeb's Last Fight and How Battle Creek got its Name," in the *Colorado Magazine,* VII, pp. 97-101.

come off, at Fort Platte,[24] between two factions of that tribe, while on a drunken spree, resulting in the death of Schena-Chischille, their chief, and several of his party.

The most acceptable item of intelligence was the probability of our reaching the buffalo range in ten days, at least, where we should find vast quantities of those animals. This led our voyaguers to expatiate anew upon the choice varieties of the feast of good things we might expect on that occasion.

Bidding adieu to our transient camp-mates, we were soon again *en route*. The day following, being unfit for travel, was devoted to overhauling and re-adjusting the freight of the waggons. Here, for the first time, I ascertained the fact, that a portion of the above consisted of no less than *twenty-four barrels of alcohol,* designed for the Indian trade!

This announcement may occasion surprise to many, when aware that the laws of Congress prohibit, under severe penalties, the introduction of liquor among the Indians, as an article of traffic,— subjecting the offender to a heavy fine and confiscation of effects. Trading companies, however, find ways and means to smuggle it through, by the waggon-load, under the very noses of government officers, stationed along the frontiers to enforce the observance of laws.

I am irresistibly led to the conclusion, that these gentry are wilfully negligent of their duty; and, no doubt, there are often *weighty inducements* presented to them to shut their eyes, close their ears, and avert their faces, to let the guilty pass unmolested. It seems almost impossible that a blind man, retaining the senses of smell, taste and hearing, could remain ignorant of a thing so palpably plain. The alcohol is put into waggons, at Westport or Independence, *in open day-light,*

[24] Fort Platte, near Fort Laramie, will receive more attention later.

and taken into the territory, *in open day light,* where it remains a week or more awaiting the arrival of its owners. Two Government agents reside at Westport, while six or eight companies of Dragoons are stationed at Fort Leavenworth, ostensibly for the purpose of protecting the Indians and suppressing this infamous traffic,— and yet it suffers no diminution from *their vigilance!* What *faithful* public officers! How prompt in the discharge of their *whole duty!*

These gentlemen cannot plead ignorance as an excuse. They well know that alcohol is one of the principal articles in Indian trade — this fact is notorious — no one pretends to deny it; not even the *traders themselves* — and yet, because no one takes the trouble to produce a specimen of the *kind* of freight taken, more or less, by all mountain companies, and FORCE them to *see, taste, touch,* and *smell,* they affect ignorance! It is thus the benevolent designs of our Government are consummated by these pensioners upon the public treasury!

Had they the will so to do, it would be no difficult matter to put a stop to all such exportations. The departure of any one of these companies for the mountains, is a thing too difficult to be effected unknown and stealthily. It becomes public talk for days and even weeks previous. Scarcely anything would be easier than for those whose business it is, to keep on the look out, and enforce the law to its full extent upon each offender. A few examples of this kind would interpose an insuperable barrier to the further prosecution of an illicit traffic in the manner it is at present carried on. A few faithful public officers, and attentive to their duty, regardless of fear or *favor,* would soon accomplish an object so desirable.[25]

[25] The liquor traffic came in for considerable attention in 1842-43. *See* L. R. Hafen and F. M. Young, *Fort Laramie,* etc. (Glendale: The Arthur H. Clark Company, 1938), pp. 86-88. For a general discussion consult H. M. Chittenden, *The American Fur Trade of the Far West* (1935 ed.), pp. 23-31, 669-74.

In subsequent pages of this work I shall have occasion to notice a few of the many evils resulting from this criminal neglect,— but at present forbear further remarks.

Our arms were now put in order for immediate use, — each individual apportioning to himself a good supply of ammunition, to be ready at all times in case of attack. Guards were ordered to be constantly on the alert. The company was divided into two parties,— one for day and the other for night guard, and these again were subdivided for alternate relieves,— thus, one of each subdivision serving a day and a night, and the reserve the day and night succeeding. The day-guard consisted of only two persons, upon duty every other day, but the night-guard numbered ten,— two being on duty for two hours were then relieved by the two next in succession, and they by the next, and so on.

Strict orders were also given to prevent any from leaving camp, or parting from the caravan while travelling. In fact, every thing began to assume a warlike aspect, as if we were really in danger and apprehensive of an immediate rencounter.

Several boxes of clothing, &c., were also opened for such as wished to purchase. But every article disposed of was sold at an enormous rate: tobacco bringing from one to three dollars per lb., according to quality; butcher-knives, from one dollar to one fifty each; hose, one dollar per pair; shirts, from three to five dollars each, according to quality; blankets, from twelve to sixteen dollars; coats, from fifteen to forty dollars; coarse shoes, four dollars per pair; six-penny calicoes, fifty cts. per yd.; beads, one dollar per bunch, etc. These were of an indifferent quality, and afforded the vender some three or four hundred per cent. advance upon purchase-price. In fact, with regard to prices, conscience had nothing to do with the matter.

CHAPTER IV.

Sept. 26th. WE are now camped upon a small creek, nearly destitute of timber, within two miles of Big Blue, or the N.W. branch of the Kansas river. The geography of this part of the country is incorrectly described upon all the published maps I have yet seen. The Republican Fork, which is the principal branch of the Kansas, is uniformly represented as the most northwesterly branch of that river, forming a junction with it at or below the usual crossing. This is not the case.

The two forks of Blue, from the northwest, united, form a large and important stream, which, according to my impression, discharges its waters into the Kansas itself, and not into the Republican. Of this, however, I am not quite positive. But be that as it may, admitting the Republican to be the main stream, Big Blue must be, as a matter of course, the most northwesterly branch of the Kansas river.

Proceeding up the Blue, the geological character of the country undergoes an entire and radical change, and the traveller is introduced to a different order of things from that previously observed.

Perhaps, therefore, it is not out of place to present a general review of the territory thus far.

The interval from the frontier of Missouri to Big Blue, a distance upwards of two hundred miles, affords great uniformity in all its more prominent characteristics. It generally comprises beautifully undulating prairies, of a most argillaceous soil, rich in sedimentary deposits and vegetable matter. It is somewhat rocky in places, but well watered by the almost innumerable streams that find their way into the Kansas, Platte and

Arkansas rivers. The creeks, with but few exceptions, are heavily timbered with oak, hickory, walnut, maple, cottonwood, and other varieties found in more eastern forests. The hills too, in some parts, are more than usually abundant in springs, and covered with stately groves, as tastefully arranged as if planted by the hand of man, while luxuriant grass and fragrant flowers usurp the place of underbrush. The prairies, hemmed in on every side by the woodlands skirting the water-courses, present to the eye proud oceans of flowery verdure, tossing their wavelets to the breeze and perfuming the air with the breath of spring.

The streams are clear, with rocky or pebbly bottoms and high, steep banks — abounding in choice specimens of the finny tribes and varieties of the testaceous order, of the *genus muscula.* The valley of the Kansas is wide and of a deep brown vegetable mould, susceptible of a high state of cultivation. The whole country is well adapted to the double purpose of agriculture and the growth of stock.

The prevailing rock is sandstone of various shades and compactness, with siliceous and fossiliferous limestone. These specifications are generally exhibited in a detached and fragmentary form, but rarely in strata as disclosed upon the surface.

Taken as a whole, the territory holds out many inducements to emigrants, and, whenever brought into market, will no doubt become speedily and thickly populated.[26]

Sept. 30th. We are again under headway. A French engagé, who had been suffering for several days past from a severe attack of the fever and ague, experienced a sudden and novel cure. Unable to travel, quarters were prepared for him in one of the whiskey waggons, where he was comfortably disposed of as we continued our

[26] By a recent treaty with the Kansas Indians, our government has become possessed of nearly the whole of this beautiful section. [Sage]

course. In passing a rough place the waggon overset, when out came the invalid head foremost, and *out came the whiskey barrels* showering full upon him! The suddenness of the fall, with the surprise and excitement of the occasion,— one, or both, or all, or some other cause unknown, effected a complete cure,— for certain it is, he did not suffer another attack of the fever and ague during the whole journey, and the next day was able to discharge his duties as well as ever.

On striking the Big Blue, the mountain road bears a north-northwest course to the head of that stream, and from thence over an interval of highlands to the Platte river. The distance travelled up the Blue requires some eight days, for heavy waggons.[27] Continuing our way, about noon we passed several Indian trails, in addition to one ten or twelve or fifteen miles back. These consist of a number of well-beaten, parrallel foot-paths, bearing a northwest and southwest direction. They are formed by the passing and repassing of the Otoes, Iowas, and Foxes, to and from their hunting grounds, towards the head-waters of the Kansas.

On the 3d of October we reached the antelope range, and saw four or five of these animals scouring the boundless expanse, or ascending some favorable eminence to gaze upon us. Slight signs of buffalo also appeared, and everything seemed to indicate the approach to a game country.

Parting a short distance from the trail, a large sage rabbit bounded up before me,— the first of his species I ever saw.[28] This animal is nearly three times the size of the common rabbit, and of a white color, slightly tinged with grey. It derives its name from being found principally in countries abounding with *absinthe* or wild sage. In the regions adjacent to the mountains,

[27] This was the Little Blue, along which the road ran. He refers to it as the main branch of the Blue. *See* his map at the end of this volume.

[28] The jack rabbit, a hare.

these animals occur more frequently,— and even among the mountains, where their tails and ears are tipped with jetty black. Their fur is soft and fine,— equalling if not surpassing that of the Russia rabbit. Their flesh is also of a superior flavor, as I have had opportunities of testing.

Towards night, three antelope appearing near the trail, our hunter made an unsuccessful attempt to approach them, which afforded me a first inkling of the nature and character of these animals.

The antelope of the grand prairie differs but little in size and shape from the common sheep, and is coated with long, brittle hair,— of a ruddy brown color, except at the tail and head, where it is short and white. The female is hornless, except an occasional blunt corneous excrescence, some two or three inches long, protruding from the head. The male, however, is equipped with hook-shaped antlers, ebony colored, and six or eight inches in length, which he sheds annually in the months of November and December.

This is the fleetest inhabitant of the prairie. No horse can compete with it in speed. Quick of sight, keen of scent, and acute of ear, it seems ever on the alert at the approach of real or supposed danger,— now swiftly advancing towards the object of its alarm or curiosity, — then circling before you with the fleetness of the storm-wind, to mount some eminence far away beyond reach, and gaze in security. Then, again, ere you have time to catch breath for admiration, it repeats its semi-gyration from an opposite direction, still nearer and swifter, till past,— as if indeed borne on the wings of lightning — and yet again surveys you in the distance. Now, running from point, to point it examines you upon all sides, as it cautiously passes round,— then, snuffing the breeze, it again calls to aid its fleetness of limb, and with the velocity of thought is lost to view in the vast expanse.

Possessed of an inordinate share of inquisitiveness, it not unfrequently falls a victim to its own curiosity. The hunter, turbaned with a red handkerchief and half concealed behind some object, first raising, then depressing his head, then withdrawing it entirely from view, then again disclosing it to the curious animal, is almost certain to allure his game within gun-shot.

I have seen numbers killed in this manner. In the spring season they appear more sensitive than at any other time, and are easily lured to their fate.

With the exhibition of this strange propensity, I have time and again been minded of its more fully developed moral prototype in man. How frequently do we see persons around us who indulge their appetites and passions, as often for mere curiosity as fancied pleasure,— venturing nearer and still nearer towards the objects that command their attention and lure them into the vortex of ruin, till, with sure and deadly aim, the shafts of the tempter pierce the waning vitals of morality, and plunge the victims headlong into a yawning abyss, where they are lost to themselves, to society, and to the world — lost forever!

Here, then, is furnished for us a moral: — Beware how you indulge a vain curiosity that lures to evil; — never parley with temptation.

These animals are found from the Big Blue to the mountains — in Oregon, California, Santa Fe, and N.W. Texas. Their flesh is tender and sweet,— quite equal to venison, though seldom fat, owing as is supposed, to their almost incessant mobility.[29]

Near our night-camp I noticed fresh beaver "cuttings," some of which consisted of trees, six inches in diameter, levelled by these sagacious animals.

The vicinity disclosed frequent boulders of red and dark ferruginous sandstone, with a soil somewhat are-

[29] Numbers of antelopes are still to be seen in various parts of the West. In Wyoming a limited "one-shot" hunt is held annually.

nose, reclining upon a changeable deposit of sand and gravel, succeeded by a substratum of parti-colored and friable sandstone. The valley of the Blue is bordered by hills of graceful slope, both green and beautiful.

I here remarked for the first time the appearance of *cacti,* which herefrom becomes quite common, and proves the pest of many places adjacent to the mountains.

The Blue is a deep, narrow stream, with a swift current, over a bed of gravel and pebbles, and is fringed by groves of oak, cotton-wood, and willow. Its valley is between one and two miles in width, with a superfice of variable fertility, but generally consisting of good arable land.

This section of country is considered very dangerous in the summer and fall months, on account of the strolling bands of Pawnees which infest it. The *voyageur* holds the latter in great dread, unless he chances to be accompanied by a sufficient force to bid defiance to their approach. A party, numerically weak and indifferently armed, meets with rough treatment at their hands while on the open prairies. Persons and property are rarely respected, and the unfortunate traveller is not only plundered, but often whipt or murdered without mercy.

This, however, may not be said of all — it is only the young warriors, when beyond the restraint of their chiefs and seniors, who perpetrate such outrages; though, to their praise be it said, instances of this kind are quite seldom, at present, compared with former years.

The courage of these Indians is held in little repute by mountaineers; and, that this opinion is not unfounded, the following incident will prove. It was related to me by an actor in the scene:

A small party of whites on their cruise down the Platte with a cargo of furs, "lay by" to make meat, near the forks of that stream. Buffalo being at some distance from camp, our adventurers were compelled to perform the duties of pack-horses in conveying the proceeds of their hunting excursions. One day, four of them left for this object, and having proceeded some six or eight miles, a war-party of Pawnees suddenly emerged from behind an eminence, directly fronting them. Alarmed at the unwelcome apparition, and imagining the whole country to be alive with Indians, they immediately ran, and were pursued towards camp. One of the number, a big, lazy fellow, and rather "green" withal, soon became tired, and sung out to his companions:

"Don't let's run so fast. Blast me, if I can keep up!"

"Come on,— come on!" cried they. "A *thousand* 'shaved heads' are upon us, half frozen for hair!"

"Pooh! I'll bet five dollars there aint thirty!"

"Done! But, who'll count the bloody varmints?"

"Why, I'll do it, just for my own satisfaction." So saying, he wheeled and advanced towards the Pawnees, as his wondering companions halted a little distance off, to learn the result of his fool-daring.

Surprised at this strange movement, the enemy also came to a stand, affording a fine opportunity to ascertain their number, which only amounted to *nineteen!*

"I've won!" exclaimed our hero. "Let's charge, and give 'em the very devil!"

The word went for command, and the four hunters dashed boldly towards the terrified savages, who in turn *fled,* with greater velocity than they had called into exercise at any time during their advance,— illustrating the truth of the saying, "tyrants are always cowards." Legs proved quite convenient articles for the Pawnee *braves!* They were out of sight in a few minutes, and were very careful not to stop until they had left their pursuers far in the rear.

A Pawnee with a defenceless enemy in his power, like some examples among the whites, is unrivalled in courage and daring; but where there is resistance offered, and fighting to be done, he, as well as the Irishman's chickens, "comes up *missing!*" He is always bravest when farthest from danger.

We were careful to observe the strictest vigilance at night, to prevent the loss of horses from lurking bands of Indians. The animals of the caravan were uniformly picketed in compact order, and sentinels, posted at suitable distances, continued to pace their rounds, from dark till daylight; while each of the company slept by his arms, in readiness at any moment to repel an attack.

Having travelled for seven successive days, we made camp late in the afternoon at the head of the right fork of Blue.

During the day we had noticed a dense smoke some distance in the rear, but, with the wind in an opposite direction, no uneasiness was felt on that account. The sentries were soon at their posts, and everything was snugly disposed of for the night. Those not on duty improved the opportunity to gain respite from the fatigues of the day, and, in a brief interval, were snoring away at an admirable rate.

The polar-star by its "pointers" had just told the hour of midnight, when these hurried words rang through camp:

"Lave, ho! Lave! [30] Prairies on fire! Quick — catch up! catch up!"

This startling announcement instantly brought every man to his feet; — and such a scene as now met the eye! How awful, and how grand! The wind, new changed and freshened, to the right and rear, was tossing the flames towards us, rapidly — lighting the heavens with their lurid glare, and transforming the darkness of night into a more than noon-day splendor!

Here was, indeed, an *"ocean of flame!"* far as the

30 "Lave" appears to be a corruption of the Spanish levar, to get up, or arouse, as from sleep. It is in common use among Mountaineers. [Sage]

eye could reach — dancing with fiery wavelets in the wind, or rolling its burning surges, in mad fury, eager to lick up every vestige of vegetation or semblance of combustible that appeared in its way! — now shooting its glowing missiles far, far ahead, like meteors athwart the sky, or towering aloft from the weeds and tall grass, describing most hideous and fantastic forms, that, moving with the wind, more resembled a cotillion of demons among their native flames than aught terrestial! — then driving whole sheets of the raging element into the withered herbage in front, like the advance scouts of an invading army, swept onward its desolating course, leaving in its track naught save a blackened waste of smoking ruins!

Altogether, it was a sublime spectacle, a stupendous scene, grand and imposing beyond description, and terrible in its beauty! Commingled with sensations of wonder and admiration, it tended to impress the beholder with feelings of painful melancholy. The broad expanse, but a few moments since arrayed in all the mourning grandeur of fading autumn, was now a naked desert, and every vestige of loveliness in an instant snatched from view!

How sudden, how awful, how marked the change! and yet, how magnificent in its career, though doleful its sequel!

We were speedily under way, with as much earnestness of advance as that of righteous Lot, in his escape from burning Sodom.[31] For a while the pursuing enemy

[31] The great peril of our situation, and the pressing necessity of a hurried flight, may be readily inferred from the fact that one waggon was freighted with a large quantity of gunpowder. None of us were quite so brave or present-minded as several Mexicans, in the employ of Messrs. Bent & St. Vrain, on an occasion somewhat similar. While journeying across the grand prairies, the powder-waggon accidentally caught fire, which was noticed immediately by the Mexican attendants, who hurriedly clasped it upon all sides, to prevent the vehicle from being blown to pieces, while one of them proceeded deliberately to extinguish the flames! Neither could we stand comparison with a lieutenant of the Mexican army, at Santa Fé, who

kept even pace, and threatened to overtake us, till, headed by the strong wind, which meanwhile had changed its course, it began to slacken its speed and abate its greediness.

About sunrise we crossed the regular Pawnee trails, (leading to and from their hunting grounds, which bore the appearance of being much frequented,) and at 10 o'clock A.M., reached the Platte river, having travelled a distance of thirty miles without halting.

The mountain road strikes the above stream at lat. 40° 41′ 06″ north, long. 99° 17′ 47″ west from Greenwich, some twenty miles below the head of Grand Island.[32] This island is densely wooded and broad, and extends for fifty or sixty miles in length. The river banks are very sparsely timbered, a deficiency we had occasion to remark during the remainder of our journey.

The valley of the Platte at this place is six or seven miles wide, and the river itself between one and two miles from bank to bank. Its waters are very shallow, and are scattered over their broad bed in almost innumerable channels, nearly obscured by the naked sand-bars that bechequer its entire course through the grand prairie. Its peculiarity in this respect gave birth to the name of *Platte,* (shallow,) which it received from the French, and *Chartre,*[33] (surface,) from the Mexicans, — the Indians, according to Washington Irving, calling

on opening a keg of powder, made use of a RED-HOT IRON in lieu of an auger, for that purpose. It is needless to say, a tremendous explosion followed. Several of the bystanders were killed, but the lieutenant miraculously escaped. He soon after received a Captain's commission from the Commander-in-chief, in consideration of his indomitable COURAGE! [Sage]

32 The Charles Preuss maps of the Fremont expeditions show the road reaching the Platte River some distance east of the 99th Meridian, but the mileage below the head of Grand Island is about the same as given by Sage. *See* the *Charles Preuss Maps of 1846,* reproduced by Nolie Mumey in 1952.

33 Early New Mexican documents call the Platte the *Chato* (Flat) River, although it was called the *Río Jesús María* by the Villasur expedition of 1720. *See* A. B. Thomas, *After Coronado,* etc., (Norman, University of Oklahoma Press, 1935), pp. 37, 134.

it *Nebraska*[34] a term synonymous with that of the French and Americans,—however, I am ignorant in reference to the latter.

The bottom upon the south bank is between three and four miles broad, and of a light, deep, and rich soil, occasionally sandy, but covered with thick and lusty vegetation. Back from the valley, ranges of broken sand-hills mark the transition to the high arid prairies in the rear, where vegetation becomes more dwarfish and stinted in its growth, and is intermingled with frequent *cacti*.

These immense plains are generally clad with a short, curly grass, (the buffalo grass,) very fine and nutritious, and well adapted to the sustenance of the countless herds of buffalo and other wild animals that feed upon it. Their soil is generally of a thin vegetable mould, upon a substratum of indurated sand and gravel.

In many places it is quite sterile, producing little other than sand-burrs and a specimen of thin, coarse grass, that sadly fail to conceal its forbidding surface; in others, it is but little better than a desert waste of sand-hills, or white sun-baked clay, so hard and impervious that neither herb nor grass can take root to grow upon it; and in others, it presents a light superfice, both rich and productive, beclad with all that can beautify and adorn a wilderness of verdure.

The springs and streams of water are "few and far between,"— an evil, however, slightly atoned for by the occasional pools formed in favoring depressions during the rainy season, which are retained in their places by the extreme hardness of the soil. Were it not for these it would be almost impossible, in many directions, to travel the vast prairies lying between the Arkansas and Missouri, from long. 22° 30′ west from Washington to the Rocky Mountains. That this section of country

[34] The Sioux have bestowed the appellation of Duck river upon the North Fork of the Platte. [Sage]

should ever become inhabited by civilized man, to any extent, except in the vicinity of large water-courses, is an idea too preposterous to be entertained for a single moment.[35]

As the reader is now inducted to the grand prairie as it is, it may not be amiss to say something relative to this phenomenon, before dismissing the subject in hand.

The *steppes* of Asia, the *pampas* of South America, and the *prairies* of the great West, so far as my information extends, are possessed of one general and uniform character. There is something deeply mysterious associated with them, that puzzles the philosopher and cosmogonist to explain. Why is it neither timber nor shrubs, as a general thing, are found within their confines? Why have not the same causes operated here which produced the stately forests of other regions?

The above questions are often asked, and as often answered; but never satisfactorily.

Some respond by a reference to their frequent burnings,— others to some chemical defect in their soil,— others, to the disgeniality of their climate,— others, to their infecund aridity,— and yet, others, to the supposition that some operation of nature or art has effected the destruction of quondam forests, and reduced them to their present condition.

Each of these answers, though, doubtless, partially true in many respects, fails to solve the problem before us.

Here we have, in many places, almost measureless extents of fertile soil, moist and abundantly watered, by rains, springs, and ever-flowing streams, with all the desiderata for the producing of trees,— and what withholds them? Other sections of country, under less favorable circumstances, are not wanting in this respect.

---

[35] He is following the appraisal of the region given by Stephen H. Long, when he officially explored the area and labeled it the "Great American Desert."

Why is it? Timber of every kind adapted to the zone and climate will grow as thriftily when planted here, as elsewhere. The frontier forests of our Western States have been observed for years past to make slow but constant encroachment upon contiguous prairies, from all sides, where, as yet, they have a foothold;— and why? Partly, because their enlargement is not circumvented by those annual burnings that formerly devoured every tender shoot daring to raise its head above ground; and, partly, through the operation of other causes, sure and gradual in their effect, which have planted the groves of other lands and taught their branches to wave in the breeze. Doubtless the same causes would produce the same results, all over these vast regions, as elsewhere.

But, why have they not — why are the prairies timberless? Simply, because a sufficiency of time has not yet elapsed for the operation of these causes,— timber has hitherto had no possible chance for generation. The phenomenon, if rightly viewed, will thus explain itself. Geology points to the time when these vast solitudes were the bed of old Ocean and the home of waves,— but, gradually emerging or suddenly elevated from the watery abyss, they now present some of the more recent formations of dry land.

Herbage and grass, being more easily propagated than trees,— sown as are their seeds by the birds and scattered by the winds of heaven,— in a brief interval, beswathed the new-born earth with smiling green. Thus clothed with verdancy, they soon became the favorite pastures of the countless herds that thronged them. With game, appeared the red man to hunt it, and with him the yearly conflagrations that now repel the intruding woodlands and confirm the unbroken sway of solitude amid her far extending domains.

Here, then, we have spread before us the prairies as we find them,— the problem of their existence needs no further solution.[36]

Oct. 12th. Still continuing up the Platte by its south bank, we made camp at night near the head of Grand Island. During our progress we saw large quantities of wild geese and cranes in the river bottoms, that presented tempting marks for our *voyageurs*. One of the latter,— a tall, raw-boned, half-crazed, and self-confident Missouri "Ned,"— good natured and inane,— sporting the familiar *soubriquet* of "Big Jim,"— wishing to prove the truth of the Dogberry axiom, that "some things may be done as well others," started to approach a large flock of sand-hill cranes, parading half obscured in a plat of grass near the road side.

The wary birds, however, caught glimpse of the approaching Nimrod and flew. Still our hero advanced, crawling upon all-fours, to within sixty or seventy yards of their recent position, when, raising up, he espyed an object which his excited imagination portrayed a crane, and promptly yielded to it the contents of his rifle.

Of course the obstinate creature remained in *statu quo*.

Re-loading with all possible speed, he again fired! But the second shot proved futile as the first.

Determined the next should count whether or no, he advanced still nearer, and had raised for his third discharge, before the naked truth burst upon his astonished vision,— he had been shooting at a bunch of dead grass! Shouldering his rifle he now rejoined the caravan, and was received by the wags who had witnessed his exploit, as follows:

"Ho, Jim! I say, Jim! Did you kill it?"

"Hang me, but it stood fire well,— didn't it?"

"Reckon you wanted a bigger charge."

[36] Omer C. Stewart, Professor of Anthropology at the University of Colorado, has marshalled the evidence in support of his thesis that "all grasslands occurring on deep fertile soil are man-made, by people who periodically set fire to the grass and kept woody vegetation from growing." – "Why the Great Plains are Treeless," in the *Colorado Quarterly,* II, pp. 40-50. *See also* his other writings, especially "The Forgotten Side of Ethnogeography," in *Method and Perspective in Anthropology,* edited by Robert F. Spencer (Minneapolis, 1954), in which a full bibliography is listed.

"Strange you couldn't knock it cold at that distance!"

"May be your gun's out of order?"

"Yes. I'll bet a stewed crane of it. Have you noticed the *"sights"* lately?"

"Why, *Jim*. Really you've had *bad luck!* What, within sixty yards and not kill? I can beat that, all day!"

"Ha, ha, Jim! Shoot him grass!"

This rally was received, by our hero, in good part, who joined in the sport with as much *gusto* as though some one else were the victim.

The day, however, was not permitted to pass without another display of the prowess of "Big Jim."

A doe antelope, attracted by the strange appearance of the moving caravan, and impelled by its innate curiosity, had ventured to a tempting proximity. Mounted upon a fleet horse and supposing he could easily ride down the antelope, our hero started in pursuit.

Intently surveying the passing scene, the agile animal permitted him to advance within a few yards of her before she took the alarm. Now was a novel race. Away went antelope and away went Jim, in full chase. The former was soon far ahead, and stopped to gaze upon her pursuer.

Supposing she had become tired and was about to yield, our hero came dashing on, impetuously, under whip and spur, fully intent upon her capture. But, again, away went antelope, and away went Jim, whose steed, ambitious as its rider, and proud in its own fleetness, strained every nerve for the crisis. Even the antelope seemed to have found a champion to contest her unrivalled and universally acknowledged superiority. With distended mouth and protruding tongue, panting in the excitement of fear, and foaming in the vehemency of effort, she gained but slowly upon the bounding charger, as both swept over the prairie almost with speed of the storm-wind!

Now, again, she stops to gaze upon her pursuer. By

this time all began to feel an interest in the result of the strange race. The word resounded:

"Go it, Jim! you'll beat the beater, yet!"

Once more, the antelope shoots from before both horse and rider, like the swift-winged arrow twanged from a giant's bow!

A broad ravine intercepting her course was cleared at a bound, and left the flying animal far upon the other side. At a bound the steed also cleared the barrier, but, in striking upon the opposite bank, it plunged headlong upon the yielding ground, tossing its rider far away in advance, all safely sprawling in a sand heap.

The luckless wight, on recovering, found his noble beast so sprained by the fall it could scarcely stand, and its every nerve vibrating with frightful tremors. Of course here was the *finale* of the race, as both now returned to the caravan,— the recent rider, on foot, leading his jaded steed,— the ridden slowly limping behind, — presenting a marked contrast between the opening and closing scene.

The ill-fated horse was too much disabled for further service during the journey.

As our hero joined the company, the joke-loving wags again broke loose:

"Well, Jim. I say,— ahem! did you catch the tarnal critter?"

"Pooh! Why didn't you hold on, and not let her slide through your fingers in that way!"

"Why, man! You wasn't spry enough, when you jumped off your horse, or you might have caught her — just as easy!"

"I'd like to know what you was diving arter in that sand-bank! — the antelope wasn't there!"

"Oh, Jim! Shoot him grass, kill horse. Me look next time he run antelope."

The passive recipient of these sallies had little peace from henceforth, and soon began to wish he had never seen an antelope or heard of a crane.

CHAPTER V.

Near camp was the site recently occupied by the Pawnee village, whose occupants had evidently deserted it with the utmost precipitancy, leaving lodge-skins, mortars, bowls, pans, and a variety of other articles strown confusedly upon all sides. They had doubtless become alarmed at the approach of some real or supposed enemy, and consulted their own safety in flight.

Having started early the next day, our hunter soon brought in two fine antelope, the sight of which again raised the ambition of Big Jim, who would fain do deeds of equal wonder; and he accordingly strolled off into the hills with that intent. After shooting at several of the wary animals without success, he began to get tired of the sport, and concluding the "poverty-stricken" creatures not worth the powder and lead, set his face for the caravan.

Plodding leisurely along, he espied a prairie snake, and, o'erjoyed at the thought of counting a *"coup,"* gathered his rifle by the small, and brought it down with such force, he not only killed the snake, but broke his gun-stock short off at the breech. With the pieces, one in each hand, he made his appearance before his comrades, who hailed him:

"Hallo, Jim. What's that you've killed?"

"Gun broke. Why, you must have overloaded it!"

"When'll you go hunting again? — 'case I want to go too!"

"Poor Jim! Shoot grass, kill horse, break gun! Wat in de wor. does him mean!"

"Never mind, Jim. Don't be skeered at these fellows. It takes you to play the devil and *break* things!"

Towards night, several buffalo bulls having made their appearance, our hunter, mounting a horse, started for the chase, and in a brief interval, returned laden with a supply of meat. Camp had already been struck, and preparations for the new item of fare were under speedy headway.

The beef proved miserably poor; but when cooked, indifferent as it was, I imagined it the best I had ever tasted. So keen was my relish, it seemed impossible to get enough. Each of us devoured an enormous quantity for supper,— and not content with that, several forsook their beds during the night to renew the feast,— as though they had been actually starving for a month.

The greediness of the "greenhorns," was the prolific source of amusement to our *voyageurs,* who made the night-air resound with laughter at the avidity with which the unsophisticated ones "walked into the affections of the old bull," as they expressed it. "Keep on your belts till we get among cows," said they, "then let out a notch or two, and take a full meal."

It was equally amusing to me, and rather disgusting withal, to see the "old birds," as they called themselves, dispose of the only liver brought in camp. Instead of boiling, frying, or roasting it, they laid hold of it *raw,* and, sopping it mouthful by mouthful in *gall,* swallowed it with surprising *gusto.*

This strange proceeding was at first altogether incomprehensible, but, ere the reader shall have followed me through all my adventures in the wilds of the great West, he will find me to have obtained a full knowledge of its several merits.

The beef of the male buffalo at this season of the year, is poorer than at any other. From April till the first of June, it attains its prime, in point of excellence. In July and August, these animals prosecute their knight-errantic campaign, and, between running, fighting and gallantry, find little time to graze, finally emerging from the contested field, with hides well gored, and scarcely flesh enough upon their bones to make a decent shadow.

It is nowise marvellous, then, that our lavish appropriation of bullmeat at this time, when it is unprecedentedly tough, strong-tasted, and poor, should excite the mirth of our better-informed beholders.

The night was a cold one, and claimed for it Big Jim as second guard. When called for "relieve," with a borrowed gun, he commenced his rounds,— but the cold soon drove him to the camp-fire.

Here, weariness and the somnific effects of a generous heat, speedily found him stretched at full length towards the fire, snoring away at a sound rate, the subject of their combined influence.

The guard time had already expired, and his partner on duty, perceiving the pleasant situation of the indomitable Jim, called the next "relieve," and retired.

These paced their rounds, and the fourth guard succeeded, but still our hero occupied the same place in which he had *lain* his "tour." The sentinels were about to take their posts, as a loud sharp voice resounded through camp.

"Quit, there! What d'ye mean?"

Hastening to the spot from which the cry proceeded, who should be seen but Big Jim, in great agony, rubbing his foot with most pitiable grimace:

His slumbers had been disturbed by a falling log, of the camp-fire, which had planted its glowing weight full against one of his feet,— becrisping the sole of his shoe and severely scorching its tenant, before awakening him. Dreaming some one had hold of his foot, and started by a sudden acuteness of pain, he exclaimed as above quoted.

The sentinels laughed at his mishap, and turning to pace their rounds, drawled out:

"What d'ye mean? Sure enough, what d'ye mean! Shoot grass, kill horse, break gun, *lay guard,* burn shoe,

and scorch foot;— all in two days and two nights! Poor devil,— why ye no born wid better luck!"

With the morning, the subject of his recent adventures called forth fresh scintillations of waggish wit,— while the unrivalled capacity of our hero, as a gormandizer, gave cue to the cuts that followed:

"Well, my head for a foot-ball, if that aint the greatest idea yet. What! – *roast foot, basted with leather,*— and his own at that! Such a meal none but Jim would ever have thought of!"

"Why, man! What put you in the notion of that dish?"

"Strange, indeed, if you can't find the wherewith to stuff your devil, without cooking your feet! Souse, to be sure! Here, you can take my hat!"

The luckless wight had now enough to engage his attention during the remainder of the journey, and began to wish he had never seen a mountain company, or left his sweet home in Missouri to cross the great prairies with such a crowd,— but all to no purpose; he was too late to retrace his steps alone.

Oct. 13th. Starting at early day, we travelled till about 11 o'clock, A.M., and halted for breakfast. The teams were scarcely turned to graze, when a dense band of buffalo cows made their appearance, from the back prairie, wending their way towards the river.

Expectation was on tip-toe, and all appetites doubly sharpened for an anticipated feast, as our hunter and his assistant started to intercept the witless animals at the river bank.

The two placed themselves in a chosen position and awaited the heavily moving throng, which soon advanced to within shooting distance. The sharp crack of a rifle now stopped their headway, and caused them to recoil a few paces, leaving one of their number struggling in death. Another discharge followed, and the affrighted herd were seen flying from their concealed enemy, with all the energy that innate dread of danger

ATTACK ON A HERD OF BUFFALOES

and death lent to their ready feet,— but not until another victim had dank the sod with the unsought libation of its heart's blood.

It pained me, as I came up, to witness the noble beasts as they lay extended upon the gore-dyed ground. But the present was no time for regret; we were to feed upon their carcases.

The process of butchering was a new development of that most useful science. The carcase was first turned upon the belly, and braced to a position by its distended legs. The operator then commenced his labors by gathering the long hair of the *"boss,"* and severing a piece obliquely at the junction of the neck and shoulders,— then parting the hide from neck to rump, a few passes of his ready knife laid bare the sides,— next paring away the loose skin and preparing a hold, with one hand he pulled the shoulder towards him and with the other severed it from the body; — cutting aslant the uprights of the *spina dorsi* and "hump ribs," along the lateral to the curve, and parting the "fleece" from the tough flesh at that point he deposited it upon a clean grass-spot.

The same process being described upon the opposite side, the carcase was then slightly inclined, and, by aid of the leg-bone bisected at the knee-joint, the "hump-ribs" were parted from the vertebræ; after which, passing his knife aside the ninth rib and around the ends at the midriff, he laid hold of the dissevered side, and, with two or three well directed jerks, removed it to be laid upon his choicely assorted pile; a few other brief minutiæ then completed the task.

Meanwhile, divers of the company had joined the butcher, and, while some were greedily feeding upon liver and gall, others helped themselves to marrow-bones, *"boudins,"* and *intestinum medulæ,* (choice selections with mountaineers,) and others, laden with rich spoils, hastened their return to commence the more agreeable task of cooking and eating.

BUFFALO HUNT.

The remaining animal was butchered in a trice, and select portions of each were then placed upon a pack-horse and conveyed to the waggons.

The assortment was, indeed, a splendid one. The "dèpouille" (fleece-fat) was full two inches thick upon the animal's back, and the other dainties were enough to charm the eyes and excite the voracity of an epicure.

The camp-fires soon presented a busy and amusing spectacle. Each one was ornamented with delicious roasts, *en appolas,* on sticks planted aslope around it, attentively watched by the longing *voyageurs,* who awaited the slow process of cooking. Some were seen with thin slices from the larder, barely heated through by the agency of a few coals, retreating from the admiring throng to enjoy *solo* their half-cooked morsels,— others, paring off bit by bit from the fresh-turned hissing roasts, while their opposite received the finishing operation of the fire,— and others, tossing their everted *boudins* into the flames, and in a few seconds withdrawing for the repast, each seizing his ample share, bemouthed the end in quick succession to sever the chosen esculent, which, while yielding to the eager teeth, coursed miniature rivulets of oily exuberance from the extremities of the active orifice, bedaubing both face and chin, and leaving its delighted eater in all the *glories of grease!*

Every man had now become his own cook, and, not to be backward, I closed in with the overture.

Seizing a frying-pan replete with tempting levies from the "fleece," I twice subjected it to its duty, and as often its delicious contents found ample store-house; and even yet my longing appetite seemed loth to cry "hold, enough!"

The agreeable odor exhaled from the drippings of the frying flesh, contained in the pan, invited the taste, — a temptation claiming me for its subject. Catching up the vessel, a testing sip made way for the whole of its contents, at a single draught,— full six gills! Strange as it may seem, I did not experience the least unpleasant feeling as the result of my extraordinary potation.

The stomach never rebels against buffalo-fat. Persons, subsisting entirely upon the flesh of these animals, prefer an assortment of at least one third solid dépouille.

The *voyageur* is never more satisfied than when he has a good supply of buffalo-beef at his command. It is then his greasy visage bespeaks content, and his jocund voice and merry laugh evince the deep-felt pleasure and gratification that reign within.

Talk not to him of the delicacies of civilized life,— of pies, puddings, soups, fricasees, roast-beef, pound-cake, and desert,— he cares for none of these things, and will laugh at your *verdancy!*

He knows his own preference, and will tell you your boasted excellencies are not to be compared with it. If you object to the sameness of his simple fare, he will recount the several varieties of its parts, and descant upon each of their peculiar merits. He will illustrate the numerous and dissimilar modes of so preparing them, that they cannot fail to excite by their presence and appease by their taste the appetite of the most fastidious. And then, in point of *health,* there is nothing equal to buffalo-meat. It, alone, will cure dyspepsy, prevent consumption, amend a broken constitution, put flesh upon the bones of a *skeleton,* and *restore a dead man again to life!* — if you will give credence to one half of the manifold virtues he carefully names in your hearing.

Oct. 14th. We were early *en route,* and made some twenty miles. Our hunter, during the day, rejoined the caravan, laden with the best portions of three other fat cows, to add to the fund of life and good humor enjoyed by each.

Late in the afternoon, we made camp opposite a

heavily wooded island, called Brady's Island, in memory of a man, so named, who was murdered upon it by his companion some eight years ago.[37]

The two were connected with a boat, laden with furs, on its passage to the States. They had frequently quarreled, and were generally upon otherwise bad terms. On the day of the fatal occurrence, they were left alone in camp by the rest of the boat's crew, who went in quest of buffalo. At their return, Brady was found lying in his blood,— killed, as his companion affirmed, by the accidental discharge of his own rifle.

The tale was received quite doubtingly, and its listeners were only deterred from the execution of summary vengeance upon the murderer by thought of the bare possibility of its truth.

The body of the unfortunate man was buried near the spot,— but being subsequently disinterred by the wolves, his bones were left to bleach and moulder in the sun and rains of heaven. Some of them were lying scattered near by, upon our arrival, which were collected by the sympathizing *voyageurs,* who bestowed upon them those rites of sepulture they had been so long and cruelly denied.

The reader will naturally enquire, what became of the supposed murderer? His was a fearful retribution, — a mournful tale of suffering, worse than death, till death itself in pity came to his relief.

Soon after the melancholy incident previously related, the shallowness of the Platte river compelled the company to abandon their boat, and make the best of their way to the States on foot,— a distance of two hundred and fifty miles to the nearest inhabitants, either Indian or white.

Their provisions running short, and no game at hand,

[37] Brady's Island is shown on the Preuss Map, *op. cit.,* being just west of the 100th meridian. Fremont in the *Report* of his expedition of 1842, p. 21, mentions Brady's Island, and says it "bears the name of a man killed on this spot some years ago."

a separation was had about midway of their journey, and each one hurried to its termination as rapidly as possible. The murderer, being but an indifferent walker, was soon left far in the rear.

His comrades, on their arrival at the Pawnee village, sent two Indians to bring him in, and continued their course to Council Bluffs.

Nothing further was known of the subject of our sketch, till some eight or nine days subsequent, when a small party of engagés in the employ of the American Fur Company, on passing the Pawnee village, were met by the head-chief, who requested them to visit a white man lying sick at his lodge.

They went. He was the murderer, at the point of death. His story was briefly told.

The night succeeding the departure of his companions, in an attempt to light a fire with his pistol, to disperse by its smoke the myriads of musquctoes that swarmed around and nearly devoured him, an unknown charge it contained was lodged in his thigh-bone — severing it to a thousand pieces. In this condition he lay helpless. To walk was impossible; — he could scarcely move, far less dress his wounds in a proper manner. He managed, however, to affix a piece of red flannel to an upright stick, to tell the transient traveller the site of his supposed last resting place, then, crawling with difficulty to the river-side, he remained six days and nights – tormented by musquitoes, reduced by pain, and wasted by continued hunger, till scarcely the wreck of manhood was left him.

It was then he longed for death to terminate his agony. Still he could not endure the thoughts of dying.

Early in the morning of the seventh day, his ear caught the indistinct murmur of sounds. Were they human voices? — No, he must be dreaming. He hears them again. It is no dream; — they are human voices!

They approach. Is it to his assistance?

O'erjoyed he beholds two Pawnees bending over him,

with compassion pictured expressively upon their countenances. They gave him meat,— they dressed his wounds, and did everything in their power to alleviate his misery.

Oh, say not there is no pity in the bosom of the red man!

Having constructed a rude litter of poles, and using their own robes for his bed, they carefully conveyed him upon their shoulders to the place he yet occupied.

But the care of sympathizing attendants failed to atone for previous neglect. Mortification had already taken place, and death claimed him for a victim. He expired in the presence of those whom the good chief had called to his bed-side;—but, before his tongue refused to speak, he confessed the *murder of Brady,* and owned the justice of his punishment in all the untold miseries he had been compelled to endure.

"Vengeance is *mine,* and I will REPAY IT, saith the Lord!"

On resuming our journey the road gradually bore towards the hills upon the left, (which presented an outline of conical eminences, rising, as the traveller advances, to an elevation of four or five hundred feet,) and finally crossed them at the point of an angle formed near the confluence of the two great forks of the Platte, upon the east side; from thence, descending to the opposite bottom, we reached a timberless spring and made camp soon after nightfall.

The lack of wood at this place was readily met by the great abundance of *bois de vache,* (buffalo-chips,) the common substitute of the prairies;[38] and, in a brief interval, the camp-fires were merrily blazing, with all the appliances of cookery about them.

Early the next morning, our hunter rejoined the cara-

---

[38] Buffalo dung, when dry, made a good fire; in fact, it was the principal fuel used on long stretches of the treeless plains.

van, bringing with him the spoils of two more cows. He had passed the night upon the prairie alone, without coat or blanket, or anything to screen him from the bleak autumn winds, that swept over the naked plains, dancing their dirges to the dying year.

The sky gave evidence of an approaching storm, and we hastily started in quest of some more sheltered spot in which to weather it. A few miles brought us to the river, and, availing ourselves of a small supply of drift wood, we made halt.

The combustibles the vicinity afforded were soon collected, and the camp-fires imparted their generous warmth despite the falling rain. Nor were they permitted to remain long unembellished by the numerous kettles, frying-pans, and roasting-sticks at command.

I here enjoyed full test of some of the many varieties of mountain fare hitherto so freely enlarged upon by our *voyageurs,*— which, as they now asserted, would make a man "shed rain like an otter, and stand cold like a polar bear!" — quaintly adding, "if he could always *live* upon such 'didins,' he need *never die!*"

I must in justice confess that the real merits of our present "bill of fare," by far exceeded my previous expectations.

The rain continued till near night; but little did we care. The choicest the prairie afforded, was now before us, and, rain or shine, we were contented. Sound in health and buoyant in spirits, we fully enjoyed ourselves, despite the frowning elements.

A little before sundown, the rain subsided into a thick fog, and an old bull, in the consequent obscurity, straggled close upon camp.

The abrupt passage of a rifle-ball through his lights, was his first *feeling* sense of the presence of danger. The affrighted customer then retreated a few steps, and, falling, surrendered himself to the resistless power of cold lead.

A large band of cows also made their appearance, in the same manner, and our hunter struck out to waylay them.

Permitting the unwitting animals to advance within good shooting distance, a discharge from his rifle brought down one of their number. The band then recoiled slightly; but, snuffing the odor of blood, they returned immediately to their prostrate companion.

This was enough,— a charm now riveted them to the spot,— a strange infatuation had seized upon them. They began by spurning the ground with their feet,— then, bellowing, gored the fallen beast, as if forcing her to rise,— then, rolling upon the grass, in demonstrative sympathy,— and, now that she had ceased to struggle and lay yet quivering in death, they licked her bleeding wounds and seemed to exercise a kind of mournful rivalry in the bestowment of their testimonials of affection.

She is encircled by her companions. An effort to approach from without is resisted by those within. A fight ensues, and all becomes confusion. Each turns against her neighbor, and continues the strife till the space around the carcase is again vacated; whereupon a general rush once more centers to the spot, and all unite to react the former scene.

In this manner they persisted in their frenzied devotion to the fallen one, as if determined to restore her to life and action, or perish by her side.

Meanwhile the hunter's rifle had been busily employed. But they heeded it not. Four more of their number lay gasping in death upon the ensanguined ground; and still they seemed no more disposed to leave the scene of slaughter than at first. Sixteen successive shots were fired, each bearing blood, wounds and death, and yet the spell was no nearer broken.

It was a spectacle vested with melancholy animation. The pawing, goring, bellowing, licking of wounds, and struggles of rival affection, remained the same, with no visible abatement of their vehemency.

The sun had set, and the sable hue of twilight empalled the blood-dank slaughter-ground. The death-dealing rifle had ceased its sharp crack, and the gore-scenting wolves, half starved and eager for their supposed prey, came flocking upon every side, mingling their wobegone howlings with the piteous moans of the spell-bound herd, and the loud whistlings of the prairie winds,— and yet, they lingered.

At last the impatient hunter advanced. More affrighted at the presence of man than the companionship of death, they now gave way, and reluctantly left the field to him, who had so unfeelingly occasioned their burthen of mourning and woe; — still, ever and anon stopping to gaze, as if longing to return and die with those they loved!

All hands were now summoned to aid at the work of butchery; but the fast-enshrouding darkness soon drove us back to camp, leaving the task not half completed.

Our withdrawal from the premises was the signal for possession by the eager wolves, whose ceaseless yelpings the livelong night, made the gloomy interval doubly dismal. By morning, nothing but bones and thick pieces of skin marked the scene of their recent revellings![39]

Thus early, I had learned, that to approach buffalo with success, the hunter should carefully maintain the leeward, such being their remarkable sensitiveness, they will sooner flee from the smell than the sight of a man. Their sense of smell, with the wind, in fact, far exceeds their scope of vision. It is so extremely acute, that even the fresh footsteps of a man crossing their path, are to them a sure cause of alarm and flight.

---

[39] Sage has given here one of our best accounts of such a slaughter scene.

Of all the diversities of game indigenous to the mountains and prairies of the great West, with the exception, perhaps, of the grizzly bear, no animal is more tenacious of life than the buffalo. To shoot it in the head, is an inane effort. No rifle can project a ball with sufficient force to perforate the thick hair and hide to its brain, through the double scull-bone that protects it. A paunch shot is equally vain. The only sure points for the marksman are, the heart, lights, kidneys, or vertebræ; and even then the unyielding victim not unfrequently escapes.

Buffalo, wounded in the skirts of the lights, have been known to live for several days afterwards. I have witnessed their escape, even after the reception of fifteen bullet-wounds, and most of them at such points as would have proved fatal to almost any other animal.

In the summer of '43, I myself killed one of them, that had been shot through the pussy surface at the *butt of the heart,* apparently four or five days previous, which doubtless would have recovered had it remained unmolested.

A gun, suitable for killing this kind of game, should never carry to exceed forty balls to the pound — a lesser bore would be almost entirely useless. The distance generally required for a shot, the smallness of the ball, its liability to variation from the wind, with its failure to "hold up" and retain its force, contribute to render the use of such a piece little else than idle waste of ammunition.

Oct. 17th. The sun arose bright and clear, and with its first appearance the caravan was in motion. Proceeding up the South Fork some ten miles we halted for breakfast, and made arrangements for fording the stream.

Near us lay the carcase of one of the cows wounded on the previous evening, and as yet scarcely dead. She had travelled thus far after being shot in the lights.

Our crossing was effected with little difficulty, but occupied till late in the afternoon. The river was full a mile wide and very shallow, with a soft sandy bed, requiring the strength of all the united teams to each waggon. The day proved cold, and the water was like an application of ice to the naked skin. Our teamsters, who were compelled to cross and recross, some dozen times, felt in not the best humor, and were better pleased than any one else at the termination of their unpleasant task.

Having safely gained the opposite bank, we travelled up the river five or six miles, and halted for the night.

During our course the bottoms upon either side presented one dense, interminable band of buffalo, far as the eye could reach. The whole prairie pictured a living mass, moved by impressive dread, as the breeze heralded our approach, and the countless multitude made way before and on either hand.

Ever and anon, an old bull would linger, as if to intimidate, and not unfrequently venture within gunshot. One fellow, in particular, passed side-long, for a mile or more, stopping at intervals to gaze upon us, shaking his shaggy head in defiance, as much as to say, "you dare not come near!"

Big Jim saw this, and his pride was wounded. The bull, in his opinion, had challenged the whole party, and there was no one stout-hearted enough to accept it.

Here was a chance for a full display of his bravery and skill. Ever since we had reached the buffalo range, his proud spirit had yearned to become the death of some one of these terrible monsters, that he might relate the deed of perilous exploit to wondering posterity and incite the rising generation to emulate his noble achievement.

But, alas, for the fadeless laurels he might otherwise have won, in an evil hour his rifle had been sacrificed for the extermination of a huge, venomous serpent. He did the deed at one fell blow; — brave, but unfortunate! Yet he had one consolation amid his troubles,— no victory is ever gained without some loss to the conquerors.

Still, he needed his gun, for without it how was he to avenge the foul insult the savage beast of the prairie was even now hurling in the very face of the shrinking crowd? Something must be done.

With these cogitations, an idea struck him,— he could borrow a rifle; so, advancing to a comrade, he exclaimed:

"Do lend me your rifle, one minute!"

"Yes, Jim," was the ready reply. "But see you don't break it over the first paltry little snake you come across!"

"That's a lie. 'Twas a big rattle-snake I broke mine over. 'Twasn't a paltry little snake!"

Thus, vindicating his assaulted reputation, he took the gun and hastened to prostrate the impudent barbarian inviting attack.

Jim looked at the bull, and the bull looked at Jim,— shaking his head, and throwing the loose sand from beneath him high into the air with his feet, and goring the ground with his horns of burnished ebony. If the creature had looked terrible before, he now looked fourfold more so, in Jim's estimation.

Thinking caution the parent of safety, our hero was unwilling to venture further, and so, prostrating himself at full length behind a cluster of *absinthe,* (sage,) he planted his battery, having his high-crowned hat for a rest, and blazed away at the bull's head.

The hardened wretch stood the shot without flinching. Looking for a moment at the spot from whence the strange salute had proceeded, and again shaking his head and snorting with scorn, he wheeled and slowly trotted off.

Eager to get a second trial to finish the work so nobly

begun, our hero commenced pursuit. Seeing him advancing, the bull thought it time to show his heels, and in a few minutes was lost in the distance.

The courageous Nimrod now, for the first time, bethought him of his hat, which, in the ardor of his bold charge, he had left at the spot chosen as his stand to hurl death and destruction to the naughty bull. He hastened to regain it — but no hat could be found; — the winds had borne it far away over the prairie, to be worn out in search of a wearer, and the unlucky *bravo,* hatless, rejoined the caravan.

Here the truth at once flashed upon the minds of the waggish clique, that had hitherto proved his sore annoyance, and they began anew:

"Now that beats me, clear out! How came you to give the bull your hat and leave yourself bare-headed? That's another wrinkle!"

"It's no such thing," said Jim. "The wind took it away; — and it's none of your business neither. *I paid for it!*"

"True. But what did the wind want with your hat? Sure, if it needed a foot-ball, to toss over the prairies, it would have been your head, the *lightest* of the two!"

"You're a fool!" retorted Jim, indignantly.

"There, now. That's the time you cotcht it, my boy. Why, fellow, Mr. Jeems took off his hat, out of pure *politeness,*— to win the good opinion of the bull. He were right. Didn't you see how the gentleman-cow *bowed* and *scraped* in turn. Why, *he throw'd the dirt clean over his back,* not to be outdone in good breeding! Ah, but the pesky wind! While Mr. Jeems were showing his brotten up, what had it to do, but to snatch his hat and *run off with it!* Mr. Jeems are no fool! and the feller what says he am,—(I want you all to understand me; Mr. Jeems have been most shamefully abused and misused, and I can whip the chaps what's done it — provided they'll let me; — I say, then, I want you all to understand me!) Mr. Jeems *are* NO fool, and the man what says he am — is,— (I can't think of words bad enough,) — is — is, as *near the mark* as though he'd drove *centre!*"

"Aye. Jim's right. You are all a pack of dough-heads to make fun of him in the way you do. Suppose you'd be struck *comical!* Then what'd you think of yourselves!"

"Poor Jim. Shoot grass, kill horse, break gun, burn shoe, scorch foot, and go bare-headed! Wat him mean?"

"I say, Jim. When're going a hunting again? —'case I want to go 'long too!"

CHAPTER VI.

Oct. 18th. BEARING to the right, over a high undulating prairie, we struck the North Fork of the Platte, after a drive of about twelve miles, and continuing up its left bank a short distance, camped for the night at the mouth of Ash Creek.[40]

The stream at this place is a broad bed of sand, entirely dry, except in the spring months. Higher up, however, it affords a generous supply of pure running water, sustained by the numerous feeders that force their way into it, from the high grounds dividing the two rivers.

The valley is of variable width, and well timbered with beautiful ash groves, from which the creek derives its name. Here are also found several varieties of wild fruits indigenous to the mountains. As a whole, it presents to the eye a pretty flower-garden, walled in by huge piles of argillaceous rock, and watered by murmuring streamlets whose banks are ornamented with shade trees and shubbery.

Near camp had been the scene of a fierce and bloody battle between the Pawnees and Sioux, in the winter of 1835. The affray commenced early in the morning, and continued till near night. A trader, who was present with the Sioux, on the occasion, describes it as having been remarkably close. Every inch of ground was disputed – now the Pawnees advancing upon the retreating Sioux; and now the Sioux, while the Pawnees gave

[40] For a discussion of routes crossing from the South Platte to the North Platte, *see* this *Series* III, p. 224. What later became known as the "Upper California Crossing" was on a route that descended the valley of Ash Creek to the North Platte.

way; but, returning to the charge with redoubled fury, the former once more recoiled. The arrows flew in full showers,— the bullets whistled the death-song of many a warrior,— the yells of combating savages filled the air, and drowned the lesser din of arms.

At length arrows and balls were exhausted upon both sides,— but still the battle raged fiercer than before.

War-club, tomahawk and butcher-knife were bandied with terrific force, as the hostile parties engaged hand to hand, and the clash of resounding blows, commingling with the clamor of unearthly voices which rent the very heavens, seemed more to prefigure the contest of fiends than aught else.

Finally the Pawnees abandoned the field to their victorious enemies, leaving sixty of their warriors upon the ensanguined battle-ground. But the Sioux had paid dearly for their advantage; — forty-five of their bravest men lay mingled with the slain. The defeated party were pursued only a short distance, and then permitted to return without further molestation to their village, at the Forks of the Platte.

This disaster so completely disheartened the Pawnees, they immediately abandoned their station and moved down the river some four hundred miles,— nor have they again ventured so high up, unless in strong war-parties.

About the same time the village on Republican fork of Kansas was also abandoned, and its inhabitants united with the Loups.

The evidences of this cruel death-harvest were yet scattered over the prairie, whose bones and sculls looked sad, indeed. One of the latter was noticed, near camp, with a huge wasp's nest occupying the vacuum once filled by the subtle organs of intellect. Strange tenant, truly, of a human scull,— but, perhaps, not an unfit antitype of the fierce passions that whilom claimed it as their dwelling place.

A specimen of the bread-root, *(psoralea esculenta,)* was procured from the creek-bank by one of the *voyageurs.* This is very common in the vicinity of the mountains, and attains a size from twenty to thirty inches in circumference. It is taprooted, and generally prefers the rich sandy soil of bottoms and ravines,—not unfrequently penetrating to the depth of five or six feet. In shape, it is much like the common beet. Its exterior is covered with a thick ligument of tough fibres, curiously interwoven, enveloping a white pulpy substance, which is very sweet and pleasantly tasted.

The day following we proceeded some twenty miles, and camped at a place called the Eagle's Nest.

A few scattering trees at the right of the bottom, here mark the transition to the high prairie. One of these was the war-eagle's eyry, upon which she rears her annual brood, and teaches it to soar far away, or levy tribute from the surrounding wilderness.

The proud bird of Jove was yet sailing aloft, in silent majesty, almost lost to vision in the long space of intervening blue that told the grandeur of her flight; and, tinged with the purple and gold of the setting sun, she seemed looking down with a jealous eye upon the unwonted invaders of her earthly home. A few light clouds, garnished with day's departing glory danced athwart the western sky, as the full moon arose, hastening to reenter her nightly pathway, and course amid the array of glittering worlds, and smile upon the wide realms of Solitude; — while countless herds of grazing buffalo covered the prairies on either side of the broad and silent river; and naught met the listening ear, save the dolesome hooting of the midnight owl, as she resumed her nocturnal ditty, to enhance the deep melancholy of loneliness; or the shrill whistlings of the prairie-winds, as they sported in mirth and chanted their requiems to the dying year; or the terrific bellowings of the hoarse-toned bison, the softening cadence of

THE WAR EAGLE

whose voices sounded trebly mournful as it swept far along and became lost in the distance; or yet, the dismal howlings of the half-starved wolves, that gathered by scores upon every hill-top and renewed, in more piteous accents, their ceaseless concert; — all these united to invest the scene, so magnificent in itself, with a savage wildness, at once incitive of terror and admiration.

In our progress during the day I remarked, at frequent intervals, bare places coated with saline efflorescences, and occasional plats of fine bluish grass, (herba salée,)[41]— appearances quite common from this onward.

Our night slumbers were disturbed by the quick discharge of firearms, which instantly brought every man to his feet, rifle in hand. The cause of this alarm was the appearance of a mad wolf among the caravan animals, and several shots were fired before the guard could despatch him. He proved one of the largest of his species, and looked fearful as his blood-red eyeballs and foaming mouth were exposed by the camp-fire.[42]

In the morning it was ascertained he had bitten nine head of horses and cattle.

The buffalo range affords every variety of wolves, common to the mountains and regions still further west. Of these there are five distinct classifications, viz: The big white or buffalo wolf; the shaggy brown, the black; the gray, or prairie wolf; and the cayeute, (wa-chunka-monet,) or medicine-wolf of the Indians. [coyote].

The white and brown wolves are the most numerous, and follow the buffalo in bands by hundreds, subsisting

[41] Commonly called Salt Grass.

[42] A mad wolf attacked the companies at the rendezvous of 1833, and several deaths resulted. See F. F. Victor, *River of the West* (Hartford, Conn., 1870), p. 143; and W. A. Ferris, *Life in the Rocky Mountains*, etc. (Denver, Old West Publishing Co., 1940), pp. 265-66.

upon the carcases of such as die of themselves or are slaughtered as their necessities demand.

These wolves behave with great sagacity in their predatory operations, and appear to exercise a perfect understanding and concert of action with each other on such occasions. First, stationing themselves by files at given distances along the course their intended victim is expected to run, two or more of them enter the herd of unconscious buffalo, and, singling out the fattest one, drive it to the track at which their companions await to take part in the grand race. This done, the victim is made to run the gauntlet between two rows of wolves. As it advances, others join their fresh numbers to the chase, till at length, tired down and exhausted in strength, the ill-fated animal falls ready prey to their greediness. The poor creature is first hamstrung to prevent its escape, and then literally devoured alive!

The black wolf is seldom met with in these parts. It nearly equals the white and brown in size, and is fully as large as the common cur-dog.

The prairie wolf is not more than half the size of the above mentioned, and much less ferocious. Its color is of a dark gray, and its fur quite soft and fine.

The cayeute or medicine-wolf compares with the common feist, and is of a grayish color, much like that of the wild rabbit of the States. Its fur is fine and thick, and might be turned to good account for the manufacture of caps, muffs, &c.

The Indians cherish many superstitious notions in regard to this animal, and hold it in great veneration. They consider it as the messenger employed by the Great Spirit, on special occasions, to herald the approach of events interesting to the welfare of his red children, and for that reason they are never known to harm or molest it.

Just at daylight, a large band of buffalo crossed the river nearly opposite to camp. It was headed by an old bull, that led the way, grunting and bellowing as he advanced, as if in mock personation of the bugleman of a corps of cavalry. Some three or four hundred cows and calves followed, side by side, with marked and regular tread, like platoons of infantry marching in set step to music, presenting a truly comical exhibition.

A *voyageur* seized his rifle and saluted with its contents the music-master and captain-general of the advancing army, as he was about to ascend the river bank. In an instant the whole detachment to "right about face," and retreat precipitately to the rearward shore, with no other music than the clatter of hoofs and the splashing of water, or order than the confused rivalry for speedy escape from the unexpected presence of danger.

Oct. 20th. Resuming our course, during the forenoon, the strange deportment of a buffalo bull near the trail arrested attention.

He was running in a circle, at the height of his speed, and narrowing its sphere at each gyration. Several of us rode out to him,—but he still, continued, (with frothing mouth and protruding tongue, swollen to the utmost distention of his jaws, rolling eye-balls, like globes of clotted gore; and bellowing for pain,) following the fast-decreasing limits of his strange course, regardless of our presence.

He soon commenced whirling round and round, with faltering, half stumbling steps, and finally fell prostrate before us, apparently in the last paroxysm of mortal agony. In vain he struggled to rise, while his tongue bled from between his jaws, chafed in fruitless effort to close them, and his head, keeping time with the convulsive throes of his fast-waning strength, tore up the prairie-sod and lashed the ground in the mad fury of effort.

The spectacle was one of the most striking exhibitions of excruciating pain I ever witnessed. Even the rough mountaineers were excited to pity, and gladly alleviated his miseries by hastening his end. A friendly bullet put a period to his sufferings, and placed him far beyond the reach of summer's heat and winter's cold, mad wolves and all the inexpressible horrors of hydrophobia.

At our noon encampment we commenced the process of "making meat," preparatory to passing a long distance devoid of game; and, as the reader may be anxious to know what kind of an operation this is, I will explain. It consists simply in cutting into thin slices the boneless parts of buffalo, or other meat, and drying them in the wind or sun. Meat thus cured may be preserved for years without salt. Ropes of raw hide were stretched around the waggons, upon which the results of our labor were left to the finishing effects of the wind and sun as we proceeded,— thus making an important saving in the item of time.

It is astonishing how long a time fresh meat may be kept without injury, upon the grand prairies, in dry weather, when it receives the free access of air. Some of that killed on our first arrival among buffalo was yet hanging to the waggons, as sweet and sound as ever. I have known it to be preserved, in this way, for ten or twelve days in the heart of summer. Meat, packed in snow, while in a frozen state, may be retained fresh for months without injury. I have known an instance of its being thus kept from January till June. The air is so pure and dry, it requires but little effort to preserve meat, for any requisite length of time, almost at any season of the year.

Our hunter, having proceeded in advance of the waggons during the afternoon, was overtaken about sundown at a place selected for night-camp, which he had ornamented with the carcases of three cows,— and there again, was soon witnessed another display of rare feasting, such as mountaineers alone know how to appreciate and enjoy.

The night proved cold and uncomfortable, and the bright-glowing camp fires presented most captivating inducements to the shivering sentinels, as they paced their dreary rounds, to step within its cheering influence. Big Jim, who was on the third "relieve," thought it too bad he should be compelled to suffer so much from cold, while a nice warm fire was permitted to waste its kind heat upon the bleak air of night, without so much as one to enjoy its beneficence.

No, it would not do. "Why mayn't I just as well stand guard at the fire, as elsewhere? I can, I'm sure. I'll *stand* this time, and not *lay* as I did before, and then there'll be no danger of falling asleep and burning one's self; nor'll they have the chance to twit me about lying guard and burning shins. I'll head 'em this time, and they wont know the difference."

So saying, he approached the fire, and, giving it a kick, extended his hands towards its blaze,— ever and anon rubbing them together and then again spreading them to receive its pleasing warmth; then turning his back to partake alike of its comforting influences and obviate the jealousy that might otherwise be engendered between front and rear.

Now, he stands attent,— he hears something move. He stretches himself to his full height, on tip-toe, and gazes in the black envelope of surrounding night, made doubly obscure in contrast with the refulgence of the camp-fire.

"How dark it has grown!" said Jim. "What can it be? Wonder if it's Indians. Pooh! it's nothing but the wind. Bless me, I can't see the use of a poor devil's standing guard on such a dark night as this! (stepping backward still nearer the fire,) he can't see nothing, if he does. Feugh,— what is it smells so? (turning round.) Good gracious, how hot my back is!"

The mystery of Jim's present predicament is easily explained. The skirts of his jeans coat, having come in contact with the wind-tossed flames, caught fire, and were burned to the shoulders before he was aware of the accident. The garment was rendered entirely useless, and even his pantaloons were burnt to his skin, in several places.

Jim began to think it as bad to *stand* as to *lay* guard, and concluded that, of the two, fire was more dangerous than Indians; — for, one thing was certain, the Indians had never yet injured him, but he could not say as much of *fire!*

In the morning, as may be supposed, our hero's last mishap was the prolific subject of comment, and the wags were promptly on the alert to amuse themselves still further at his expense:

"Say, would you believe it! — That's the way Jim's hit upon to *shine* in this crowd,— he burns up his old coat to make a *light!*"

"Ah, ha! So he means to shine by the light of his old clothes, and come it over us in an underhand manner! Jim, that'll never do; — I tell you, once for all."

"Wonder if he wont burn up himself next?"

"He? No. He's too *green* and *sappy* to burn himself, and so he takes his old clothes!"

"Poor Jim. Shoot grass, kill horse, break gun, burn shoes, scorch boot, lose hat, stick coat in him fire! Poor fellow. No can do without Jim, no how."

The third day succeeding the last mentioned adventure, we passed a stream, called by the traders Johnson's creek, in memory of a man by that name who was murdered in its vicinity, several years since, by the Indians.

He was a missionary, and on his way to Oregon, with a party headed by one John Gray. As they were about to raise camp, one morning, a band of Yanktau-Sioux came charging over the hills, and preparations were made to resist them. Such a course Mr. Johnson felt scrupulous of acceding to, and stoutly protested against it,— affirming it to be wrong.

As the savages approached, the ill-fated man stepped forward to meet them unarmed, despite the remonstrances of his comrades,— imagining the Indians would not kill him, as he was a missionary and had come to do them good.

They, however, proved regardless of him or his intended good, and he fell the victim of his own foolish credulity. Three Indians fell in the conflict that ensued, and he and they filled the same grave.[43]

Oct. 24th. About noon we crossed Gonneville's creek,[44] a large easterly affluent of the Platte. This stream also derives its name from a trapper, killed near it in an Indian fight, some eight years since.

Upon the south bank of Gonneville's creek, ten or twelve miles from the river, is a singular natural formation, known as the Court House, or McFarlan's Castle, on account of its fancied resemblance to such a structure.[45] It rises in an abrupt quadrangular form, to a height of three or four hundred feet, and covers an area of two hundred yards in length by one hundred and fifty broad. Occupying a perfectly level site in an open prairie, it stands as the proud palace of Solitude, amid her boundless domains.

Its position commands a view of the country for forty miles around, and meets the eye of the traveller for several successive days, in journeying up the Platte. We have been in sight of it for three days, and even now seem no nearer than at first, notwithstanding our course, meanwhile, has borne not far from a direct line towards it.

---

[43] W. H. Gray, Oregon missionary, does not report this incident in his *A History of Oregon,* etc. (Portland, 1870).

[44] Now called Pumpkin Creek.

[45] Courthouse Rock, well known landmark on the Oregon Trail, is located about four miles south of Bridgeport, Nebraska.

Here, for the first time, I remarked the deceptiveness of distance, on the high prairies and in regions adjacent to the mountains. Sometimes an object will appear as if within a mile, at most, which cannot be reached short of fifteen or twenty miles; then, again, objects will seem to be much further off than they really are.

I attribute this, in part, to three several causes:— First, the variable state of the atmosphere, in regard to density. Second, the absence or plenitude of humid exhalations and effluviæ in the air of different regions. Third, the peculiar locality of some places in regard to the reception of the sun's rays.

In passing from Gonneville's creek to Fort Platte,[46] we encountered no more buffalo,— these animals having been driven back into the high prairies by bands of strolling Indians.

If the prospect had hitherto been lonesome, it now seemed threefold lonely. The hard-beaten footpaths that had furrowed the bottoms and plains, in all directions, ever since our first entrance to the buffalo range, were still seen; but, unhonored by the presence and unmarked by the footprints of their whilom travellers, they looked like the once oft-trodden streets of some deserted city.

Late in the afternoon we were joined by two engagés from Fort Platte, whose object it was to hasten our advance. Soon after, we entered upon a stretch of burnt prairie, and were compelled to travel till daylight the next morning, before a sufficiency of grass could be found for a camping place.

Oct. 25th. Resuming our course about midday, we had proceeded only a few miles, when a mounted Indian appeared upon the opposite bank of the river, and accosted us:

"Chay, cullo! — Hanno chaum-pa-monet ha Mena-

[46] A trading post to be discussed in fn. 61.

huska tour?" (Tell me, friend! — Are those the Long-knife's [47] waggons?)

On being answered in the affirmative, he commenced crossing to join us.

Plunging into the river with his horse, he had proceeded about midway of the stream, when the panting beast suddenly sank into the quicksand, throwing its rider head foremost into the water. At length, having effected a ford, he hurried up to us, profusely dripping with wet as evidence of the thoroughness of his recent drenching.

First shaking hands with the company, he began to inquire about liquor, affirming the waggons contained that article, and adding, it was "right the Long-knife should bring the fire-water to *give* to the red man," as did the Bad-medicine,— but it was wrong to sell it. For his part he would not buy the fire-water. He would buy blankets, knives, beads, and ammunition,— not the fire-water; but the Long-knife should give it to him.

The personage thus introduced was one of the chiefs of the Brulé Sioux, and sported the name of Marto-cogershne, or Brave Bear. He was a turbulent fellow, that proved the pest of his village traders. Slim and spare-made in person, he was somewhat pale and sickly looking, and seemed about thirty years of age. His arms were a short fusee, with a bow and arrows slung to his shoulders, and a butcher-knife affixed to his belt. His hair was long, parted in front, and turned backwards; that upon the occiput, being bound in a cluster with panther's skin, hung in a plated cue and almost trailed

[47] This term seems to call for a word of explanation. Our company was designated by the Indians as the Long-knife, or American company, – a term by which all Americans are known among them. The American Fur Company, employing almost exclusively Frenchmen, or individuals speaking the French language, receives the appellation of Wah-ceicha, or the Bad-medicine company, – a phrase universally applied to the French among the mountain tribes. – [Sage]

CHIEF OF THE BRULÉ SIOUX

the ground, while a lone eagle's plume completed his head-dress. A robe enveloped his body, which, with moccasins, leggins, and breech-cloth, constituted his full costume,— a description of dress responding to that almost universally common among mountain tribes.

We were soon joined by others of his people, who eagerly enquired respecting the amount of liquor brought with us.

Among these were several individuals recognized by our *voyageurs* as old acquaintances; particularly one, an old chief called Bull Tail, (Tah-tunga-sana,) who was distinguished in attire from all his fellows by the addition of a hair-seal cap and a frock-coat, which he had received as presents from the whites.

One of our party gave a favorable account of the old fellow, and related a story much to his credit.

The narrator, during the previous winter, while searching for stray horses among the hills, had become so bewildered he was unable to find his way back to camp. He thus wandered for four successive days, unarmed, without food, and with but a single robe for covering. His destiny would, doubtless, have been to perish, had not the kind hearted Tah-tunga-sana discovered him, and, pitying his forlorn condition, taken him to the village, upon his own horse, some twenty miles off, going himself on foot the entire distance. Here, the lost one was treated to the best the lodge of his deliverer afforded, and, when sufficiently recovered, he was escorted to the nearest station of the whites.

I turned for another look at the worthy chieftain, who now rode up and greeted his protegé with much cordiality.

He appeared to be about eighty years of age, and was gray-headed, spare-visaged, and much wrinkled. His coat, buttoned close around him, served for a robe, while his matted ear-locks disclosed upon the one side a raven's and upon the other a hawk's feather, for ornaments. His face, like those of his companions, was liberally bedaubed with vermilion, and each cheek embellished with alternate spots of white and black, by way of variety. His only weapons were a bow, arrows, and a tomahawk-pipe.

As a whole, he presented rather a shabby and ludricrous appearance, that, were it not for the recollection of his worthy conduct, would have excited, in the mind of the beholder, far more of contempt than interest.

A Sioux squaw, the wife of a French engagé, accompanying us on her return from the States, now received the marked attention of our visitors. It is rare that an Indian will shake hands with a woman; but now, they might break through the restraints of custom; this was a special case; she had visited the white man's lodge, and could tell them many interesting things,— she was something more than a common squaw,— they might shake hands with her. She was accordingly greeted in a most flattering manner, and found tedious employment in answering the numerous questions with which she was plied.

Continuing for a few miles further, we made camp just at nightfall, and were promptly joined by a new recruit of inquisitive visitors, from an adjoining village.

The whole throng of Indians now numbered some thirty,and demanded a "talk" with the Long-knife. Upon this a circle was formed, with the whites upon one side and Indians upon the other, when Marto-cogershne opened the harangue in behalf of his people.

He commenced in a low, distinct tone of voice. His robe, drawn loosely around him, was held to its place by the left hand, exposing his right arm and shoulder. As he proceeded he became more animated, and seemed to enter into the full spirit of his discourse. The modulations of his voice, its deep intonations and expressive cadences, coupled with a corresponding appropriateness of every look and gesture, presented one of the most perfect specimens of delivery I ever witnessed.

His speech, as imperfectly translated upon the occasion, ran as follows:

"Long-knife: We are glad to see you — we are glad to see your people, and shake you all by the hand, that we may smoke together and be friends.

"Long-knife: We are glad the Great Spirit has put it into your heart to return with the road-travellers, (waggons,) and the white buffalo, (oxen), and the medicine-dogs, (horses,) bearing fire water, (whiskey,) blankets, and many other good things, ere yet the chill winds and snows have compelled His children to light the lodge-fires of winter. The Long-knife brings choice things to the red man, and it is good that we trade. (Applause.)

"The Great Spirit is good to His children. To us He has given the buffalo, the elk, the deer, and the antelope, that we may be fed and clothed, and furnished with lodges to shelter us from the storms and cold. To us He has given the mountains and prairies, for hunting grounds. For us He has taught the streams to flow, and planted trees upon their banks, to give us food and drink, that we may meet around our lodge-fires with comfort and rejoice in His goodness, even while he spreads his white robe upon the hills, and lays the couch of winter upon the plains.

"All these — all this country — *everything* that the Long-knife beholds are ours. The Yellow-hair [48] said truly,— all, all belong to us; — we have them — the Great Spirit has given them to us,— they are ours! (Great applause.)

"Long-knife: You have come to trade with us: — it

[48] This is the name applied, by the Indians, to Gen. Clarke, one of the leaders of the first party of whites that ever crossed the mountains. An allusion is here had to an expression made use of in his talk to the Sioux on that occasion. – [Sage]

is good. Your people are wise, and make many things; — you bring them to us, and we take them; but we give you robes and horses in their stead; — we pay you for them all. Yet, the Long-knife pays not for all he takes from us.

"Do I say the Long-knife steals? No. The Long-knife will not steal. He says, none but *bad* men steal, and the Long-knife is not bad. *But yet he takes our property without paying for it! He* kills our game, *he* eats our meat, *he* burns our wood, *he* drinks our water, and *he* travels our country,—and *what* does *he* give the red man in exchange for all this? (Unbounded applause.)

"Long-knife and friend: My people are generous,— they are brave,— they are all soldiers. The Long-knife bears the fire-water in his road-travellers, (waggons;) — we have heard of it and are glad.

"My people would drink of the fire-water that their strong hearts may become stronger. It is good that they should drink it,— it is good that the Long-knife should give it to them; that we be twice glad to see him, and bless him in our hearts while we drink around our lodge-fires. (Applause.)

"Long-knife: Would you be our friend? Then give us the fire-water. My people are generous, but they are brave. The Long-knife has *taken our property,* let him refuse not the fire-water, lest they be angry and rise like the mountain bear, nerved for conflict. Then will they take it to themselves and avenge the wrongs of the red man!" (Great applause.)

Upon this, the Brave Bear resumed his seat, and the commandant began his reply, which was rendered into the Sioux language, by their interpreter. The purport of it was:

"It is true, the Great Spirit is good to His children. He made all things of which the Brave Bear speaks, and He has given them to his children. The white and the red man are alike his children; the buffalo, the elk, the deer, and the antelope, with the wood, the water, and the whole country around, equally belong to both.

"I and many people have come as friends, to trade with you. We have smoked with you before. The Long-knife takes nothing from you he pays not for. He buys the things he bears to you in a far distant country, and throws for them the white-iron.[49] He brings them to you and swaps them for robes and horses.

"He takes nothing without paying for it, unless it be that which the Great Spirit has given equally to his children,— the white and the red man.

"Would the Brave Bear and his people be friends to us? We are friendly — we are generous. We will give tobacco to the Brave Bear, that he and his people may smoke and be our friends. But the Long-knife will not here give him the fire-water. Let him come to the Long-knife's lodge, then shall he have of it a little, that he may bless the Long-knife in his heart. The Brave Bear can have none now.

"The Brave Bear says, his people are generous, but they are brave,— they are all soldiers. Be it so. My people are generous,— *they* are brave — *they* are all soldiers! Does the Brave Bear wish for fight? My people are ready to either smoke or fight! The Brave Bear says, unless I give him the fire-water for his people, *they* will nerve their arms for conflict, and take it! Will they? Let them try! The Long-knife says, *let them try!"*

The conclusion of this reply was received with a bad grace by those to whom it was addressed, and created great excitement among them. Several left for the village, obviously for the purpose of arming and returning with increased numbers to the meditated attack.

Meanwhile our arms were put in a proper condition

[49] Silver. This phrase is the Sioux mode of expressing the act of paying money for any article. – [Sage]

for resistance, and all needful arrangements made to give the assailants a warm reception should they commence upon us. This done, our commandant brought a few plugs of tobacco, and, laying them before the Brave Bear said:

"It is good that the Brave Bear and his people should smoke. Here is tobacco,— let him take it to his warriors that we and they be friends;— or would he rather fight?"

Bull Tail, (Tah-tunga-sana,) who had hitherto remained silent, now arose and addressed his companions:

"Tah-tunga-sana is grieved at the words of the Brave Bear. Would my brothers fight the Long-knife, and rob him of what he has brought to us, that they may become fools by drinking the fire-water?

"Who shall then bring us medicine-irons (guns) to kill our meat; or knives to butcher it; or blankets and beads for our squaws; or the red earth (vermilion) to paint our faces when we arm for war? And, who shall bring us all the other things so needful for us?

"The Long-knife will not do it. You rob him. No one will bring them to us. We shall be without them! We shall be poor indeed!

"Brothers: Why would you drink the fire-water, and become fools? Would it not be better that the Long-knife no more bring it to us? We give for it our robes and our horses;— it does us no good. It makes us poor. We fight our own brothers, and kill those we love, because the fire-water is in us and makes our heads bad! The fire-water is the red man's *enemy!*

"Brothers: Tah-tunga-sana is old;— will you listen to him: He has been always the friend of the pale-face. When first the Yellow-hair (Gen. Clarke) came to the red man's lodge, Tah-tunga-sana took him by the hand. He will always take the pale face by the hand. He loves the pale-face. The pale-face is his brother,— he is *our* brother! — He brings us many good things.

"Brothers: The Long-knife has spoken well. It is good that we smoke,— that we, and the Long-knife, and his people may be friends. Let us accept his present, and go to our lodges, and there tell to our children how kind the Long-knife is to the red man."

The speech was received in silence,— no one expressing either approbation or dissent, as the old man resumed his seat. The Brave Bear hung his head sullenly, but said nothing.

The talk had evidently come to a close. At last, Bull Tail arose, and, shaking hands with the commandant and each of the company, took the tobacco and left for the village. The others soon after, one by one, followed his example, and we were finally rid of their unwelcome presence; — not, however, until they had stolen an axe and several other articles, despite the strictness of our vigilance.

CHAPTER VII.

Oct. 26th. RAISING camp at daylight we resumed our way, and soon afterwards arrived opposite the "Chimney," an extraordinary natural curiosity that had continued in view and excited our admiration for some four days past.[50]

This singular formation surmounts a conical eminence which rises, isolated and lonely, in the open prairie, reaching a height of three hundred feet. It is composed of terrene limestone and marl, quadrangularly shaped, like the spire of some church, six feet by ten at its base, with an altitude of more than two hundred feet,— making, together with the mound, an elevation of five hundred feet.[51] A grand and imposing spectacle, truly; — a wonderful display of the eccentricity of Nature!

How come such an immense pile so singularly situated? What causes united their aid to throw up this lone column, so majestic in its solitude, to overlook the vast and unbroken plains that surround it?

The "Chimney" is situated about three miles to the left of the mountain trail, though it seems no more than eight hundred yards distant. Upon this question our party entertained no small diversity of opinion. Some of the less knowing were confident it could not exceed a half mile; and one fellow offered to bet five dollars he could run to it in fifteen minutes.

---

[50] Famous Chimney Rock, sentinel of the Oregon Trail.

[51] Formerly the "Chimney" was much higher than at present, and could be distinctly seen in a clear day as far as Ash creek. The wind and the rain are continually reducing it; and it is said to be full fifty feet less than it was nine years ago. Calculating from this datum, what must have been its altitude no longer remote than a couple of centuries! – [Sage]

The banter was promptly accepted, and the "greenhorn," doffing his coat and hat, started in full expectation of winning the wager. But, instead of fifteen, it took him forty-five minutes to reach the spot!

The day after passing the "Chimney," we entered a broad defile of lofty ridges, and made camp. This locality is known as Scott's Bluff,[52] which is, properly speaking, a wing of the Rocky Mountains.

From Ash creek to this place, an almost precipitous wall of arenaceous rock, limestone, and marl, shuts the high prairie from the river bottoms. As the traveller proceeds, this wall or ledge gradually increases in height, and recedes from the river, sometimes to a distance of thirty or forty miles, till it unites in a chain of hills, many of which are covered with sturdy pines, and others are mere heaps of naked sand or indurated earth. The ridge then continues its course until it at length becomes united with the lateral chain of the Rocky Mountains, which bounds the "Plains of Laramie" upon the southeast.

At Scott's Bluff these hills crowd themselves abruptly towards the Platte, where they present a most romantic and picturesque scenery.

Our camp was in a rich opening, or valley, two miles wide, and walled in upon the right and left by perpendicular masses of earth and rock, that tower to a height of from three to eight hundred feet. In reaching it, the trail bore leftward from the river, about seven miles, through a level prairie, by which we were inducted to the valley, without any perceptible variation of its general surface.[53]

---

[52] Scott's Bluff is now a National Monument with a museum near its base, housing the famous collection of authentic paintings done by W. H. Jackson, the pioneer photographer. The famous bluff is across the river and southwest of the city of Scottsbluff, Nebraska.

[53] The road was thus much farther south than the present one that goes through Mitchell Pass, immediately at the south base of the bluff. The road Sage was following was through Robidoux Pass.

Near the entrance, upon our left, the spectacle was grand and imposing beyond description. It seemed as if Nature, in mere sportiveness, had thought to excel the noblest works of art, and rear up a mimic city as the grand metropolis of her empire.

There stood the representations of palaces, with their domes and balustrades; churches, with their spires and cupolas; and streets, with their gigantic dwellings, stores, work-shops, and ware-houses. And there, also, were parks, pleasure-grounds, and public squares, all so admirably defined by the agency of the winds and rains of ages, that the traveller might readily imagine himself to have arrived within the precincts of the deserted city of some peopleless country, whose splendor and magnificence once more than vied with the far-famed Palmyra of the desert, even in its best days.

To the right arose a pile of sand-rock and marl in pyramidal form, three hundred feet high, that occupied its prairie site detached from hill or other eminence.

Near this stood a more singular natural formation than any previously noticed. It described a complete circle, of one thousand feet in circumference, and attained an altitude of not far from four hundred feet. Its sides were of great regularity, and represented masses of solid mason-work, rising abruptly till within sixty or seventy feet of the summit, where they accline in a blunt, cone-like manner, reducing the periphery to one third that of its base. At this point is reposed a semi-spherical form, regularly jutting with a gradual swell upon all sides — then tapering to an oval shape till near the apex, at which the whole mass is surmounted by a rude imitation of sculptured flame, pointing upwards to the sun, as if this strange monument of nature had been erected in honor of the great source of light and heat!

Still further to the right, upon the river bank, is another immense pile, exceeding either of the before described in altitude. It is an oblong square, and presents erect lateral walls upon three sides, leaving upon the fourth a gradual acclivity which faces the river. Its summit expands into a beautiful terrace containing an area of several acres, which at the proper season is adorned with herbs, flowers, shrubbery, and grass, like a pleasure garden upon some house-top, and commands a view of the whole country, lending enchantment to the neighboring scenes. Its base is about one mile long by twelve hundred yards wide, and points endwise from the river towards the valley.

Then comes the continuous wall which bounds the locality upon the right. This likewise presents a level summit, varying from fifteen yards to a half mile in breadth, for a distance of ten miles, when, slowly sinking in its course, it finally becomes lost in the prairie. Covered with grass and shrubs, it is the favorite home of the mountain sheep, where she breeds and rears her young, secure in her inaccessible fastness; and oftimes from its precipitous edge, at elevations of six or eight hundred feet above the adjacent prairie, will her head and mammoth horns be seen, peering in wonder upon the rare traveller, as he passes adown the valley.

The interval between the two mural ridges is of uniform width for about ten miles, and is watered by a beautiful stream nearly the whole distance, when it inducts the traveller to the open prairie,— leaving the immense wall which bounded it upon the leftward, at his entrance, transformed to high conical hills, covered with pines, and almost lost to view in the growing space; while that upon his right, diminishing in size, gradually disappears and unites with the far-spreading plain.

Most of the varieties of wild fruits indigenous to the mountains are found in this vicinity, and also numerous bands of buffalo, elk, deer, sheep, and antelope, with the grizzly bear.

In the summer months the prospect is most delightful,

and affords to the admiring beholder an Eden of fruits and flowers. No higher encomium could be passed upon it than by employing the homely phrase of one of our *voyageurs*. In speaking of the varied enchantments of its scenery at that season, he said: "I could die here, then, certain of being not far from heaven!"[54]

Before leaving this romantic spot, feelings of gloom and melancholy usurped those of pleasing admiration, by the death of one of our number.

The deceased was on his way to the mountains for the recovery of his health, with a frame fearfully reduced by the ravages of that fell destroyer, consumption. For several days past he had declined rapidly, owing to the weather and the unavoidable exposure incident to our mode of travelling. To-day the cold was more than usually severe, and an uncomfortable rain and sleet commenced soon after camping. In an attempt to pass from the waggons to the fire, he staggered and fell;—before any one of us could arrive to his assistance, he had breathed his last.

We buried him upon the bank of the stream that wends its course through the valley. Darkness, with its sable pall, had enveloped the scene as we covered him from view, and left the winds and the wolves to howl his requiem, until the voice of spring shall bid the wild-flowers grow and bloom upon his grave.

This lovely valley had before this witnessed the death-scene of one who left his bones to bleach within its limits. His name was Scott, from whom the neighboring eminences derive their present appellation.

Attracted by the enchanting beauty of the place and the great abundance of game the vicinity afforded, he wandered hither alone and made it his temporary residence. While thus enjoying the varied sweets of soli-

[54] This area is now "Wildcat Hills Recreation Grounds."

tude, he became the prey of sickness and gasped his life away; — and none were there to watch over him, but the sun by day and the stars by night; or fan his fevered brow, save the kindly breezes; or bemoan his hapless fate, other than the gurgling stream that sighed its passing sympathy beside the couch of death![55]

There is a mournful interest and a touching melancholy associated with this simple story, that must thrill with emotion the finer feelings of our nature. The incident, which had so recently transpired, contributed to enhance these gloomy sensations to an extent I never before experienced. I felt — I cannot tell how. I felt like giving vent to my feelings in verse.— Yet, I cannot write poetry. I made the attempt, however, and here is the result before the reader:

THE WANDERER'S GRAVE

Away from friends, away from home,
And all the heart holds dear,
A weary wand'rer laid him down,—
Nor kindly aid was near.——

And sickness prey'd upon his frame
And told its tale of woe,
While sorrow mark'd his pallid cheeks
And sank his spirit low.

Nor waiting friends stood round his couch
A healing to impart,—
Nor human voice spoke sympathy,
To sooth his aching heart.

The stars of night his watchers were,—
His fan the rude winds' breath,
And while they sigh'd their hollow moans,
He closed his eyes in death.

[55] For another version of the Scott tragedy and for a biography of the man, *see* Merrill Mattes, "Hiram Scott, Fur Trader," in *Nebraska History,* XXVI, pp. 127-62.

Upon the prairie's vast expanse
This weary wand'rer lay;
And far from friends, and far from home,
He breath'd his life away!

A lovely valley marks the spot
That claims his lowly bed;
But o'er the wand'rer's hapless fate
No friendly tear was shed.

No willing grave received the corse
Of this poor lonely one; —
His bones, alas, were left to bleach
And moulder 'neath the sun!

The night-wolf howl'd his requiem,—
The rude winds danced his dirge;
And e'er anon, in mournful chime,
Sigh'd forth the mellow surge!

The Spring shall teach the rising grass
To twine for him a tomb;
And, o'er the spot where he doth lie,
Shall bid the wild flowers bloom.

But, far from friends, and far from home,
Ah, dismal thought, to die!
Oh, let me 'mid my friends expire,
And with my fathers lie.

Oct. 27th. The day being clear and pleasant, we travelled rapidly, and in the course of the afternoon reached Horse creek. This stream is a large affluent of the Platte, heading in the Black Hills, and, tracing its way in a northeasterly direction, through a timberless country, (in many places mere barren wastes,) makes its debouchment nearly fifteen miles above Scott's Bluff.

The region adjacent to its head is represented as being rich in minerals, among which is gold; and from my limited information respecting its geological character,

I am inclined to accredit the rumor. The story runs thus:

Six or eight years since, Du Shay, an old French hunter, while ranging in the parts above alluded to, on crossing one of the two principal forks that unite to form the main stream, observed a singular looking something in the creek bed, which he picked up. It was apparently a fragment of rock, very heavy, and contained numerous yellow specks.

Having deposited it in his bullet-pouch for preservation, subsequently, in approaching a band of buffalo, its weight became so annoying he thoughtlessly threw it away. The year following he visited Santa Fe, at which place his pouch was accidentally emptied, and, among its contents, several bright particles, that had become parted from the rock, attracted the attention of the Mexicans. These were carefully gathered up, and, upon due examination, proved to be virgin gold.

The old man, on his return, searched diligently for the spot that afforded the treasure he had so foolishly thrown away,—but (not being intellectually one of the brightest gems of nature's casket, and feeble and childish withal) he was unable to find it, or even to decide upon which of the two streams it belonged.[56]

Upon one of the affluents of Horse creek, thirty or forty miles south of the Platte, is a beautiful valley, shut in by two ridges of precipitous hills, known as Goche's hole.[57]

This locality, in wildness and picturesque beauty,

---

[56] This purported gold discovery was repeated in the press following the initial gold discoveries of 1858 in the Colorado region.

[57] Now known as Goshen Hole. Theodore Talbot, who accompanied the Thomas Fitzpatrick contingent of the Fremont party, traveled from the South Platte forts to Forts Platte and Laramie in 1843. He tells of going through "Goshen's Hole, or the Valley of Goshen." *See* C. H. Carey (ed.), *The Journals of Theodore Talbot,* etc. (Portland Metropolitan Press, 1931), pp. 33-34.

claims affinity to the neighborhood of Scott's Bluff. Its area is broad and of several miles extent,— inaccessible except at two or three points. The surrounding hills are generally composed of marl and earthy limestone. Towering in vertical walls to the height of many hundred feet, they present the appearance of a strongly fortified place. The soil is remarkably rich, well watered, and timbered,— strikingly contrasting with the nude sterility and desolation of the circumjacent country.

A heavy fall of snow during the night prevented our leaving camp until the fourth day subsequent, when were again *en route*. Having passed the night of Nov. 1st at Morain's Point, the next day we arrived at Fort Platte.[58] This latter place is situated a short distance above the mouth of Larramie river, and is our point of present destination.

From Horse creek to the Larramie river, the bottoms, in many places, afforded dense groves of heavy timber — the more agreeable as we had been so long accustomed to open and woodless prairies.

The geological character of the country is nearly the same with that previously described — though possessed of greater humidity of soil. The formations, noticed in the vicinity of Scott's Bluff and Goche's hole, have merged into strata of limestone of various shades and compactness, with occasional layers of primitive sandstone.

The prairies were beautifully undulating, and covered with lusty growths of dried vegetation. The hills, now and then, were ornamented with a few scattering pines and cedars, which stood like lonely sentinels to watch the progress of changing seasons.

As some of my readers may entertain the design of visiting these remote regions, or passing beyond them to the more distant shores of the Pacific, it may not be

[58] To be described presently.

deemed a digression for me to present a few hints as to the most advisable mode of travelling upon this long and wearisome journey.

A caravan of waggons should make only two camps per day. Travellers should adopt the rule to start at daylight and continue until ten o'clock, A.M.,— then, having halted some six hours, (if it be summer, if spring or fall, four only,) again resume their way till after sundown.

Fifteen miles, upon an average, are as far as an ox team should travel per day,— mules or horses might keep on for twenty miles.

Caravans ought always to lay by in rainy weather, as the wet and irritation consequent upon draught, gall the neck and shoulders of their animals and soon render them unfit for service;— every precaution should be taken to preserve their strength and soundness, as upon them rests the sole dependence of a travelling company.

A mounted party ought, as a general thing, to observe the same rules, and not think of averaging over twenty-five miles per day. They might travel later; but in such cases, they should always proportionally lengthen their noon halt.

In the above manner the entire journey from Independence to the Pacific may be performed without injury to animals, or the expenses attendant upon a relay.

Fort Platte, being next to Fort Hall, the most important point on the route to Oregon, calls for a brief description. This post occupies the left bank[59] of the North Fork of Platte river, three-fourths of a mile above the mouth of Larramie, in lat. 42° 12′ 10″ north, long. 105° 20′ 13″ west from Greenwich,[60] and stands upon the direct waggon road to Oregon, *via* South Pass.

59 The left bank as one ascends the river.

60 Obs. Lt. Fremont, in 1842.– [Sage]

It is situated in the immediate vicinity of the Oglallia and Brulé divisions of the Sioux nation, and but little remote from the Chyennes and Arapaho tribes. Its structure is a fair specimen of most of the establishments employed in the Indian trade. Its walls are "adobies," (sun-baked brick,) four feet thick, by twenty high — enclosing an area of two hundred and fifty feet in length, by two hundred broad. At the northwest and southwest corners are bastions which command its approaches in all directions.

Within the walls are some twelve buildings in all, consisting as follows: Office, store, warehouse, meat-house, smith's shop, carpenter's shop, kitchen, and five dwellings,— so arranged as to form a yard and *corel,* sufficiently large for the accommodation and security of more than two hundred head of animals. The number of men usually employed about the establishment is some thirty, whose chief duty it is to promote the interests of the trade, and otherwise act as circumstances require.

The Fort is located in a level plain, fertile and interesting, bounded upon all sides by hills, many of which present to view the nodding forms of pines and cedars, that bescatter their surface,— while the river bottoms, at various points, are thickly studded with proud growths of cottonwood, ash, willow, and box-elder, thus affording its needful supplies of timber and fuel.[61]

---

[61] John Bidwell, who reached Fort Laramie on June 22, 1841, recorded in his *A Journey to California, op. cit.,* p. 8: "there is another fort, within a mile and a half of this Place [Fort Laramie] belonging to an individual by the name of Lupton." Many of the descriptions and references to Fort Platte by overland emigrants, official explorers, and military men from 1841 to 1845 are quoted or referred to in Hafen and Young, *Fort Laramie and the Pageant of the West* (Glendale, Arthur H. Clark Company, 1938), pp. 95-111. Accurate measurements of the deserted post were made by Thomas Bullock of the pioneer Mormon band in 1847. He drew the ground plan and gave the measurements of the post, exclusive of the bastions, as 144 feet by 103 feet, 2 inches. *See* Hafen and Young, *op. cit.,* pp. 125-27, for the ground plan and a detailed description.

One mile south of it, upon the Larramie, is Fort John,[62] a station of the American Fur Company. Between these two posts a strong opposition is maintained in regard to the business of the country, little to the credit of either.

At the time of our arrival at the Fort, two villages of Indians were encamped near by. Their lodges, being the first I ever saw, proved objects of great interest to me.

The lodge of a mountain Indian consists of a frame work of light poles, some twenty-five feet long, bound together at the small ends, and raised by planting the opposite extremities aslope, at given distances apart, so as to describe a circle, at the base, converging to a triangular apex, for roof and sides; — over this is spread a covering of buffalo robes, so nicely dressed and seamed, it readily sheds rain and excludes the fierce winds to which the country is subject. A small aperture at the top, affords passage for smoke emitted from the fire occupying the centre ground work. The entrance is at the side, where a large piece of undressed buffalo skin (hung from the top and so placed as to be opened or closed, at pleasure, upon the ingress or egress of the inmate) furnishes the simple substitute for a door.

These lodges (some of them containing quantities of roofage to the amount of ten or fifteen buffalo skins) are large and commodious; and, even comfortable, in the severest weather; the heat from the centre fire, being refracted on striking the sloping sides, communicates an agreeable warmth to every part.

An Indian lodge, in the summer, is admirably adapted

62 This is the fort that was named Fort William at the time of its founding, in 1834. When rebuilt with adobes in 1841 it was called Fort John, presumably in honor of John B. Sarpy, an officer of the company that built and owned it. This name was not generally accepted, and the post soon became known as Fort Laramie. See Joseph Williams' account in this *Far West and the Rockies Series*, III, p. 226. Hafen and Young, *Fort Laramie, op. cit.*, gives the history of the fort.

to the pleasure of its occupants,— by raising the lower extremeties of the envelope and securing them at a proper elevation, a free passage of air is obtained, which greatly contributes to increase the merits of the delightful shade afforded by the superstructure.

A lodge of the largest size may easily be made to accommodate fifteen persons. The interior is arranged by placing the fixtures for sleeping at the circumference of the circle, which afford seats to the inmates, and thus a sufficient space is left vacant between them and the centre fire.

This kind of dwelling is the one almost universally adopted by the mountain and prairie Indians, and is, perhaps, better suited to their condition and mode of life than any other that could be devised.

Dependent solely upon the chase for a subsistence, the various Indian tribes inhabiting the mountains and countries adjacent can occupy no fixed residences. Contrary to the habits of more eastern nations, among whom agriculture commands attention to a greater or less extent, they are continually necessitated to rove from place to place in pursuit of game.

Give to one of them a bow, arrows, knife, lodge, and running horse, and he is rich, happy and contented. When the erratic propensities of the buffalo (upon which is his almost exclusive dependence) compel him to change his location, he has only to pull down his lodge, saddle his horse, and away.

So accustomed are they to this incessant rambling, they regard it more as a pleasure than an inconvenience. I have frequently seen hundreds of families moving together,– presenting to the unsophisticated beholder a novel and amusing spectacle,— with their horses, mules, dogs, men, squaws, children, and all the paraphernalia of savage domestic economy, and the rude accoutrements of peace and war, commingled indiscriminately.

The Sioux tribe, to whose country we have now introduced the reader, is, perhaps, the largest Indian nation upon the continent of North America, with the exception of the ancient Mexicans, if indeed they may be called Indians. This tribe occupies a territory extending from the St. Peters, of the Mississippi, to the Missouri, and from thence to the forks of the Platte, and up that river to its head-waters. They are supposed to number not far from eighty thousand men, women, and children, and are divided into many fractional parts, each bearing its own name, yet speaking the same language and claiming a common nationality.

Of these divisions are the Brulés, Oglallas, Yanktaus, Piankshaws, Minecosias, Blackfeet, Broken-arrows, and Assenaboins, with many others whose names have escaped my recollection. The only perceptible difference in language is, in the pronunciation of words like the following, *meallo, appello* and *Lacota,*– those upon the Mississippi, and some in the vicinity of the Missouri, pronouncing them *meaddo, appeddo,* and *Dacota.*

The members of this nation, so far as my observation extends, are a cowardly, treacherous, thieving set, taken as a body — and are well deserving the appellation of mean and contemptible; though there are some honorable exceptions to the remark.

Any effort to civilize them must necessarily prove tedious, if not altogether impracticable, while they adhere to their present roving habits; — though three several missionary stations have been recently established among them, with slight success; viz: at St. Peters, Lac qui Parle, and Traverse des Sioux. But the Indians of those sections, being under the more direct influence of the U. S. Government, have begun to abandon their former wandering habits, and betake themselves to agricultural pursuits.

The term Sioux, as applied to this nation, is of Franco-Canadian origin — being a corruption of the word *sued,* and means *drunk or drunken,*— in allusion to their excessive fondness for liquor and predilection to inebriacy. The name by which they call themselves, and are known among other tribes, is *Lacota,* or *Cut-throats,*— for such is the literal meaning of the term; and rarely, indeed, were ever a pack of scoundrels more justly entitled to the appellation.[63]

The night of our arrival at Fort Platte was the signal for a grand jollification to all hands, (with two or three exceptions,) who soon got most *gloriously drunk,* and such an illustration of the beauties of harmony as was then perpetrated, would have rivalled Bedlam itself, or even the famous council chamber beyond the Styx.

Yelling, screeching, firing, fighting, swearing, drinking, and such like *interesting* performances, were kept up without intermission,— and woe to the poor fellow who looked for repose that night,— he might as well have thought of sleeping with a thousand cannon bellowing at his ears.

The scene was prolonged till near sundown the next day, and several made their egress from this beastly carousal, minus shirts and coats,— with swollen eyes, bloody noses, and empty pockets,— the latter circumstance will be easily understood upon the mere mention of the fact, that liquor, in this country, is sold for four dollars per pint.

The day following was ushered in by the enactment of another scene of comico-tragical character.

The Indians encamped in the vicinity, being extremely solicitous to imitate the example of their "illustrious predecessors," soon as the first tints of morning began to paint the east, commenced their demands for firewater; and, ere the sun had told an hour of his course, they were pretty well advanced in the state of "how came ye so," and seemed to exercise their musical

63 For Sioux names and their interpretations, *see* F. W. Hodge, *Handbook of American Indians* (2 vols., Washington, D.C., Government Printing Office, 1907-10).

powers in wonderful rivalry with their white brethren.

Men, women, and children were seen running from lodge to lodge with vessels of liquor, inviting their friends and relatives to drink; while whooping, singing, drunkenness, and trading for fresh supplies to administer to the demands of intoxication, had evidently become the order of the day. Soon, individuals were noticed passing from one to another, with mouths full of the coveted fire-water, drawing the lips of favored friends in close contact, as if to kiss, and ejecting the contents of their own into the eager mouths of others,— thus affording the delighted recipients tests of their fervent esteem in the heat and strength of the strange draught.

At this stage of the game the American Fur Company,[64] as is charged, commenced dealing out to them, gratuitously, strong drugged liquor, for the double purpose of preventing a sale of the article by its competitor in trade, and of creating sickness, or inciting contention among the Indians, while under the influence of sudden intoxication,— hoping thereby to induce the latter to charge its ill effects upon an opposite source, and thus, by destroying the credit of its rival, monopolize for itself the whole trade.

It is hard to predict, with certainty, what would have been the result of this reckless policy, had it been continued through the day. Already its effects became apparent, and small knots of drunken Indians were seen in various directions, quarrelling, preparing to fight, or fighting,— while others lay stretched upon the ground in helpless impotency, or staggered from place to place with all the revolting attendencies of intoxication.

The *dram*-a, however, was here brought to a temporary close by an incident which made a strange contrast in its immediate results.

[64] The American Fur Company owned Fort Laramie, the trade rival of Lupton's Fort Platte.

INDIAN FUNERAL.

One of the head chiefs of the Brulé village, in riding at full speed from Fort John to Fort Platte, being a little too drunk to navigate, plunged headlong from his horse and *broke his neck* when within a few rods of his destination. Then was a touching display of confusion and excitement. Men and squaws commenced bawling like children; — the whites were bad, very bad, said they, in their grief, to give Susu-ceicha the fire-water that caused his death. But the height of their censure was directed against the American Fur Company, as its liquor had done the deed.

The body of the deceased chief was brought to the Fort, by his relatives, with a request that the whites should assist at its burial; but they were in a sorry plight for such a service. There, however, were found sufficiently sober for the task, and accordingly commenced operations.

A scaffold was soon erected for the reception of the body, which, in the mean time, had been fitted for its last airy tenement. This duty was performed by the relatives of the deceased in the following manner: it was first washed, then arrayed in the habiliments last worn by Susu-ceicha during life, and sewed in several envelopes of lodge-skin, with the bow, arrows, and pipe once claiming him as their owner. This done, all things were ready for the proposed burial.

The corpse was then borne to its final resting place, followed by a throng of relatives and friends. While moving onward with the dead, the train of mourners filled the air with their lamentations and rehearsals of the virtues and meritorious deeds of their late chief.

Arrived at the scaffold, the corpse was carefully reposed upon it facing the east, while beneath its head was placed a small sack of meat, tobacco and vermilion, with a comb, looking-glass, and knife, and at its feet, a small banner that had been carried in the procession. A covering of scarlet cloth was then spread over it, and the body firmly lashed to its place by long strips of raw hide. This done, the horse of the chieftain was produced as a sacrifice for the benefit of his master in his long journey to the celestial hunting ground.

The above mode of sepulture is that commonly practised by the mountain tribes. It is seldom indeed they ever dispose of their dead in any other way than by placing them either upon scaffolds, branches of trees, or in some elevated position, not unfrequently covered by lodges, where they are left to moulder and waste in the winds and rain, till the bones falling one by one upon the prairie, are gathered up by surviving friends, and finally entombed in mother earth.

The corpse of the ill-fated man being thus securely fixed in the airy couch assigned it, to await the speedy process of dissolution, and mingle with its kindred earth, that its bones might find their proper places beneath the prairie sod, the village once acknowledging him as its head now met round the scaffold, men, women, children, and little ones, to bewail the sad fate that had bereaved them of their loved chieftain.

First, encircling it at a respectful distance, were seated the old men, next the young men and warriors, and next the squaws and children. Etespa-huska, (Long Bow,) eldest son of the deceased, thereupon commenced speaking, while the weeping throng ceased its tumult to listen to his words:

"Oh, Susu-ceicha! thy son bemourns thee, even as was wont the fledgelings of the war-eagle to cry for the one that nourished them, ere yet thy swift arrow had laid him in dust. Sorrow fills the heart of Etespa-huska; sadness crushes it to the ground and sinks it beneath the sod upon which he treads.

"Thou hast gone, oh Susu-ceicha! Death hath conquered thee, whom none but death could conquer; and who shall now teach thy son to be brave as thou was brave; to be good as thou wast good; to fight the foe of thy people and acquaint thy chosen ones with the war-song of triumph! to deck his lodge with the scalps of the slain, and bid the feet of the young move swiftly in the dance? And who shall teach Etespa-huska to follow the chase and plunge his arrows into the yielding sides of the tired bull? Who shall teach him to call for his prey from the deer, the elk, and the antelope, as thou hast done, or win honors from the slaughtered bear?

"None. Etespa-huska has no teacher. He is alone. Susu-ceicha is dead!

"But thou wilt soon gain the happy country. Thy journey is short. There wilt thou bestride the fleet horses that never tire, and roam amid the fruits and flowers, the sweet waters and pleasure-groves of that lovely clime; for thou are worthy.

"And, oh, Wakantunga! (Great Spirit,) do thou pity Etespa-huska. Do thou teach him to be brave and good like his father, for who is there to pity or teach him now he is left alone!"

Then, turning to the audience he continued:

"Brothers: Strong was the arm of Susu-ceicha, and fleet was the arrow shot from his bow. Thirty and five of the enemy hath he slain in battle, whose waving locks were the trophies that ofttimes measured the quick step of the scalp-dance. Fourscore and ten were the medicine-dogs he brought from the land of the foeman, that their shrill neighings might greet the ears, and their strong backs carry the people he loved; for brave was the heart of Susu-ceicha!

"What warrior ever came to his lodge and went hungry, or naked, or needy away? What widow or orphan of his people blessed not their chief, when he returned from the chase and apportioned to them their wonted dues from the choice spoils of the buffalo? for generous was the soul of Susu-ceicha.

"Brothers: Susu-ceicha is dead. No more shall his voice be heard in your councils, or his courage lead you to victory, or his generosity rejoice the hearts of the needy, the widow, and the orphan. Etespa-huska laments a father and a teacher. The Burnt-thighs[65] a mighty chieftain; and the nation its bravest warrior! We all mourn him; sorrow fills the hearts, and tears wash the cheeks of his people. It is good that we bemourn him, and mingle with the winds the voices of our lamentation, for who shall now stand in the place of Susu-ceicha.

"Brothers: Let us stamp his memory upon our hearts and imitate his virtues, that our acts may rear to him a living monument, which may endure till time itself shall die!"

No sooner had the orator ceased, than a tremendous howl of grief burst from the whole assemblage, men, women, and children, which was renewed in quick succession for several hours, when finally the bewailing multitude retired to their lodges.

[65] This is the interpretation of the Indian name which the French have supplied by the word Brulé. – [Sage]

CHAPTER VIII.

THE events of the day had for the present put an effectual stop to dissipation among the Indians, and not long aferwards they began to pull down their lodges and remove to the neighborhood of buffalo, for the purpose of selecting winter-quarters.

The disgusting scenes connected with our arrival at the Fort had pretty much ceased on the evening of the second day, and everything, with a few exceptions, began to assume its wonted aspect.

The winter trade was now considered fully opened. Parties were sent with goods from the Fort to different villages, for the purpose of barter, and affairs began to show a business-like appearance.

Some two weeks subsequently, a band of Brulés arrived in the vicinity. They had come for a drunken spree, and soon opened a brisk trade in liquor.

Our visitors crowded the Fort houses in quest of articles of plunder, and became an incessant source of annoyance to the engagés. One room, in particular, was thronged almost to the exclusion of its regular occupants. The latter, losing all patience, at length hit upon a plan to rid themselves of the intruders.

After closely covering the chimney funnel, by aid of some half rotten chips a smoke was raised; the doors and windows being closed to prevent its egress. In an instant the apartment became filled to suffocation,—quite too much so for the endurance of the wondering savages, who gladly withdrew to gain the pure air of the exterior. On being told it was the Long-knife's medicine,[66] they replied:

"Ugh! Wakea sutiello ha Mena-huska tour!" (Ugh! The Long-knife's medicine is *strong!*)

During their stay at the Fort, an incident occurred which will serve to illustrate a singular trait in the character of these Indians.

A brave, named Bello-tunga, (Big Eagle,) received a blow over the head from a half crazed drunken trader, which came very near terminating in serious consequences. What would have been the result, it is hard to tell, had not the whites promptly interfered, and, with much effort, succeeded in pacifying the enraged savage by presenting him a horse.

At first he would admit of no compromise short of the offender's blood — he had been struck by the pale-face, and blood must atone for the aggression,— unless that should wipe out the disgrace, he could never again lift up his head among his people,— they would call him a coward, and say the white man struck Bello-tunga and he dared not to resent it.

The services of his father, hereupon, were secured in behalf of the offending party, which, after great ado, finally effected an adjustment of the difficulty.

An Indian considers it the greatest indignity to receive a blow from any one, even from his own brother; — and, unless the affair is settled by the bestowment of a *trespass offering* on the part of the aggressor, he is almost sure to seek revenge, either through blood or the destruction of property. This is a more especial characteristic of the Sioux than of any other nation. In fact, the Snakes, Crows, Arapahos, Chyennes, and most other tribes are far less nice in its observance,—

66 This word, in Indian signification, means any person or thing possessed of extraordinary or supernatural powers, as well as any act for conciliating the favor and obtaining the assistance of the Great Spirit. That medicine is the strongest which is the most efficient for its intended purposes. – [Sage]

though all regard the like an insult that justly calls for revenge.

Soon after, an expedition was detached to Fort Lancaster,[67] on the South Fork Platte, and another to White river, an affluent of the Missouri, some eighty miles northwest of the main trading post. The latter party included myself with its number.

Our purpose was to build houses in the vicinity of White river, and thus secure the trade of several villages of Brulés that had selected their winter quarters in the neighborhood, and were anxiously awaiting our arrival.

On the last of November we were under way with two carts freighted with goods and liquor, accompanied by only six whites, one negro, and an Indian.

Crossing the Platte opposite the Fort, we continued our course, west by north, over a broken and tumulous prairie, occasionally diversified by thick clusters of pines and furrowed by deep ravines, and abounding in diminutive valleys, whose tall, withered grass gave evidence of the rich soil producing it. To our left the high, frowning summits of the Black Hills began to show themselves in the long distance, like dark clouds, and planted their dense pine forests upon the broken ridges whose irregular courses invaded the cheerless prairie far eastward.

A ride of twenty miles brought us to Rawhide,[68] where we passed the following night and day.

This creek traces its course over a broad sandy bed, through a wide valley of rich clayey loam, slightly timbered and luxuriant in grasses. Towards its head,

---

[67] Fort Lancaster, generally called Fort Lupton, and named for Lancaster P. Lupton, was located about a mile north of the present site of the town of Fort Lupton, Colorado. For an account of the fort, *see* L. R. Hafen, "Fort Lupton and its Founder," in the *Colorado Magazine,* VI, pp. 220-26.

[68] Rawhide Creek still carries the same name. It enters the North Platte near the town of Lingle, Wyoming.

it is shut in upon both sides by high pine hills; but, in passing on, these mural confines are exchanged for the prairies, and the creek finally debouches into the Platte.

An abundance of prelée and rushes afforded fine pasturage to our animals, and a kindly grove of dry cottonwood gave us requisite fuel for camp-fire.

Before leaving, we were joined by another Indian mounted upon a dark bay horse, the noblest animal of its kind I remember to have seen among the mountain tribes. It had been stolen from the Snakes during the past summer, as its present owner informed us, and he seemed not a little proud of the admiration we bestowed upon it.

The new comer proved Arketcheta-waka, (Medicine Soldier,) a brother of Bello-tunga, the brave referred to on a former occasion. Seating himself by the fire, he looked dejected and melancholy, and his face bore indubitable evidence of a personal encounter with some one.

On enquiring the cause of this, we learned that he had left his father's lodge by reason of a quarrel he had had with his eldest brother,— the latter having struck him with a fire-brand and burnt his body in several places during a drunken spree,— he was now on his way to White river, there to await the suitable time for revenge, when he should kill his brother.

We told him this would not be right; — it was liquor that had done him the wrong, and not his brother; — liquor was bad!

He seemed to acknowledge the truth of our suggestions, and asked "why the pale-faces brought the fire-water to do the red man so much harm?" Our trader replied, "The whites want robes, and can get them for liquor when nothing else will do it."

The answer evidently perplexed him, while he sat gazing silently into the fire, with his arms akimbo upon his knees, and palms supporting his chin, as if striving to work out to his own satisfaction this strange problem in morality.

The third day we resumed our course, and after a drive of six or eight miles, came upon a large band of buffalo. Here, at our request, the Medicine Soldier doffed his robe, slung his arrow-case over his naked shoulders, mounted his horse bow in hand, and started for the chase.

At first he rode slowly, as if reserving the speed of his charger till the proper time. The buffalo permitted him to approach within a few hundred yards before they commenced flight. Then was a magnificent spectacle.

The affrighted beasts flew over the ground with all the speed that extreme terror lent to their straightened nerves, and plied their nimble feet with a velocity almost incredible — but they were no match for the noble steed the Indian bestrode. He was among them in a trice, and horse, Indian, and buffalo were lost in identity, as they swept over a snow-clad prairie, in one thick, black mass, like the career of a fierce tornado, tossing the loose drifts upwards in small particles, that, in their descent, pictured white clouds falling to the earth, ever and anon enshrouding the whole band from view.

Now their course is turned and makes directly towards us. They pass, all foaming with sweat — with lolling tongues and panting breath — but they still seem loath to abate from the energy of their wild terror.

Soon the Indian and his gallant steed part from them. He has selected the choicest of the band and pursues her singly. Side by side both cow and horse keep even pace, while the ready archer pours in his arrows,— some of them, forcing their entire way through the bleeding beast, fall loosely to the ground upon the opposite side.

At length, spent by the toilsome flight, exhausted by

CHASING A BUFFALO.

loss of blood, and pierced through her vitals by the practised marksman that follows her, she halts for fight.

Now, she plunges with mad fury at the horse,— the well-trained steed clears the force of her charge at a bound. Again, she halts,— the blood spouts from her nostrils and mouth — she staggers. Again, she musters her expiring energies for one more desperate onset at her enemy, as if determined, if die she must, not to be unavenged. Her charge proves futile as the former. A death-sickness comes over her. Her life is fast ebbing from within her. She reels,— she totters — she falls,— and breathes her life away upon the blood-dyed snow.

A few moments' delay put us in possession of an ample supply of fresh meat,— the Indian reserving the robe only as his share. The cow proved a most excellent selection, and did honor to the judgment of the hunter.

As we travelled on, the snow, which scarcely an hour since had first attracted our attention, became deeper and deeper, and our progress more tedious and difficult.

From bare ground and comparatively moderate climate, we were fully inducted to the region of snow, ice, and winter. The prairie was high and undulating. To our left an immense wall of secondary rock surmounted a ridge of naked hills, that described in its course the curve of a rainbow, enclosing upon three sides a large valley facing the east,— thence, stretching westward and raising higher and higher, hastened to mingle its heads among the cloud-capped summits and snows of the neighboring mountains.

From a light coating of loose snow our course soon became obstructed by still deepening layers, covered with a thick crust, scarcely strong enough to bear our weight, but quite sufficient to wrench and jar us at every step, and make our advance threefold tiresome.

The cold was so intense, we were forced to walk to

keep from freezing. Our difficulties thickened the farther we progressed. Night closed in upon us, and we could no longer distinguish our course. Yet we kept on, in hopes of reaching some creek or spring where we might await the coming day.

Slowly, onward,— plunge, plunge, at every step; — now prostrate at full length upon the hard crust, and then again staggering in resistless mimicry of drunken men.

The chill winds sweeping over the dreary expanse pierced us through at each whiff, and seemed to penetrate every nerve, and joint, and muscle as if to transform our hearts' blood into icicles. But still it was plunge, plunge along; onward, plunge, fall; but yet onward! There is no stopping place here,—'tis push on or die!

Thus, travelling for three or four hours, not knowing whither, we came finally to the leeward of a high hill. The agreeable change produced by the absence of wind, called forth a hearty response. "Camp, ho," was echoed upon all sides. But here was no water for ourselves or our animals. We must yet go on. Still we lingered — loath to leave the favored spot. The Indian, who had been absent for a brief space, now came up, shouting:

"Mine washtasta!" (Water, very good!)

"Tarkoo mine?" asked the trader. (What water?)

"Mine-loosa. Tunga warkpollo." (Running-water. A large creek.)

It proved L'eau-qui-court,[69] the stream upon which we had intended to pass the night.

Pushing on, a few moments brought us to its banks, in a deep valley covered with snow. A fire was then promptly built from a small quantity of wood we had the precaution to take with us from Rawhide, and all

[69] Running Water, a stream now called Niobrara. It flows eastward and enters the Missouri near the town of Niobrara, Nebraska.

hands were soon as comfortably conditioned as circumstances would admit.

A hearty supper served to appease the appetites so keenly sharpened by a toilsome journey of thirty miles, occupying from sunrise till ten o'clock at night. This over, each one cleared for himself a place upon the frozen ground, and, spreading down his bed, quickly forgot his cares and sufferings in the welcome embrace of sleep.

L'eau-qui-court, or Running-water, heads in a small lake under the base of the first range of Black Hills, and following an easternly course, empties into the Missouri, about one hundred and fifty or two hundred miles above Council Bluff. It derives its name from the rapidity of its current, which rolls over a pebbly bed with great velocity.

At this place it is narrow and deep, with steep banks, and not a stick of timber is to be found on it, above or below, for twenty miles. At the lake where it heads, there is an abundance of timber; large groves of cottonwood are also found at some distance below our present camp.

The intermediate country, from Rawhide, is a cold and cheerless expanse almost at all seasons of the year. From the commencement of fall to the very close of spring, it is subject to frost and snow; — for what cause, it is hard to conjecture. Its surface, though quite elevated, is not sufficiently so to make such marked difference in climate between it and adjoining sections.

The next day proved cloudy; we, however, resumed our course which led over a rough, tumulous country, covered with snow and darkened by occasional clusters of pines.

Early in the morning our Indians left us and took a nearer route to the village. Soon after we became bewildered in the obscurity of the atmosphere, and travelled till night unconscious whether right or wrong. Finally, coming to a deep ravine that obstructed further progress, we turned to a neighboring grove of pines, at the point of an eminence, and made camp. It was a bleak airy place, but by aid of a huge fire of dry pine we were quite comfortable, despite a heavy fall of snow during the night.

With the morning our perplexities were renewed. Directly in front lay a broad and impassable ravine, beyond which a high mountain range arose to view. Should we go up or down? After much debate we decided upon the latter, and, bearing northward during the day, struck the head of a stream which subsequently proved White river.[70]

This stream traces its way through a broad valley, enclosed upon either side by high pine hills. Its banks are studded with thick groves of cottonwood, elm, ash, box-elder, and willow,— with nearly all the varieties of fruit-bearing shrubs and trees indigenous to the mountains. In the item of plums and cherries, it gave evidence of exuberant fecundity. The bushes, in many instances, yet bore the dried relics of their burthen, as if to tempt the beholder's taste,— while the tall grass and rosebuds,[71] every where attested the summer-verdure and beauty of the valley in which they grew.

The snow that had hitherto impeded our progress, now gradually became less as we advanced down the valley, and soon gave place to bare ground. Game

[70] White River flows northeastward into South Dakota and then eastward to reach the Missouri River a few miles south of Chamberlain, South Dakota. It is mistakenly shown on Sage's map as a branch of the Niobrara.

[71] Rosebuds are found in great quantities in many places, throughout the mountains, during the winter, and attain a large size. They are highly esteemed by many as an article of food, and have not unfrequently been the means of preserving life in case of extreme hunger and lack of other eatables. – [Sage]

appeared in great numbers, attracted from the adjoining hills to pass the winter in this inviting locality.

A journey of two days brought us to the site selected for houses, and, consequently to a halt, for the present.[72]

The place was surrounded by wild and romantic scenery. Directly in front, upon the opposite side of the creek, arose a perpendicular wall of marl and half formed sandstone, towering, stratum above stratum, to a height of three or four hundred feet, and overlooking the valley above and below,— while further on, a steep hill-side, covered with tall, straight, and almost branchless pines, burst upon the view.

Rearward a gradual acclivity led to a high plateau, some two miles broad, coated with long, tall grass, when a ridge of abrupt pine hills introduced the more distant mountains, with their rugged sides and frowning summits,— and, higher up, an immense pile of earthy limestone, surmounting a wing of hills as it approached the river, presented a medley of curious and fantastic shapes,— objects alike of amusement and wonder.

One of the latter, denominated the "Devil's Teapot," [73] exhibited externally an almost perfect facsimile of that kind of vessel. It was of gigantic proportions, — being one hundred feet high, and, occupying a conspicuous position, may be seen for a distance of many miles.

---

[72] This would be in the vicinity of present Harrison, Nebraska.

[73] For an identification of this landmark and the area described by Sage we are indebted to Dr. Eric G. DeFlon and the Museum of the Fur Trade (Charles E. Hanson, Director) at Chadron, Nebraska. Dr. DeFlon, who has fished the upper White River many times, gave us generous aid. Upon receipt of our letter of inquiry (March 27, 1955), Dr. De Flon, with the Sage book in hand, traversed the region of the bluffs along the White River near present Crawford. He concludes that Sage's "Devil's Tea-pot" is the large butte near Crawford now known as Saddle Rock. He points out that the formation, being sandstone, may have changed shape somewhat in more than a century. Also, he says that the army at nearby Fort Robinson used for years some of these buttes as targets for artillery practice.

The Indians from a near village, immediately upon our arrival, came flocking around for the threefold purpose of begging, trading and stealing; and, from this forward, we rarely experienced an interval free from their annoyance.

Prompt arrangements were here commenced for building a store room and trading house; — but meanwhile, we were forced to keep strict guard both night and day.

Two braves were secured to "act soldier," and assist in keeping the thieving propensities of their people in check. Yet, notwithstanding the united vigilance of all hands, the latter would frequently perpetrate their petit larcenies under our very eyes, without being detected in the act,— so adroit were they at the business. An instance of this kind happening to myself is perhaps worth relating.

Previously to the erection of houses, we were necessitated to sleep in the open air. Wearied by the lateness of the hour, one night I spread down my couch by the camp-fire with the intention of retiring. The weather being very cold, I had scarcely turned to warm myself, when a backward glance revealed the sudden disappearance of my sleeping appendages — robes blankets and all!

Informing the trader of my mishap, and catching a glimpse of the thief as he dodged past a knot of Indians at the further extremity of the camp, gun in hand, I started after the nimble lark; but the thick bushes and darkness soon shut him from view and left me in fruitless pursuit.

At length, relinquishing the hope of ever regaining the stolen articles, and vexed at the impious savage, who, instead of obeying the Scripture injunction of "take up *thy* bed and *walk,*" had snatched MY bed and RUN! I returned to camp. Here I was shown a robe, by the trader, that had been brought in scarcely a minute before and offered in barter for liquor; — it was one of the two I had lost.

The bearer was now promptly charged as being accessory to the theft. This he stoutly denied, alleging that the robe had been given him by another Indian for the purpose he had offered it.

Upon this the affair was referred to our soldiers, who, after much parleying and no little threatening, succeeded in causing him to return the missing articles. The fellow then demanded of me a cup of liquor as pay for bringing them back. Mustering to my aid a few words of Sioux, I replied: "Mea warche yau wechacha ceicha, opata-ne ha warktash-ne coga! — I neither like bad men, nor will I pay for doing bad."

Marto-nazher, (Standing Bear,) one of our soldiers, on hearing my answer, arose and addressed the crowd in an earnest and impressive manner. He was grieved on account of the many depredations continually committed by his people upon the property of the whites. It is wrong — very wrong, said he, to conduct in this manner; — if such wickedness is allowed, the whites will abandon the country. Whites do not steal from us. — Something must be done — an example must be had — the perpetrators of these outrages must be punished.

"You, Schena-sarpah," he continued, throwing his piercing glance full upon the chop-fallen culprit, who hung his head for shame at being caught in a manner so little to his credit, "Aye, you Scena-sarpah do carry a bow and arrows; you call yourself a brave; and yet you steal from our friends, the pale-faces!

"Do brave men steal from their friends? No! Schena-sarpah should alone steal from his enemies, if he be a brave man and a soldier.

"Who are they that steal from their friends? Squaws and children, as Schena-sarpah well knows. Then he is no better than they! Why should he carry a bow? Why go to war, or follow the chase? Squaws and children do neither. None but brave men go to war — none but they should follow the chase.

"Schena-sarpa needs no bow. Let him go to his lodge. There let him make robes and moccasins for braves, and take care of children with squaws,— for such should be his occupation, and only such should be his companions!"

So saying, he approached the unresisting thief, and, taking from him his bow, arrows, and panther-skin quiver, resumed his seat. Then, breaking the arrows and shooting them away, one by one, among the trees, he snapped the bow across his knee and threw it into the fire. The bright flame from the burning bow had barely died away, when the quiver was consigned to the same fate. As the last fragments of the effeminate's weapons mouldered to ashes, a smile of satisfaction played upon the countenance of the Standing Bear, at the thought of having avenged the wrongs of the white man.

And, truly, this was an infliction of summary punishment. The amount of property destroyed exceeded the value of a horse, and, in the estimation of an Indian, constitutes a man's chief wealth. The offender was thus not only left disarmed by the operation, but made poor, and reduced to a level with the squaws and children to whom he was set apart. He bemoaned his loss most piteously, and started for his lodge, bellowing like a motherless calf.

Another instance of theft occurred soon after, almost as remarkable. A robe was stolen from off one of our party, while he was asleep, and bartered for whiskey, without his knowing it!

Our Indian soldiers were of great service in conducting the trade. If any difficulty occurred, they were always at hand to assist in its adjustment, and preserve order and quiet so far as lay in their power. If any visitor became troublesome, they at once ordered him to his lodge, and enforced their commands in case of resistance.

Every trader is necessitated to employ one or more braves to assist him in his business at the villages. An Indian considers it a great honor thus to receive the confidence of a white man and "act soldier" for him, as he denominates it. Some of them have not unfrequently gone so far as to kill those of their people who proved guilty of misusing the traders by whom they were employed.

They exercise a kind of supervisory office in the management of affairs which could not well be dispensed with,— and very often have the lives of traders been preserved by the judgment and discretion of these men.

Dec. 25. Christmas finds us in our new residence, which, with the exception of a chimney, is now completed.

This great annual festival is observed with all the exhilarating hilarity and good cheer that circumstances will allow. Several little extras for the occasion have been procured from the Indians, which prove quite wholesome and pleasant-tasted. One of these, called *washena,* consists of dried meat pulverized and mixed with marrow; another is a preparation of cherries, preserved when first picked by pounding and sun-drying them, (they are served by mixing them with *bouillie,* or the liquor of fresh-boiled meat, thus giving to it an agreeable winish taste;) a third is marrow-fat, an article in many respects superior to butter; and, lastly, we obtained a kind of flour made from the *pomme blanc,* (white apple,)[74] answering very well as a substitute for that of grain.

The above assortment, with a small supply of sugar and coffee, as well as several other dainties variously

[74] Also known as Indian turnip (*Psoralea esculenta*).

prepared, affords an excellent dinner,—and, though different in kind, by no means inferior in quality to the generality of dinners for which the day is noted in more civilized communities.

The day following our turbulent neighbors were augmented in number by the accession of another village of Brulés, and Marto-cogershne, of whom I have spoken upon a former occasion, became with his family our constant annoyance.

Visiting us at one time, squaws and all — as was his daily custom — to beg liquor, (which, some way or other, he always obtained,) the brother of our tormentor demanded a quantity of that article to take with him to his lodge. This, after many sharp words, was offered; but, having no vessel for its conveyance, he extended his demands to a kettle,—which, of course, was refused; whereupon he threatened vengeance unless both were forthcoming upon the *mocosco*,[75] (prairie,) and required still farther the gift of a pair of moccasins.

Our trader replied, "The liquor is for you, and here are the moccasins, (pulling off his own and passing them to him,) but the kettle you cannot have."

The affair thus ended for the present, and the modest beggar retired to his lodge. The next morning, however, two of our horses were found pierced with arrows, and so badly, that they died soon after.

At another time, Marto-cogershne became so enraged at being refused a whole keg of liquor "on the prairie," he rushed upon the trader with his butcher-knife to kill him. What would have been the result, it is hard to tell, had I not stayed the descending weapon by seizing the fellow's arm. Here our soldiers interfered and

[75] This expression implies the bestowment of anything as a free gift. It is also used to denote a random way of speaking with regard to truth. – [Sage]

put him out of the house,— closing the door upon him. The exasperated savage then commenced shooting upon us through the door; — two Indian boys passing in the interval also furnished marks for his gun, and not long subsequently a mule and an ox belonging to us fell to appease his insulted dignity.

However, the *chef d'ouvre* of his rascality was exhibited in stealing our whole *cavallard,*[76] consisting of ten head of horses and mules, which he drove into the mountains. We were compelled to give a quantity of liquor and ammunition, two blankets, and several other articles before we could secure their return.

From the movement of things, he was evidently instigated by the American Fur Company traders to do us all the mischief in his power. Certain it is, he was their regular "soldier," and received from them numerous presents in consideration of his good conduct.

The employees of this company are frequently guilty of such disgraceful conduct. In connection with this conclusion I might cite instance upon instance, and string out a volume of proof, were it necessary.

Soon after Christmas we commenced erecting our chimney. The materials for it were procured from an adjoining bank. While engaged in quarrying them, the operator came to a crevice filled with a strange fleshy substance, coiled together like the folds of a huge rope. "Hallo!" cried he, with astonishment, "here's the Devil, himself!"

The extraordinary announcement brought all hands to the spot to get a peep at "Old Nick," and the Indians, also witnessing the unusual commotion, came hurrying up to learn its cause.

The result proved, that, if not the Devil, it was his

[76] This is a mountain phrase of Spanish origin, (cave lardo,) and means a band of horses or mules. – [Sage]

great prototype,— it was that "Old Serpent," with all his progeny.

By means of a stick, *thirty-six large snakes*[77] were exposed to view,— some of them six feet in length. They were in a torpid state, the result of the severe cold of winter.

Having drawn them out, one by one, it was proposed to treat them to a warm bath. Accordingly, after placing them in a hole for the purpose, a kettle of scalding water was thrown upon them. The vivifying effects of this unwonted application restored them to a sudden animation, when, wriggling and twisting for a few moments in all the contortions of agony, they at last tacitly curled up and expired.

The Indians were much shocked on seeing this, and expressed their astonishment at our reckless presumption by their deeply accented "tula,"— turning away from the spot with evident emotions of terror.

On inquiring the cause, I learned in answer, that the various Indian tribes in the vicinity of the mountains are accustomed to regard the snake with a kind of superstitious veneration, and consider the act of killing it a sure harbinger of calamity. In the observance of this singular notion, they are scrupulously exact; — but, in despite of repeated inquries, I have been unable to obtain the reasons upon which the whim is based.

These tribes cherish many religious tenets, rites, and customs,— some general and others peculiar only to individuals.

An Indian will never pronounce the name of the Big Medicine, or Great Spirit, other than in a reverential manner, nor upon trivial occasions.

This being is considered the Great Superintendent of

[77] It is common for snakes to gather in dens and hibernate in this fashion. *See* A. M. Woodbury, "A Snake Den in Tooele County, Utah," in Herpetologica, VII, pt. I, pp. 4-14.

all things, whose power sustains the universe,— causing day and night with the varying seasons,— making the grass to grow, the water to run, and the rains to fall, for the good of man and beast.

Some imagine He lives in the sun; others, in the air; others, in the ground; and others in the immensity of His works.

The animal or thing possessed of wonderful or extraordinary powers, such as their ignorance ascribes to be the attributes of the Supreme Being, they look upon as endowed with a greater or less share of His presence, and venerate it accordingly. Thus, the sun, fire, lightning, thunder, fountains of peculiar medicinal qualities, extraordinary localities, and various other things are alike objects of religious regard.

Although their theological sentiments are generally the same, the manner of showing their respect for this Overruling Providence differs with different tribes, families, and even persons. For instance,— some tribes shave their heads in token of their submission to Him. Others mark themselves for His own by some peculiar manner of cutting their ears for the reception of ornaments; — while others burn their thighs, tattoo their breasts, scar their arms, or flatten the heads of infants, for a like purpose.

The instrument, with which such ceremonies are performed, is invariably thrown away. In case of cutting the ears of an infant, the gift bestowed upon the operator is regarded as indicative of its success during life; — parents have been known to give as high as ten horses on like occasions.

Some make indelible marks of a blue color upon their chins and foreheads,— or the figures of lizards, snakes, arrows, or other objects upon their arms.

Some show their reverence in the peculiar manner of receiving the pipe and passing it to another; —

others by certain ceremonies before smoking,— thus, pointing the pipe-stem to the zenith, then towards the ground, then horizontally upon either side, as if saying, "Oh thou, whose habitation is immensity, accept this as the willing tribute of homage from thy child."

They will never allow a bone of any kind to be broken within their lodges, and express great consternation and alarm at such an occurrence. Some will not permit a stick of wood to be struck with a knife or other edged tool while burning, and others exhibit their devotion by some peculiarity in the structure of their lodges, or the mode of placing their medicine-bags, the length and shape of their arrows, their fashion of hair-dressing, and various minutiæ of like character.

Others again will never eat unless they bestow the first mouthful as an offering to the prairie,— believing that, as the prairie affords water, grass, and game, for the good of the red man, it is the fullest embodyment of the Essence of Good; therefore, in the observance of this practice, they not only acknowledge their faith in the existence of the Great Spirit, but set apart the first of their substance as test of their piety.

Their ideas of the existence of a principle, or being, who is the author and prompter of evil, are crude and indefinite.

They are ready to acknowledge its reality, but seem to consider its person more manifest in man himself than any other creature or thing. Their enemies they esteem as the more special incarnation of this principle, and next to them they regard a worthless, mean, and cowardly individual of their own people. They also look upon creatures of an injurious and harmful nature, as the greater or less impersonation of evil.

Their notions of right and wrong are equally simple.

It is right to be brave, to do good to friends, to relieve the needy, to feed the hungry, and to worship the Great

Spirit,— these are acts of general morality. There are various other duties taught by their code relative to intercourse with each other,— to children and parents, husbands and wives, deference to age, chastity, etc., the performance of which is essential to virtue.

The line of demarkation between virtue and vice is yet more simple and comprehensive; — every thing derelict of right is wrong.

I shall recur to several points, connected with the foregoing subjects, in another place.

CHAPTER IX.

THE difficulty and danger, not to say crime and bloodshed, connected with the illicit trade in alcohol, as conducted among our western Indians, is great and imminent. To illustrate this point, I need only to place before the reader a summary of facts which occurred, many of them under my own observation, during the winter of 1842.

Soon after our arrival at White river a man was sent to a neighboring village with a keg of diluted alcohol, for the purpose of barter. The Indians, feeling more disposed to drink than pay for it, demanded the keg as a gift "on the prairie." This was refused. They threatened — a fight ensued, (the soldiers and trader defending the keg and the Indians trying to take it.) Weapons were used, and the result was, both soldiers and trader were beaten off,— the latter, after being dragged through the lodge-fire three or four times, narrowly escaped with his life.

A party of Indians under the excitement of strong drink, attacked and took a trading house of the American Fur Company, near by,— robbing it of both liquor and goods.

Two parties in the Fur Company's employ, from different posts, met at a neighboring village,— one having goods and the other alcohol. The Indians, as usual, got drunk, and commenced a fight among themselves; — because the goods-trader happened to be in the lodge of one of the weaker party, they attacked him. He was compelled to flee, and barely escaped with his life through the friendly interference of the squaws. His goods were all stolen; — while one of the Indians who defended him was brutally murdered, and several others wounded.

Not long afterwards, our trader was shot at, three or four times, while engaged in this dangerous traffic, and one of his soldiers severely wounded.

About the same time, the trader of another company received a deep stab, while dealing out the vile trash, and would have been killed but for the energetic efforts of his soldiers.

Previously to the above, the Indians seized upon a trader and compelled him to stand over a hot fire until he was nearly roasted alive,—meanwhile, helping themselves to his stock in hand.

Soon after, two warriors came to trade for a blanket at our post,—one of whom was drunk. While being waited upon, the latter drew his knife and was in the very act of stabbing the unsuspecting clerk, as I caught his wrist and arrested the blow.

At another time, as our trader was standing surrounded by us all, he was shot at by a drunken Indian, who, by the merest accident, missed his object.

Again, one night a party of drunken Indians undertook to fire the house in order to consume us alive, but were providentially prevented, owing to its being constructed of green pine logs.

The most dangerous time I experienced during the winter was near the close of it. An Indian employed as our soldier, became crazed upon the drugged liquor of the American Fur Company, and made his appearance before us in a high state of excitement. This fellow had been denominated by his people the Bull Eagle, (Tahtunga-mobellu,) and was a chief,— highly esteemed as a medicine-man, and regarded as the greatest brave in the Sioux nation. He was a tall, well-made, noble-looking person — and,— such eyes! I never saw the like planted beneath the brows of any other mortal. They glared like lightning, and, as they fell upon the

Bull Eagle drinking the Fire-Water.

individual to whom directed, seemed to penetrate the very soul and read the embryo thoughts of his heart.

Through the misrepresentations of those in the interest of the Fur Company, he fancied himself misused by our trader, and came determined on revenge. Arms in hand and stripped for the contest, accompanied by his wife and two or three friends, he confronted us,— his strange appearance told for what. In the fury of passion his every look gave evidence of the raging demon within.

Here, lest he should be misunderstood, he premised by a full statement of his grievances. They were many, but the chief of them was, that our trader had employed another to "act soldier" in his stead, while he was too drunk to perform the duties of that appointment. "I have been dressed [78] as a soldier," said he, "to be laughed at, and now Peazeezee [79] must die!"

The room was full of Indians, and one of them, an old man, exclaimed:

"When Peazeezee dies, let me go under,[80]— I must live no longer!"

"Is this your love for the pale-face?" returned the infuriated chieftain. "Then die you first!"

Upon this, seizing the defenceless old man, he drew his knife and made a heart-thrust. The intended victim, however, grasped the descending blade in his bare hand and arrested its course — but his fingers were nearly severed in so doing. Here the wife of Bull Eagle rushed up to her husband and seized him by both arms, while others interfered, and the scene of conflict was removed from the apartment to the space in front.

Now was a general fight. The women and children, crying for terror, ran about in the utmost confusion

78 Previously, he had been presented with a citizen's dress to secure him for the company's interest. – [Sage]

79 Yellow-hair. The Indian name for our trader. – [Sage]

80 This term implies death, or the act of dying. – [Sage]

and dismay,— while raving combatants yelled and whooped, as knives, clubs, and tomahawks were busily dealing wounds and scattering blood.

Soon after, the parties retired to their village, and the melée ended with only six wounded.

In a brief interval the Bull Eagle again returned, accompanied by his wife,— the latter earnestly endeavoring to dissuade him from his purpose.

A shot was his first salute, on entering the door, which a timely thrust from the squaw averted from its object. The kind-hearted creature then grasped the bow. Relinquishing it in her hands, the madman made a pass at the trader with his tomahawk,— this blow was dodged, and the heroine, rushing between the two, prevented its repetition. Dropping his tomahawk, he then fell upon the object of his hatred, butcher-knife in hand.

But here he found himself in the firm grasp of several friendly Indians, by whom he was borne from the room.

This state of affairs was the signal for another engagement between Bull Eagle, at the head of his partizans, and the friends of the whites,— more desperate and bloody than the former. With great difficulty we retained our arms from the forcible grasp of the contending factions. This, to us, was a moment fraught with extreme peril — not knowing friend from foe, and instantly apprehensive of the knives and arrows of the avengeful throng. It was, indeed, a moment when the agony of suspense quivered with thrilling intensity upon every nerve, and vibrated in every sinew. To fight, would have been a relief. But, whom should we fight? It might have been our best friends — for who could discriminate? The death of one connected with either party, at our hands, would have proved the signal for our instant slaughter. Both would have united to exterminate us,— and, beset as we were, upon all sides, prudence dictated a strict neutrality. Sometimes fifteen or twenty would be struggling for our arms at once,—a strong temptation, as the reader may rest assured, for us to use them in self-defence.

Meanwhile the conflict continued with unabated fury. Several attempts were made upon the life of Bull Eagle, but without success. Two were killed and others wounded, when a final stop was put to the further effusion of blood by the withdrawal of the chieftain to his lodge.

In about an hour subsequent, he returned for the second time,— but reason had now resumed her sway, and he came to apologize for his bad conduct. Calling our trader his "very good, his best friend," he cried for grief that he had attempted to kill him. He averred that liquor had made him a *fool,* and said he should never cease to regret the great wickedness he had thought of doing to his "best friend." Ever after this affair, he remained our steadfast friend, and presented our trader with six super-fine robes, in evidence of the sincerity of his repentance.

The foregoing results of this infamous traffic, are only a few of the many instances of like nature I might cite, in proof of its imminent danger to those engaged in its prosecution; — but this is not the darkest part of the picture. There are yet scenes in reserve, more bloody and dreadful than those above recited, though not, perhaps, quite as perilous to the whites themselves. They all occurred in the winter of 1842, during the brief period of two months, and resulted immediately from the sale of liquor.

I shall not enter into details, but content myself by laying before the reader a mere synopsis of facts.

In November, the American Fur Company, from Fort John, sent a quantity of their drugged liquor to an Indian village, on Chugwater, as a gift, for the purpose of preventing the sale of that article by their competitors in trade. The consequence was, the poor creatures all got drunk, and a fight ensued, which ended in the death of two head chiefs, Bull Bear and Yellow Lodge, and six of their friends,— besides the wounding of fourteen others, who took part in the affray.

Soon after, an affair occurred from the same cause, resulting in the death of three.

About the same time, another of like nature took place in the Chyenne village, and three more were killed.

Several were also killed, in the interval, in the vicinity of the Chyenne and Missouri rivers, by their friends and companions, while under the maddening influence of intoxicating drink,— the precise number is not known.

The very last trade at the close of the season, produced its usual deeds of bloodshed and murder. Two Indians were killed, and the person who sold to them the vile article narrowly escaped with his life.

I might go on still further with the sickening sketch; but, as enough has already been said to shock the sensibilities of the reader, in endeavoring to afford him some idea of the enormities and untold horrors connected with this criminal traffic, I must forbear.

The liquor used in this business, is generally third or fourth proof whiskey, which, after being diluted by a mixture of three parts water, is sold to the Indians at the exorbitant rate of three cups per robe,— the cups usually holding about three gills each.

But, notwithstanding the above unconscionable price, a large share of the profits result from the ingenious roguery of those conducting the trade.

Sometimes the measuring-cup is not more than half full; — then, again the act of measuring is little other than mere feint, (the purchaser receiving not one fourth the quantity paid for.)

When he becomes so intoxicated as to be unable to distinguish the difference between water and liquor, (a thing not rare,) the former is passed off upon him as the genuine article.

Another mode of cheating is, by holding the cup in such a manner that the two front fingers occupy a place upon the inside, and thus save to the trader nearly a gill at each filling.

Some have two cups, (one of the usual size, and the other less,) which are so exchanged as to induce the purchaser to believe he is obtaining a third more than he actually receives; and others, yet more cunning, fill the measure half full of tallow and deal out the liquor from off it,— the witless dupe, not thinking to examine the bottoms, supposes he receives the requisite quantity.

No wonder the Indian, with such examples before him, learns to hate the white man, and despise and abhor his boasted civilization. No wonder he looks with an eye of suspicion, alike upon his religion and his learning, and revolts at the thought of either, as the ingenious devices of scientific roguery. He is taught all the white man's vices before he learns any of his virtues. The emissaries of Satan, by their untiring efforts, effectually stop his ears, blind his eyes, and harden his heart, ere yet the heralds of the Gospel set foot upon his soil, to tell him of the blessings of Christianity, and the way to happiness and to heaven.

If the Indian is bad, it is because the white man has made him so. Uncontaminated by intercourse with the offscouring of civilization, who come to cheat and despoil him of his property, and deprive him of his comforts, you find him quite a different being. You find him brave, generous, and hospitable, as well as possessed of many exemplary moral qualities. If he is a savage, he might, in many respects, prove a safe and worthy teacher to those who pride themselves upon a more enlightened education.

He has a heart instinctive of more genuine good feeling than his white neighbor — a soul of more firm integrity — a spirit of more unyielding independence. Place the white man in his condition, divested of all the restraints of law, and unacquainted with the learning and arts of civilized life — surrounded by all the associations of the savage state — and the Indian, by comparison, will then exhibit, in a more striking light, that innate superiority he in reality possesses.

No: The Indian should not be despised. He holds weighty claims upon our pity, our compassion, and our respect,— but never should he be despised.

Old Bull Tail, of whom I had occasion to speak in a former chapter having forgotten wholesome sentiments he advanced at the time referred to, took it into his head to have a spree. But, as he was not possessed of the means to obtain the wherewith, he adopted a somewhat novel substitute.

He had an only daughter, and she was handsome — the pride of her family and the boast of her village. She was lovely, and all the high qualities of a princess were exhibited in her deportment. But, Bull Tail must drink; why not give his daughter to the Yellow-hair and receive from him a keg of liquor as a marriage present?

This thought was acted out, and one morning the old chief came to us, followed by his daughter, who, aware of her father's designs, gave vent to her grief in a flood of tears.

As he entered the door, our trader addressed him:

Trader. Bull Tail is welcome to the lodge of the Long-knife; — but, why is his daughter, the pride of his heart, bathed in tears? It pains me that one so beautiful should weep.

Bull Tail. Chintzille is a foolish girl. Her father loves her, and therefore she cries.

Trader. The contrary should prove a greater cause for grief!

Bull Tail. The Yellow-hair speaks well, and truth only falls from his lips.

Trader. How, then, can she sorrow? Bid her speak and tell me, that I may whisper in her ear words of comfort.

Bull Tail. Nay, pale-face; but I will tell thee. Bull Tail loves his daughter much — very much; he loves the Yellow-hair much! — he loves them both, very much. The Great Spirit has put the thoughts into his mind that both might be alike his children; then would his heart leap for joy at the twice-spoken name of father!

Trader. What do I hear? I know not the meaning of thy words.

Bull Tail. Sure, pale-face, thou art slow to understand! Bull Tail would give his daughter to the Yellow-hair,— for who like him is so worthy to take her to his lodge? Bull Tail has for a long time called the pale-face his brother, and now he would claim the Yellow-hair as his son. Loves he not Chintzille?

Trader. Were I to deny my joy at the words of Bull Tail, my tongue would lie! The Yellow-hair has no wife, and who, like the lovely Chintzille, is so worthy that he should take her to his bosom? How could he ever show his gratitude to her noble father!

Bull Tail. The gift is free, and Bull Tail will be honored in its acceptance,— his friends will all be glad with him. But, that they may bless the Yellow-hair, let him fill up the hollow-wood [81] with fire-water, and Bull Tail will take it to his lodge; — then the maiden shall be thine.

Trader. But, Chintzille grieves,— she loves not the Yellow-hair!

Bull Tail. Chintzille is foolish. Let the Yellow-hair measure the fire-water and she shall be thine!

Trader. Nay, but the Yellow-hair may not do this.

[81] Keg. – [Sage]

Chintzille should never be the wife of him she loves not!

The old man continued to plead for some time, in order to bring to a successful issue the negotiation by which he hoped to "wet his whistle" and gain a son-in-law,— but all to no purpose. Our trader could not be persuaded to form an alliance so entangling upon any such terms, and the chieftain left with all the lineaments of disappointment and chagrin depicted upon his countenance.

The mode of marriage prevalent among the mountain and prairie tribes would seem rather strange and somewhat unfair to the better informed of civilized communities.

The lady has little to say or do in the business. When an Indian takes it into his head to get married and meets with the squaw suiting his fancy, he wastes no time in useless courtship, but hastens to her father and demands of him to know how much he loves his daughter and what gift of horses will make his heart rejoice in a son-in-law?

The father, after consulting with his daughter and her mother, states the terms. If these prove agreeable to the suitor, he immediately accepts them, and the twain "become one flesh" without further ceremony.

In case the woman has no father, her eldest brother fills his place,— and if she have neither father nor brother, her next nearest relative assumes the responsibility of bestowing her in marriage.

If she be the eldest daughter, and has unmarried sisters, the bridegroom becomes equally entitled to them, and is looked upon as their common husband.

The first year succeeding this new relation, the bride's family consider all the horses and other valuables of the new-made husband as their own; the second year he is permitted to retain his personal property for the use of himself and wife; — but the third year he enjoys an equal right with his relatives to everything in their possession.

The decision of parents in the bestowment of a daughter in marriage is generally controlled by the largeness of the amount offered; thus showing that civilized life is not the only condition in which individuals are sometimes governed by sordid motives in pronouncing upon questions of such vital importance to the welfare of others.

The female is the only party upon whom the marriage contract is considered binding.

The man may sunder it at any time suiting his convenience or caprice. He has the power, even, to dispose of his wife to another, or, at a mere word, to absolve himself from all obligation to her. In case of the latter, the discarded one returns to her father's lodge,— ready again to test the realities of this uncertain relationship, whenever an opportunity presents itself meeting with the approval of those who assume to make barter of her affections and person.

A woman, to be happy in this state of society, should never indulge in that fancied passion, pictured in such glowing colors by crack-brained poets and novel-writers, called *love;* — or, if she has the assurance to do otherwise, it should be of that more versatile and accommodating order, so often exhibited in more refined circles, which may be reclaimed and transferred as interest or circumstances suggest. Her affections are not at her own disposal, and, to render life tolerable, she must learn to love *only* as she is loved, and to love herself above all others.

Next to horses, women constitute an Indian's chief wealth.[82] This circumstance not unfrequently results in

[82] The Arapahoes, according to Col. Henry Dodge, listed the good things of life in this order: whiskey, tobacco, guns, horses, women.

one individual appropriating to himself six or eight.

The squaw is compelled to dress robes and skins, make moccasins, cure and take care of meat, attend to the horses, procure fire-wood, and perform sundry other little drudgeries that an Indian will not do. Through her he becomes possessed of the means of procuring from the whites such articles as his necessities or fancy may require. A plurality of wives with him, therefore, is more a matter of economy than otherwise.

CHAPTER X.

AMONG our daily visitors was Tahtunga-egoniska, a head chief of the Brulé village.

Years had bleached his locks with their taming frosts and taught him self-government. Well disposed as a man, he never became a participant in those disgusting scenes of intoxication that almost continually transpired around us. He was a mere looker on — a moralizer; and, as he witnessed the blameworthy conduct of his people, an ill-suppressed sigh was frequently audible, and the inward workings of regret were plainly defined upon his countenance. Melancholy too had left her traces upon him, and, as he sat day by day in gloomy silence, he seemed the very impersonation of grief.

Whenever the throng dispersed for a few moments, he would improve the opportunity of conversation with us; for in the benevolence of his heart he loved the whites, and was greatly pained at the injuries and injustice it was so often their lot to endure.

But he had a story of his own to tell; it was a tale of affliction — a stab at the best feelings of a father's heart! And, by whom? By the very whites he loved! Aye, by the very men whose business it was to degrade his people and ruin them by the contaminating effects of an unhallowed intercourse!

Six months had scarcely yet passed since the old chief had been called to mourn his youthful hope, and the pride and joy of his declining years — his first-born son! And that son had fallen by the hand of the white man!

Still, the sorrow-stricken father harbored no thought

of revenge; he sought nothing for himself save the locks of that son, that he might hang them within his lodge, and gaze upon them and weep!

His simple tale was so touching in its nature it served to enlist the deep sympathies of our hearts. We began to regard him with much deference, and felt quite at home in his company. He would frequently entertain us with his anecdotes as occasions suggested, and at such times he invariably proved both agreeable and communicative.

The history of his own life, too, was far from uninteresting. He was the only one of the Brulé chiefs, then living, who had signed the first treaty with the whites, since which he had ever observed its stipulations with scrupulous exactness, and still carefully retained a silver medal bestowed upon him by the Government agent at that time.

Some of his stories were garbed with a strange romance, and though they may appear foreign to truth in many respects, I cannot resist the temptation of presenting a few of them to the reader.

One day, several Indians had betted largely upon a "game of hand;" [83] this called forth from the old man the following story:

"When a young man I delighted in war, and seldom did a party of our people visit the enemy that included me not with its number. These scars tell where I stood when arrows flew thick — hastening to spill the blood of the brave.

"Rarely did we return empty-handed from the foeman's land — without horses to ride or scalps to dance.

[83] This is a common game with the mountain Indians. It is commenced by one of the players who encloses a gravel-stone or a bullet in the curve of his two hands by placing the palms together, then, after sundry tosts and evolutions, suddenly parting them. If the opposing party is shrewd enough to guess in which hand the stone is retained, he wins; if not, he loses. Large amounts are often wagered upon the result of this play. – [Sage]

Yet, at times we came back like fools, and were ashamed to appear at the soldiers' feasts.

"One of these times I well recollect, and I will tell of it to my white children, that they also may remember it.

"We were proceeding against the Crows, and, like experienced warriors, had sent our spy in advance to look for the enemy. Hurrying on, in momentary expectation of a conflict, the stout hearts of our braves were appalled by his return without robe or arms, and scalpless — and with a face suffused in blood.

"This was his story: The enemy, aware of our approach, were awaiting us in great numbers. Encountering their scouts, he had been robbed and scalped, and left for dead. In this situation he lay till darkness shut down upon the mountain and the night-breeze gave him strength to meet us and advise our speedy return.

"Believing the strange tale, we hastened to revisit our lodges, and be laughed at.

"Three moons sped, and we again penetrated the land of the foemen. The scalpless warrior, far in advance of the main party, once more discharged the duties of a spy.

"This time a whoop of triumph announced the result of his mission, as he made his appearance with the scalps of two, waving from his spear.

"He tarried not to relate his adventure, but urged us instantly onward. Following him, we were led to the enemy; — we fought and were victorious.

"Among the slain was one whose scalp was wanting. Who has done this? asked the wondering braves. But none answered. Our spy, smiling, at length broke silence:

" 'Behind yon hill,' said he, 'a fountain chants melody fit for warriors' ears,— let's to it, that we may drink.'

"Following his direction, he led to a silvery spring overhung by crags and shaded by cottonwoods.

" 'Drink, warriors,' he exclaimed; when, withdrawing abruptly, he soon returned, and with the arms and robe which were his own in other days.

" 'Warriors,' resumed the spy: 'you wondered at my mishap, and lamented my hard lot when last we visited the Crowman's country; — you wondered at the condition of one among the recent slain, and asked for a reason; — and, doubtless, you wonder still more that I now stand before you bearing the store of which I was deprived! — and fain you would know in what manner I obtained the hair of two.

" 'Three times has the night-queen turned her full face to smile upon the prowess of Lacota [84] arms, since at this very spot I met an enemy. We rushed towards each other for the attack. 'Twas then he cried:

" 'Are we not both braves? why should we fight? When our people meet in the fray, then may we join arms,— till then, a truce.'

" 'To this I replied,

" 'Says Crowman peace? — then, be there peace.'

" 'Thus said, we shook hands and sat down by the fountain.

" 'Willing to amuse the foe, I gathered a pebble and proposed a game of hand. The challenge was accepted, and we played,— first, arrow against arrow, then bow against bow, robe against robe, and scalp against scalp.

" 'I was unsuccessful and lost all,— arrow, bow, robe, and scalp. I gave up all, but with the extorted promise that we should here meet again for another trial of skill.

" 'True to the word, we did meet again. We played, and this time, the Good Spirit showed me kindness.

" 'Winning back arrows, bow and robe, I staked them all against the lost scalp. The game was a close one; but again the Good Spirit favored me, and I won.

" 'Crowman,' said I, 'scalp against scalp.'

---

[84] Lacota or Dakota, another name for the Sioux.

" 'The banter was accepted, and the play continued. He lost, and I, with my winnings, arose to leave.

" 'Warrior,' exclaimed the luckless player, 'meet me in the fight, that we may try the game of arms.'

" 'Thy words please me,' I answered. 'Will the Crow-man name the place?'

" 'A valley lies beyond this hill,— there my people await their enemies, and there let me hope to see you with them.'

" 'To that place I led you. We fought and conquered. My opponent at play was among the slain. Need I tell you who took his scalp?' "[85]

The old man seemed to take pleasure in acquainting us with the manners and customs of his people, and was ever ready to assign a reason for any of them, whenever such existed. He repeated to us the names of all the streams, mountains, and prominent localities of the country, and explained the causes of their several christenings.

Some thirty miles to the westward of us, flowed a large creek, called by the Indians, "Weur-sena Wark-pollo," or Old Woman's creek. This stream is an affluent of the Chyenne river, and takes its rise at the base of a mountain bearing the same name.

The mountain is an object of great veneration with the Sioux, who rarely enter into its neighborhood without bestowing upon it a present of meat. The old man entertained us with the following explanation of a custom so singular:

"My grandfather told me a tale he had received from the old men before him, and it is a strange one.

"Many ages past bring us back to the time when the

---

[85] This story was subsequently told by G. F. Ruxton in his *Life in the Far West* (1951 edition), pp. 101-102. But Ruxton has Tahtunga-egonisk (Tahtunga-nisha) instead of the Brulé spy as the principal in the gambling and scalping story.

Lacotas lived in a country far above the sun of winter.[86]

"Here, then, the Shoshone reared his white lodge, and scoured the prairies in pursuit of game; while, as yet, the whole country abounded with lakes and ponds of water, and only the highlands and mountains were left for the buffalo and deer.

"But years passed on,— the mountains and highlands continued to prey upon the waters, and the creeks and rivers gradually reduced the limits of their possessions.

"Years again fled. The Shoshones, attracted by some better region, far away, or driven from their homes by the hostile encroachments of other tribes, gave place to the Scarred-arms.[87]

"In the course of generations, the Lacotas and the Scarred-arms warred with each other; they fought with varied success for many years.

"Once a party of the Lacotas penetrated into the heart of the enemy's country; on their return, they fell into an ambuscade, and only six of them were left to tell the fate of their companions.

"Hotly pursued by the Scarred-arms, they sought refuge in a mountain. There an obscure passage led to a recess in the mountain's side, which they entered, and were pleased to find within it a gravelly floor, and a pure fountain of sweet water.

"Tempted by the conveniences and security of the place, they thought to remain for a few days that they might recover their strength. A small fire was built accordingly, and the six braves seated themselves around it, recounting to each other their perils and dangerous exploits, and planning some mode of extrication from their present difficulties.

"Thus busied, a rustling noise from a dark corner of the apartment startled them,— but still more were

---

86 The north.– [Sage]

87 Chyennes. The name owes its origin to the practice of scarring the left arm crosswise yet adhered to by the males of that nation. – [Sage]. These Indians were also called "Cut Arms."

they aroused by the half-disclosed form of a person moving in the distance. Words gave place to silence, as the warriors, seizing their arms, awaited the feared assault. But the figure, on advancing nearer, proved that of a feeble old woman, who addressed the wondering group in their own language.

" 'Children,' said she, 'you have been against the Scarred-arms,— you have fought them,— and of a strong party, you alone survive. I know it all.

" 'You seek in my lodge a refuge from your pursuers, — and the sound of your voices with the heat of your council-fire has disturbed my rest and awoke me from a long, long trance.

" 'Your looks enquire my story.

" 'Many ages have gone, (for days, moons, seasons, and ages are painted before me as they pass,) since the Shoshones, who lived where now live the Scarred-arms, visited the lodges of the Lacotas, and bade the prairie drink the blood of slaughtered braves. I was their captive, and with the scalps of the slain I was taken from the graves of my people, many days travel.

" 'The Shoshone brought me to this country, when yet the buffalo grazed upon the hills and mountains, only; for the valleys and plains were the home of waters.

" 'Living with the Shoshone, I was not happy. I thought of my people, with all those dear to me, and prayed the Good Spirit that I might again behold them ere my passage to the death-land.

" 'I fled, hoping to reach the home of my birth; — but age had enfeebled me, and being pursued, I sought refuge in this cave. Here, having passed a night and a day in earnest communion with the Big Medicine,— a strange feeling came upon me. I slumbered, in a dreamy state of consciousness, from then till now.

" 'But your looks again ask, who are the Shoshones? — what became of them? And from whence were the Scarred-arms?'

" 'The Lacotas will soon know the Shoshones, and bring from their lodges many scalps and medicine-dogs. Divided into two tribes, that nation long since sought home in other lands. One crossed the snow-hills towards the sun-setting; — the Lacotas shall visit them, and avenge the blood and wrongs of ages. The other journeyed far away towards the sun of winter, and now live to the leftward of the places where the Hispanola [88] builds his earth-lodge.[89]

" 'Then came the Scarred-arms from a far off country, a land of much snow and cold. Pleased with the thickly tenanted hunting grounds that here met them, they stopped for the chase, and, by a possession through successive generations, have learned to consider these grounds as their own. But they are not theirs.

" 'The Great Spirit gives them to the Lacotas, and they shall inhabit the land of their daughter's captivity.

" 'Why wait ye here? Go and avenge the blood of your comrades upon the Scarred-arms. They even now light their camp-fire by the stream at the mountain's base. Fear not,— their scalps are yours! Then return ye to my people, that ye may come and receive your inheritance.

" 'Haste ye, that I may die. And, oh Warkantunga! inasmuch as thou hast answered the prayer of thine handmaid, and shown to me the faces of my people, take me from hence.'

"The awe-struck warriors withdrew. They found the enemy encamped at the foot of the mountain. They attacked him and were victorious; — thirty-five scalps were the trophies of their success.

---

88 The Spaniards. The adobe houses of New Mexico.

89 It is a singular fact, that the Cumanches and Snakes, (Shoshones), though living nearly a thousand miles from each other, with hostile tribes intervening, speak precisely the same language, and call themselves by the same general name. They have lost all tradition, however, of having formed one nation, in any previous age. – [Sage]

Ethnologists generally consider the Comanches and the Shoshones (Snakes) as being both of the Shoshonean Family.

"On reaching their homes the strange adventure excited the astonishment of the whole nation. The Scarred-arms were attacked by our warriors, thus nerved with the hope of triumph, and were eventually driven from the country now possessed by the Locotas as their own.

"The grateful braves soon sought out the mountain, to do reverence to the medicine-woman who had told them so many good things. A niche in the mountain-side, from whence issued a sparkling streamlet, told their place of refuge; but the cave and the woman alike had disappeared.

"Each successive season do our warriors visit the Shoshones for scalps and medicine-dogs,— and each of our braves, as he passes the Old Woman's mountain, fails not to bestow upon it his tribute of veneration, or quench his thirst from the creek that bears her name."

A place on White river — where the stream pours its full force against the base of a lofty peak, and the powerful attrition of its waters has formed a rocky precipice of several hundred feet in height — is known as "The Death Song." The singularity of this name led me to enquire the reasons which prompted its bestowment. Ever ready to answer questions of this nature, the old chief related the following story:

"Once, on a time, the Oglallas and Burnt-thighs held their encampment upon the river, opposite the high point of which my son enquires. While there, a dog-soldier[90] of the Burnt-thighs received the offer of six horses from an Oglalla brave, for his only daughter — a sweet flower — such an one as oft pierces the warrior's heart with her charms, when the arrows of enemies fall harmless at his feet. The offer was quickly accepted — for the dog-soldier was poor.

[90] This is the title of those selected to superintend the civil affairs of a village. – [Sage]

"When Chischille (for that was the name of the fair one) heard she was to become the wife of the Oglalla, she cried for grief,— and so obstinate was her resistance, the marriage was deferred for several days on that account.

"But, why did Chischille grieve? She had looked upon a handsome warrior of her own village, and she loved him. She forgot her duty, as a daughter, to love only at her father's bidding. Her heart had been playing truant and had lost itself in the labyrinths of girlish fancy. Bitter were the fruits of that presumption.

"Chischille, in the interval, contrived to meet the one of her choice, and the two fled towards a distant village, there to live in the undisturbed enjoyment of their youthful loves.

"But, alas, for them! They were pursued, and overtaken. The life of the young warrior atoned for his temerity,— while Chischille was cruelly beaten and brought back to her father's lodge.

"The Oglalla had already paid the purchase price, and ere the morrow's sunset, was to receive his fair prize at the hand of the dog-soldier.

"Chischille, arising with the dawn, fresh-plaited her hair, and arraying herself in her proudest attire, left the lodge. No one thought strange at seeing her thus gaily dressed for her wedding day, and, as she tripped along, many a warrior's heart beat high and loud at the thought that a creature so lovely was to become the bride of another.

"Directing her course to the river, she crossed it and ascended the high peak upon the opposite side. There, seating herself upon the utmost verge of the precipice, she gazed calmly from its dizzy height.

"In her lofty station, with her raven locks streaming in the winds, and the matchless beauty of her person so enchantingly exposed to view, she seemed more like a being of the Spirit-Land than aught human. The sweetest prairie-flower was ne'er half so lovely.

"Her strange attitude arrested the eyes of all.

" 'Why sits she there? — she will fall and be dashed to pieces!' was the general cry. 'But listen – she sings!'

" 'Why should I stay,— he is gone. Light of my eyes, — joy of my soul,— show me thy dwelling! —'Tis not here,—'tis far away in the Spirit Land. Thither he is gone. Why should I stay? Let me go!'

" 'Hear you that?' said one. 'She sings her death song. She will throw herself from the cliff!'

"At this, a dozen warriors, headed by him who claimed her hand, started to rescue the sweet singer from intended self-destruction.

"Again she chants:

" 'Spirit of Death, set me free! Dreary is earth. Joyless is time. Heart, thou are desolate! Wed thee another? Nay. Death is thy husband! Farewell, oh sun! Vain is your light. Farewell, oh earth! Vain are your plains, your flowers, your grassy dales, your purling streams, and shady groves! I loved you once,— but now no longer love! Tasteless are your sweets,— cheerless your pleasures! Thee I woo, kind Death! Wahuspa calls me hence. In life we were one. We'll bask together in the Spirit Land. Who shall sunder there? Short is my pass to thee. Wahuspa, I come!"

"Upon this she threw herself forward, as the warriors grasped at her; but, leaving her robe in their hands, she plunged headlong and was dashed to pieces among the rocks below! [91]

"E'er since, the young warrior sighs as he beholds this peak, and thinks of the maiden's death song."

Conversing upon the subject of medicine-men, he was

[91] A tale which went the rounds of the public prints, several years since, entitled the "Maiden's Leap," affords a seeming coincidence in the mode of suicide; but, by comparing the two, the reader will observe a broad dissimilarity of detail. In penning the above I was guided solely by the leading incidents as related in my hearing.– [Sage]

asked, why those individuals are so highly esteemed by his people? To this he replied:

"These men are regarded as the peculiar favorites of the Great Spirit, to whom is imparted a more than ordinary share of His power and wisdom. We respect them, therefore, in proportion to the abilities they receive, even as we reverence the Great Spirit."

Here the question was proposed, how are their abilities above those of others?

"The Yellow-hair counts as his soldier Tahtunga-mobellu,— a man of strong medicine. To him the Great Spirit has imparted the power of healing, by imbibing, at pleasure, the diseases of the sick, and discharging them from his eyes and nose in the form of live snakes.[92]

"On a time, years past, our young men went to the Pawnees and came back crying; for sixteen slain of their number were left to grace an enemy's triumph.

"It was winter, and the moans of men and maidens mingled with the howling winds. Sorrow beclouded every brow, and brave looked upon brave as if to enquire, 'Who shall wipe out this disgrace?' Then it was a medicine-chief stood up, and his words were:

" 'Be it for me to consult the Good Spirit.'

"So saying, he entered his lodge alone, nor suffered any to come near during the long fast that followed. Darkness had closed four times upon the prairie, and the sun again hastened to hide behind the mountain peaks, when, calling the young men to him, the medicine-man said:

" 'Fetch me now meat and water, with a new robe, and bid my people come near, that they may know the words that I would speak.'

"The obedient braves made haste and did as bidden. Folding the robe, he sat upon it and partook of the refreshments placed before him. After eating he arose, and six large snakes, crawling from the robe one after

[92] Tahtunga-mobellu receives the averment of all his villagers in proof of this strange feat. – [Sage]

AN INDIAN CONJUROR.

another, sprang to his shoulder, and, whispering in his ear, vanished from sight. The last snake had just told his message when the chief began:

" 'The Good Spirit wills it, that we remove from hence. Three moons being dead, let three hundred warriors return, and their hearts shall be made glad with medicine-dogs and the scalps of enemies.'

"The village left, and, at the time appointed, the warriors returned. They met the enemy,— fought, and were victorious. Sixty-three scalps and one hundred medicine-dogs were the fruits of their success."

Before dismissing the subject, many other particulars were cited in proof of the extraordinary abilities of different medicine-men, but the above being the most remarkable, I have thought proper to pass over the remainder in silence.[93]

---

[93] An account, still more wonderful than either of the foregoing, was subsequently narrated in my hearing, while among the Arapaho Indians; and, without vouching for the truth of all its particulars, I am unwilling to withhold it from the reader.

The performance alluded to is said to have occurred, some three years since, in the presence of the whole Arapaho village, incredible as it may seem. The actor was a Riccaree by nation, and is well known to the mountain traders.

In the centre of a large circle of men, women, and children, stood the subject of the appended sketch, stripped to the waist, as the gunner's mark. A shot perforated his body with a bullet, which entered at the chest and emerged from the opposite side. He instantly fell, and the blood flowing in streams dyed the grass where he lay, and everything seemed to prefigure the reality of death.

While in this condition, his wife approached and besprinkled his face with water; soon after which he arose, as from a slumber – the blood still pouring from him. Beplastering his wound with mud before and behind, the blood ceased to flow, when he commenced yawning and stretching; in a few minutes the plaster was removed by a pass of the hand, and neither blood, nor wound, nor the sign of a scratch or scar appeared! There stood the self-restored medicine-man, before the wondering throng, alive and well, and in all the pride of his strength!

He then brought his naked son into the ring, a lad of some eight years, and, standing at a distance of several yards, bow in hand, he pierced him through and through, from diaphragm to vertebrae, at three successive shots.

The boy fell dead, to every appearance, and the thick blood freely coursed from his wounds.

The performer then clasped the body in his arms and bore it around the ring for the inspection of all, three times in succession. Upon this he breathed into his mouth and nostrils, and, after suffusing his face with water and covering his wounds with a mud plaster, he commenced brief manipulations upon his stomach, which soon ended in a complete recovery, nor left a single trace of injury about him.

Both of these feats, if performed as said, can scarcely admit the possibility of trick or slight of hand, and must stand as the most astonishing instances of jugglery on record. – [Sage]

CHAPTER XI.

A LARGE grove of cottonwood near us, day after day was graced by groups of village squaws, armed with axes, for the procurement of horse food.

The bark of this tree is eaten freely by both horses and mules, and answers well as a substitute for corn or oats. Animals will thrive upon it in a remarkable manner, and even in the summer months they prefer it to grass. The bark of red elm is also used for the same purpose.

The operations of the squaws at such times contributed greatly to our amusement. Climbing fearlessly to the topmost branch of the highest tree, they would there lop off the surrounding boughs, with as much apparent ease as though footed upon *terra firma.*

And then, the enormous loads they would carry, lashed together with cords and slung to their backs, were enough to make a giant stagger. Dogs, harnessed to travées, had their part to perform, and ofttimes were they a source of vexation to their mistresses.

A squaw, trudging along under a full donkey-load of cottonwood, and followed by a squad of half-naked children, presented a spectacle quite interesting; but this was rendered rather comical, withal, when two or three draught-dogs with their heavy-laden travées reluctantly brought up the rear — every now and then lying down for weariness, or squatting to loll and gaze at their companions.

Now, she coaxes and caresses to urge them forward — they still delay. Then she turns briskly towards them with a stick,— get out, dogs! —"Yierh! Warktashne ceicha," cries the squaw, accompanying her denunciation with blows, and away go the yelping troop as fast as legs can carry them.

Dogs are the necessary appendage of every Indian lodge, and generally form an equal portion of the village population. They present almost all the different varieties of the canine species, from the wolf to the spaniel, and from the spaniel to the hairless dog of Africa. The wolf, however, is predominant, and, taken together, they more assimilate a gang of wolves than anything else. Indeed, the different varieties of prairie wolves hold familiar intercourse with the village dogs, and associate with them on friendly terms.

The species used for draught, is a large, stout-built, wolfish-looking creature, of the Exquimaux breed. Trained to his duties in early life, he is generally both submissive and tractable. The drudgery of a squaw, which is at all times onerous, without his ready aid would prove past endurance.

But these dogs are also useful in another respect. Their flesh furnishes an article highly esteemed for food, and which almost invariably graces the soldiers' feast and every other scene of conviviality. However much the squamishness of the reader may revolt at the suggestion, justice impels me to say, the flesh of a fat Indian dog, suitably cooked, is not inferior to fresh pork; and, by placing side by side select parts of the two, it would be no easy task even for a good judge to tell the difference, by either looks or taste, unless he were previously informed.

Towards the last of January, [1842], buffalo having left the vicinity, the Indians, as a necessary consequence, were compelled to move. A great scarcity of provisions prevailed among them, and we ourselves were scarcely better off than they.

Our stock in hand was nearly exhausted, and an abandonment of the post became absolutely necessary,

— a thing, however, which could not be performed without a fresh supply of horses and cattle from Fort Platte. For this purpose, I volunteered my services, and, accompanied by two engagés, was promptly under way.

A few hours' ride brought us to the head of White river, where, consuming at a meal our scanty eatables, from that onward we were left entirely destitute.

This was the first occasion subjecting me to the pains of hunger for so long a time. The second day I experienced the greatest annoyance, and then it was I felt some of the realities of starvation. The third day, however, I awoke in the morning scarcely thinking of breakfast. In fact, my appetite seemed quite passive, and the only sensation I felt was a kind of weakness and lassitude, evincing the lack of proper nourishment.

The morning was cloudy and threatening. Soon after leaving camp, snow began to fall, thick and fast. The day proved so dark, objects were indiscernible at the distance of a hundred yards in advance. Travelling, as we were, over a trackless prairie, with nothing to guide us but the wind and the position of the grass, it was by the merest accident we reached our destination a few minutes before nightfall.

Our sudden appearance was the occasion of general surprise to the Fort hands, and, after a brief explanation, we began to make amends for previous abstinence.

At first, a few mouthfuls sufficed,— but soon I again felt hungry and could be satisfied only with a double quantity,— in an equally short time my stomach demanded a still further supply, and, by the next day, hunger became so keen it seemed almost insatiable. An interval of three or four weeks was requisite before it assumed its wonted tone.

During our stay here, an Indian family, occupying one of the Fort rooms, indulged themselves in a drunken spree.

Having procured a quantity of the American Fur Company's liquor, the effects of their lavish potations soon became manifest to all within hearing distance. But the din of drunken revelry erelong assumed the wail of mourning and sorrow.

Hearing the strange commotion, I entered the room to ascertain the cause. There lay, helpless upon the floor, and apparently at the point of death, a squaw of some eighteen years: — she, in her eagerness, had swallowed nearly a pint of the vile stuff, undiluted, and now experienced its dreadful consequences.

But most conspicuous in the throng was a large, obese, cross-eyed Indian, earnestly engaged in his medicine-performances for her recovery.

A breech-cloth was his sole garb, as, with eyes half strained from their sockets and volving in a strange unearthly manner, he stood, first upon one foot and then upon the other, alternately — then, stamping the floor as if to crush it through, and meanwhile, grunting, screeching, and bellowing, and beating his breast or the wall with his clenched fists,— then, with inhaled breath, swelling like a puff-ball, he would bend over his patient and apply sugescents to her mouth, throat and breast.

This done, sundry ejections of saliva prepared his mouth for the reception of an ample draught of water, with which he bespatted her face and forehead.

But yet, all these extraordinary efforts failed to produce their designed effect. The poor squaw grew weaker, and her breathing became fainter and more difficult.

Some powerful restorative must be adopted, or she will soon be beyond the reach of medicine,— so thought the officiating doctor; or, at least, his succeeding antics indicated that such were the cogitations of his mind. Standing for a minute or two in the attitude of reflection, an idea stuck him. Ah, he has it now! This cannot fail.

Snatching a butcher-knife and hastening with it to the fire, he heats the point to redness upon the coals,— then balancing it between his teeth, at a toss he flings it vaulting above his head and backward upon the floor, — then, re-catching it, he goes through the performance a second and a third time.

Thus premised, he addresses himself with threefold energy to the grotesque and uncouth manœuvres before described. If he had stamped his feet, he now stamps them with a determination hitherto unknown; — if he had thumped his breast and beat the walls, he now thumps and beats as if each blow were intended to prostrate the object against which it was directed,— if he had grunted, screeched, and bellowed, he now grunts, screeches, bellows, and yells, till the very room quakes with the reverberations of demoniac noise! — if he had gagged, puffed, and swelled, he now gags, puffs, and swells, as if he would explode from the potency of his extraordinary inflations.

Then, with an air of confidence, he hies to his patient and commences a process of manipulation from her breast downwards, and reverse,— and then again he repeats his previous operations, with scrupulous exactness and unsparing effort, in all their varied minutiæ.

But, alas for the medicine-man! — the squaw died, despite the omnipotence of his skill!

Then was enacted another such a scene of piteous wailing, as Indians alone have in requisition, as vent for their grief.

After the usual preliminaries, the corpse of the deceased was placed upon a scaffold beside that of Susuceicha, the old chief of whom I have spoken in a former chapter. Each member of the bereaved family deposited a tuft of hair in the sack containing the meat and trinkets placed beneath her head. A smooth piece of cottonwood slab was then affixed to the scaffold, upon which were traced, in vermilion, certain quadrangular characters of unknown meaning,— answering well to the idea of an inscription of name and age.

A difficulty occurred about this time between a trader of the American Fur Company and an Oglalla chief, known as Little Lodge.

The latter had become crazed by liquor, and, being rather turbulent, was put out of the Fort. But, effecting a re-entrance, he again proved equally annoying. The trader then commenced quarrelling with him, and undertook to seize his arms. This the Indian resisted, when the trader discharged a pistol at him, but missed his object. Here was a deadly affront, that blood alone could wipe away.

With great difficulty, the Indian was finally disarmed and bound. He was thus secured till the next day, when he was liberated; — still, however, he muttered threats of revenge.

Two or three weeks subsequently, Little Lodge was present at a soldiers' feast, and the question of war with the Americans was a prominent subject of consideration.

Several speeches were made, both for and against it; and, though the prevailing sentiment seemed to be of an adverse kind, it scarcely required a half dozen words to turn the scale upon either side.

Little Lodge arose to address the council, and the friends of the whites, knowing the vengeful spirit that yet rankled in his bosom at the remembrances of his recent injuries, began to fear for the continuance of peace.

Contrary to the universal expectation, he contended for its maintenance. "But," said he, "Little Lodge has grievances of his own, and they call for redress.

"There is one among the pale-faces whose blood must wash away the foul blot that rests upon the name of Little Lodge. I know him well. He is not a Long-knife. The Long-knives are all the friends of Little Lodge.

Let the Lacota take them by the hand whenever he meets them upon the prairie. It is good that he do so. They are very many and exceedingly rich. Their country is a large one, and far away towards the sunrising. They, too, are strong for war. They have big hearts and strong, and they are very good to the red man. They bring to him many good things; why, then, should the Lacota hate the Long-knife?

"Do my brothers ask who it is of the pale-faces the Little Lodge would remove from the light of day? Know, then, he is not of the Long-knives,— he is of the Warceichas, (Frenchmen.) The Warceichas are not Long-knives!

"And, do my brothers ask, who are the Warceichas?

"Aye, who are they? Little Lodge cannot tell; — who of all the Lacotas can? Who ever heard of the country of these men? No one. They have no country, — they are no people. They are as the wandering dogs [94] that infest our hunting grounds and prey upon the game formed by the Good Spirit for the red man's sustenance. They steal into the land of the red man, and sneak around from place to place; — for they have no home; they have no country; they are no people!

"One of these it was who bade the medicine-iron speak its death-word to Little Lodge, and sought to spill the blood of a Lacota brave, after that he had made him a fool by means of his thickened [95] fire-water!

"Should Little Lodge fall by the hand of the Warceicha? He might fall by the hand of a Long-knife, and the nation would honor his memory,— but *never,* should the Warceicha bring him low!

"Then, is it not good that Little Lodge should be avenged upon this lost dog — this outcast of the world — that the whelps of a motherless breed may cease to

[94] Chunka-monet, or traveling dogs, is the name applied by these Indians to wolves. – [Sage]

[95] Allusion is here made to the drugged liquor supposed to have been palmed upon him by the trader. – [Sage]

insult and wrong the Lacotas? Which of all my brothers will say nay?"

The address was received in silence,— no one presuming to oppose an answer to its sentiments. Whether the speaker executed his threats of vengeance against the offending trader, I am yet unadvised.

Having remained two nights and a day at Fort Platte, we again started for White river, taking with us three yoke of oxen and several horses, one of which was laden with dried meat.

The snow greatly retarded our progress from the first, and so obscured the trail we were compelled to travel mostly by guess. The sun, too, was shut out by a tenebrous atmosphere, and we could judge of our proper course only by observing the movements of the clouds,[96] with the general range of the hills and ravines, or inclination of the grass.

The broad expanse of unbroken snow lying from Rawhide to L'eau-qui-court, brought a chill tremor with the thought of crossing it. Yet, go we must! It was no time to falter when the fate of others, perhaps, depended upon our prompt advance.

But the effort was no child's play. If we had experienced a tedious time during a former journey, what could we expect now? The whole interval of thirty miles was covered with snow, that grew deeper and deeper as we proceeded. Every hollow and ravine was filled, and the route otherwise seriously impeded by huge drifts and embankments.

We were frequently compelled to break foot-paths for our animals, and ever and anon pull them by main

[96] The idea of directing our course by the movements of the clouds is doubtless a novel suggestion to most readers; but its philosophy will be readily comprehended by a bare mention of the fact, that the winds of these regions almost invariably blow from a west-southwest point; and, as they are usually high, it is no very extraordinary performance to calculate the bearing of north or south, even in the most obscure weather. – [Sage]

strength from the deep pitfalls into which they would plunge and become almost lost to view. In this manner our progress was slow,— the average depth through which we waded being but little less than two feet.

The rising of a fierce head wind, piercing as the blasts of Nova Zembla, drove the snow into our faces with mad fury and added immeasurably to our sufferings.

In this manner night shut down upon us, while yet far distant from any camping-place. And, such a night! Oh, storms and deadly winter, foul and fierce! how swept ye "through the darkened sky," and with your awful howlings rendered "the savage wilderness more wild!"

The creeping cold on every nerve played freely, in haste to sting our vitals, and lay us each

> "———— along the snows a stiffen'd corse,
> Stretch'd out and bleaching in the northern blast!"

The impress of this event can never be effaced from my mind. It was midnight ere we arrived at the timberless L'eau-qui-court and struck camp. Our animals needed water, but we had neither axe or tomahawk to cut through the thick ice with which the creek was coated. As a remedy for this lack, all three of us advanced upon it, and, by our united efforts at jumping, caused a lengthy fissure with gentle escarpments towards each shore, that left midway an ample pool.

Having driven the cattle to this, in their clumsy movements upon the ice, two of them fell, and, sliding down the inclined plain, lay struggling in the freezing water, unable to rise. Our only resort was to drag them to the shore by main strength; for, left in their then condition, they must have frozen to death in a very short time.

Here commenced a series of pulling and wrenching, that, in our chilled and exhausted state, we were ill-prepared to endure.

For a while our efforts proved vain. A backward-slide succeeded each headway-pull, and vexed us with useless toil. Thus we worried for nearly three hours in water knee-deep!

At length, having procured a rope and fastened one end to their horns and the other around a pointed rock upon the shore, and gathering the slack at each successive thrust, we finally succeeded in placing them both, one after the other, upon dry land.

But, now we were in a thrice sorry plight. Not a stick of wood could be raised, far or near, of which to build a fire, and *bois de vache,* the great substitute of the prairies, was too deeply covered with snow for procurement. Our clothes, wet to the waist, were frozen upon us, and the merciless wind, with stinging keenness, pierced us through at every breath, and stood us forth as living monuments of *ice!*

Could men of iron endure such incomprehensible hardships,— such inexpressible sufferings? Yet we survived them all!

Spreading a few robes upon the snow, we lay down for sleep, dinnerless and supperless. I was now seized with a chill, which lasted for two hours or more; and so violent were its actions I could scarcely keep the covering upon me.

My companions, however, though not similarly afflicted, were worse off than myself. One had his hands and ears frozen, and the other his hands and feet,— the painful consequences of which, as the frost began to yield to the influence of generated warmth, were too apparent in their groans and writhings.

Morning at length came, and the sun arose bright and clear. The winds had ceased their ragings, and a clement atmosphere seemed pouring upon us the balm of sympathy for miseries so recently endured.

But their direful effects were not thus easily eradicated. The feet of one poor fellow were so badly frozen, it was three months before he entirely recovered; while another lost a portion of one of his ears. As for myself, a severe cold settled in my teeth, producing an intensely painful ache and swoollen face, that continued for eight or ten days.

It seems almost miraculous that we should have escaped so easily, and often, even after so long an interval, I shudder at the recollection of this anguishing scene.

Two days subsequently we reached our destination, and found all things pretty much *in statu quo*.

CHAPTER XII.

OUR intended evacuation of the post was postponed till the week following, and, meanwhile, the few customers, that still hung on, were careful to improve the passing opportunity of steeping their senses in liquor.

Another general drunken frolic was the consequence, ending as usual in a fight and still further attempts upon the life of our trader.

Soon after this, our catalogue of disasters was increased by the death of two horses, which fell a prey to wolves.

The case was an aggravated one, and provoking in the extreme. Both of them were "buffalo horses," and the fleetest and most valuable in our possession,— in fact, they were the only ones of which we ventured to boast. We had others of little worth, so poor and feeble they could oppose none resistance to magpies,[97] and much less to the rapacity of wolves.

But, no. These blood-thirsty depredators, desirous of a feast of fat things, were determined to have it, reckless of cost,— and, the encrimsoned tracks, coursing the snowy plain in every direction where passed the swift chargers in vain effort to escape, proved that they won their supper at an enormous expense of leg-wear.

Feb. 4th. All things being in readiness, we bade farewell to winter-quarters, and commenced our journey.

Crossing the river soon after, on ascending the opposite bank, a cart upset and deposited its contents in the water. The load, consisting of robes and powder,

---

[97] The magpie of the mountains is the torment of all sore-backed horses, particularly during the winter season. Despite opposition it will feed upon their skinless flesh, often to the very bones. – [Sage]

HORSE ATTACKED BY WOLVES.

became thoroughly saturated, and we were employed a full hour in fishing it out. The stream being waist-deep and filled with floating ice, amid which we were forced to plunge, our task was far from a pleasant one.

The freight needed drying, and we were detained two days for that purpose. Meanwhile the drenched powder was subjected to the experiments of one of our engagés. Having spread it to dry, he was carelessly bending over it, when a spark from the camp-fire struck the ready ignitible; a sprightly flash, enveloping the luckless wight in a sheet of flame, told the instant result. Springing to his feet, he exclaimed:

"Bless my stars! That's what I call regular *blowing up!*"

"Aye, aye, my lad," says one. "You was always a *bright* youth,— but never before did you appear half so *brilliant.* 'Tis a fact, or I'm a liar!"

Resuming our course, the second night following was passed at a pool of water between L'eau-qui-court and Rawhide. Here, having placed my shoes under my head for better security, I slept soundly till morning. Rising at an early hour, I turned for them, but one was missing, and, after searching far and near, it could not be found.

The mystery of its disappearance, however, was fully solved by the numerous wolf tracks that appeared on all sides; — some straggling marauder had stolen it during the night, and quietly deposited it in his empty stomach as the substitute for an early breakfast.

Our camp at Rawhide was beset with a throng of Indians from an adjoining village, who, as usual, were loudly clamorous and importunate for liquor. A beautiful young squaw was brought in, to exchange for that article. However, their solicitations were of no avail and their vitiated appetites went unappeased.

On the 12th of February we reached the Fort, and thus ended our disastrous and eventful expedition.

Winter in the neighborhood of the Platte had been remarkably mild, and at no time during the season had the snow remained upon the ground to exceed a day. Vegetation, even thus early, was beginning to put forth, and bring to view the beauty and loveliness of spring.

Preparations were already on foot for building a boat for the transportation of furs to the States by way of the river, and, at the solicitation of the company's agent, I reluctantly consented to take charge of it during the voyage,— thus deferring, for the present, my design of visiting Oregon. The timber used in its construction was procured from the neighboring pine hills, and prepared by a laborious process of hand, with the aid of a pit-saw. The ribs and other timber were obtained from an ash grove, a few miles above the Fort, and three men were busily engaged in putting all things in readiness for the expected spring rise — an event which seldom occurs before the 15th of May.

The winter's trade having closed, an interval of nearly three months' leisure followed, which resulted in a hunting expedition that included my self with six others.

Anxious to explore the mountains, we set our faces westward; but, owing to the reported closeness of game *en route,* very little provisions were taken with other necessaries.

Keeping the river bottom by a rocky ridge for some ten miles, our course led through several beautiful groves and broad stretches of rich alluvial soil, that presented an encouraging prospect to agriculturists. After a few hours' ride we came to a point at which the stream sweeps round the ridge's base, causing a vertical wall of lias and sandstone nearly one hundred and fifty feet high.

Abandoning the river bottom at this place, we ascended to the high prairie on the left, where an interesting plateau greeted us, extending far away to the south and west, till it became lost in the neighboring mountains. Continuing on a short distance, we again struck the river, at a small opening between two hills, and made camp in a grove of willows.

Opposite this place is a large heavily wooded island, of a blueish loam, upon a subtratum of fossiliferous limestone.

Above and below are lofty walls of limestone and ferruginous rock, that, in many places, overhang the sweeping waters at their base, and form roofage beneath which swarms of prairie swallows are wont to raise their annual broods.

Consuming our scanty supply of provisions at a single meal, each soon disposed of himself for the night. A mild atmosphere invited to repose; and, enwrapped in a single robe, my troubles were speedily forgotten in a quiet slumber.

But during the succeeding interval, a change came over the spirit of my dream. I was suddenly aroused by the crash of a huge tree, that fell across my bed, and only a providential curve arching upwards, had saved me from instant death!

"Hurra, for me!" I exclaimed, as my startled campmates came clustering around,—"It's better to be born *lucky* than RICH!"

The wind was now blowing a perfect hurricane, and the trees tottered around us, threatening every moment to fall. In an hour or so, however, the gale abating, we again addressed ourselves to sleep.

Towards morning, feeling a disagreeable warmth and superincumbent pressure, I was induced to uncover, and, looking out, the cause was explained by the presence of a dense snow that covered the ground to the depth of several inches. The fallen snow was melting fast, and that yet descending soon merged into rain.

A pretty-looking set of fellows were we, in a comparatively short time! — blankets, robes, clothes, and every article about us were wet — soaking wet — and covered with mud. It required an effort of several hours to kindle a fire, so thoroughly saturated was everything with water; — this done, we all gathered around it, and — such a group! — Oh, the beauties of mud and water! A painter might describe it,— I cannot.

If the reader imagines we felt in a superlative good humor while standing there, breakfastless, shivering, and wet, he has conjured up a strange illusion.

It having ceased raining about mid-day, in the course of the afternoon we enjoyed a beautiful sunshine for a couple of hours, which enabled us to assume a better traveling plight; and, favored by a mild atmosphere and clear sky, on the following morning, we again resumed our course.

Striking upon an Indian trail, we bore leftward from the river, and, in a short ride, came to a sand creek shut in by precipitous embankments of limestone, through which our road led by a narrow defile. A transparent spring gushes from the right bank with considerable noise, furnishing a beautiful streamlet to its hitherto high bed, which is known as the "Warm Springs." [98]

A short distance above the mouth of this creek, the Platte makes its final egress from the Black Hills through a tunnel-like pass, walled in upon either side by precipitous cliffs of red-sandstone and siliceous limestone, sometimes overhanging the stream at their base, and towering to a height of from three to five hundred feet. The high table lands constituting these immense walls, are surmounted with shrubs and occasional pines and cedars, that unite to present a wild romantic scenery.

Continuing on, and bearing still further leftward, we passed a beautiful valley, graced with several

[98] Warm Spring was visited by Fremont in July, 1842, and is described in his *Report, op. cit.*, p. 46.

springs and a small grove of cottonwood, with cherry and plum bushes, near which rose a conical hill abundant in fossiliferous limestone of snowy whiteness. A diminutive pond in the vicinity afforded several varieties of the testaceous order, both *bivalves* and *univalves* — a circumstance quite rare among mountain waters. The soil of this locality appeared to be a compound of clay, sand, and marl, and well adapted to agriculture.

Passing this, our course led over a gently undulating prairie, bounded on either side by pine hills. The soil was generally of a reddish, sandy loam, intermixed with clay; and, judging from the long dry grass of the preceding year, it was both rich and productive.

Towards night we arrived at a large creek, bearing the name of Bitter Cottonwood,[99]— so called from the abundance of that species of poplar in its valley.

These trees generally grow very tall and straight with expansive tops,— averaging from twenty-five to one hundred and fifty feet in height.

The creek occupies a wide, sandy bed, over which the water is dispersed in several shallow streams. The valley is broad and of a jetty, vegetable mould, variegated, at intervals, with layers of gravel deposited by aqueous currents, and is bounded on both sides by abrupt acclivities leading to the beautiful plateaux and lofty pine hills so abundant in the neighborhood.

The remains of three or four Indian forts were situated adjoining the place selected for our encampment. These were built of logs, arranged in a circular form, and enclosing an area, sufficient for the accommodation of twenty or thirty warriors. The walls were generally about six feet high, with single entrances, and apertures in various places for the use of their defenders in case of attack.

---

[99] On the Preuss Map *(op. cit.)* it is called Bitter Creek. Fremont, *op. cit.,* p. 48, calls it *Fourche Amère,* and the timber upon it, *liard amère.* It is the longleaf, or bitter, cottonwood.

All Indian forts, meeting my observation in subsequent travels, with one or two exceptions, were of the same general description. Some, however are almost entirely roofed in by an arched covering, presenting a coniform appearance. The only exception to this mode of fortification was of a quadrangular form, and in a solitary instance the materials were of rock. The latter structure I shall take occasion to describe in due course.

The valley gave abundant indication of wild fruit at the proper season,— such as plums, cherries, currants, goose and buffalo berries, *(shepherdia argentea.)* The signs of game were very plentiful, particularly elk; — after camp two or three of us sallied out with our rifles in quest of these wary animals, while others were busily employed in digging for roots to appease the gnawing of appetite, which began to make itself most sensibly felt by all.

About sundown both parties came in,— the hunters quite dispirited, not having seen any thing in the shape of elk or other game,— but the root diggers had been more lucky and brought with them a small supply of nutritious aliments, which were divided equally among the company,— and, though scarcely a half dozen mouthfuls were apportioned to each, they answered, to some extent, the designed object.

These roots consisted of two varieties, viz: *pomme blanc,* and *commote.*

The *pomme blanc,* or white apple, is a native of the prairies and mountains, oval shaped and about three and a half inches in circumference. It is encased in a thin fibrous tegument, which, when removed, exposes an interior of white pulpy substance, much like a turnip in taste. It generally grows at a depth of three or four inches, in the soil of hill-sides and plateaux, where is found a reddish clay loam abundant in fragmentary rocks and gravel. The stalk attains a height of about three inches, and in general description is quite like a well known article, common to the States, called "sheep-sorrel." At the proper season it bears a handsome white blossom, that would suffer no disparagement when placed in juxtaposition with many of the choicer specimens of our gardens.

The *commote*[100] is a root much like the common radish in size and shape, while a brownish skin envelopes a substance of milky whiteness, soft and nutritious, and of an agreeable taste. It is found most abundant in river bottoms, and requires a rich alluvial soil, well mixed with sedimentary deposits and vegetable matter. It generally penetrates to a depth of about four inches. Its leaves resemble those of the carrot in shape and color, and seldom grow to exceed two inches from the ground, while a stalk equally unpretending, bears a blueish blossom, not without some just claim to beauty.

The *pomme blanc* and *commote* are equally good whether boiled or raw, and are uniformly harmless, even with those unaccustomed to their use as an article of food.

Making way with our scanty supply, a fire was struck and a kettle of tea prepared from wild cherry bark, which proved quite wholesome.

This, as I ascertained, is a drink quite common among mountaineers and Indians in the spring season, and is used for purifying the blood and reducing it to suitable consistency for the temperature of summer. As the successful performer of the task assigned, I most cordially attest to its virtues, and recommend it as the most innocent and effective medicine, if medicine it may be called, that can be employed for a result so necessary to general health.

Early on the succeeding day we resumed our journey.

I now for the first time noticed a gradual change in the geological character of the country. The soil in

[100] I am ignorant of the meaning or derivation of this name. – [Sage]

many places appears to be sterile, and is generally a red clayish nature, mixed with sand and fragmentary rock, and strongly impregnated with mineral salts, among which nitre forms a prominent component. Some spots, for a considerable extent, are entirely destitute of vegetation, and present a surface whitened by saline efflorescences, among which nitre and sulphate of soda form a predominant part.

The character of the various moulds (with the exception of the alluvion in the vicinity of the rivers and creeks) is almost entirely primitive, like numerous strata of rocks upon which they repose.

The grass, from the dry specimens of the previous summer's growth, appeared to be of a longer and a coarser kind, and more sparse and isolated. The short buffalo-grass of the grand prairie had almost entirely disappeared,— in some places a blueish salt grass (herba salée) showed itself in plats uncropped by game. *Artemisie,*[101] or rather *greasewood* of the mountaineers, became quite abundant, as did *absinthe,* or wild sage, together with several specimens of the *cacti* family, which are the common pest of the mountain prairies.

The purifying effects of saline exhalations, with the odor of the *greasewood* and *absinthe* of the prairies, plateaux and table lands, and the balsam and cedar of the adjacent mountains, afforded an atmosphere, even at this unfavorable season, as aromatic as the air of Eden and as wholesome as the deathless clime of Elysium.

Eastward lay a broad expanse of prairie, bounded

[101] Lt. Fremont, in his report relative to the proceedings of the expedition of 1842, '3, and '4, has designated some three varieties of shrubs by the general term artemisie, among which are greasewood and prairie sage. Although the latter are of the same family, the difference in their appearance is so marked, I have thought it proper to observe a nominal distinction, and for that reason, they are called in subsequent pages by terms familiar to the mountaineers. – [Sage]

only by the horizon, while westward and upon either hand, the high summits of the Black Hills, with their pines and snows, told our ingress to other and wilder scenes.

Our course for some twenty or twenty-five miles led through a broad valley, though occasionally winding among rugged hills of red-sandstone and primitive rock, with denuded sides and level summits, covered with shrubs and dwarfish pines.

Towards night, on reaching a small stream, called Horse-shoe creek,[102] we struck camp. One of the party having killed a buck deer, we were promptly on hand, and not at all backward in obeying the calls of appetite, sharpened by a continuous abstinence of three days.

Deer-meat at this season of the year is very poor eating,— especially that of the buck,— it being both lean and tough; but, indifferent as it was, we were too hungry to be nice.

Previous to reaching camp I rode along the base of a small mountain, some distance to the right of the main party, in quest of game; there I caught glimpse of the first panther [103] I had yet met with. Jumping from my horse, I thought to give him a passing shot,— but he, neither liking my looks nor the smell of gunpowder, made hasty retreat to his mountain home.

Passing leisurely on, my course led through a large village of prairie-dogs, which reminds me of having heretofore neglected a description of these singular animals.

I am at a loss to imagine what it is in the habits or looks of the prairie-dog that entitles him to that appellation.

---

[102] Shown on the Preuss map. It enters the North Platte southeast of Glendo, Wyoming.

[103] The American panther (*Felis concolor*), frequently called "painter" by the trappers. – Chittenden, *op. cit,* p. 820.

In appearance and size he more approximates a large species of the *sciurus* family, commonly called the fox-squirrel, than anything I can name. His tail, however, is but an inch and a half long, while his ears and legs are also short; — as a whole, perhaps, he is a trifle larger and more corpulent than the fox-squirrel. His "bark" is precisely like the occasional chatterings of that animal, and his color is of a brownish red.

His habits are quite inoffensive and lead him to procure his food from roots and grass. Clumsy in his motions, he seldom ventures far from home — fearful of the numerous enemies that beset him on all sides, both from birds and beasts of prey.

These animals congregate together in large villages, and dig their burrows adjoining each other; — the dirt thrown from them often forming cone-like elevations three or four feet high, in whose tops are the entrances. The latter are nearly of a perpendicular descent for two feet, and then slope away to a great distance under ground.

These villagers locate without regard to the vicinity of water, and it is gravely doubted, by many persons, whether they make the same use of that fluid as other animals; — I have seen large settlements of them in high arid prairies, at a distance of fifteen or twenty miles from either stream or pool of water, and in regions subject to neither rain nor dews.

They are keen of sight and scent, and seemed governed by some code of federative regulations for mutual safety. Their guards are regularly posted at the suburbs of every village, whose duty it is to be continually on the alert and give timely warning of the approach of danger.

This the cautious sentinels discharge by standing erect at the slightest tainture of the air, or startling noise, or strange appearance; and, having ascertained by careful observations its nature and cause, they sound the sharp yelp and chatter of alarm, in a hurried manner,— then, betaking themselves to the watch-towers that protect the entrances to their burrows, from the verge of the steep parapets they again renew their warning notes, when the whilom busy populace, bescattered at brief distances for amusement or food, return with all possible despatch to their ready holes and disappear from view.

The faithful sentinels are last to retreat from their posts, and not unfrequently maintain their ground at the hazard of individual safety.

On the disappearance of the cause of alarm, they are the first to communicate the pleasing intelligence, and soon the reassured community again betake themselves to their business and sports.

The prairie-owl and rattlesnake maintain friendly relations with these inoffensive villagers, and not unfrequently the three heterogeneous associates occupy the same subterranean appartments; — a strange companionship of birds, beasts, and reptiles!

The prairie dog is extremely tenacious of life, and can seldom be killed with a rifle, unless by a brain-shot; and then, even, it is difficult to secure him, as his companions will immediately convey the carcase into their holes beyond reach.

The flesh of these animals is tender and quite palatable, and their oil superior in fineness, and absence from all grosser ingredients, to that of any other known animals; it is highly valued as a medicine in certain cases.

CHAPTER XIII.

HORSE-SHOE creek is a stream of considerable size, that traces its way through a broad valley of rich alluvion, well timbered with cottonwood and box-elder, and affording all the usual varieties of mountain fruit. The grass of the preceding year's growth was quite rank and stout, giving evidence of a fertile soil.

Resuming our course, we again bore towards the river with the design of crossing, and, after a few hours' ride came to its banks, through a broad opening between two ridges of hills that communicated with it from the high prairies and table lands upon the left.

Here, however, fording was impracticable, the stream being too high and the current swift.

The Platte of the mountains retains scarcely one characteristic of the river with which the reader has hitherto become so familiarized. It is now confined to a bed of rock and gravel, not exceeding two hundred yards in width, and is of unwonted clearness and transparency. Its banks are steep, and the attrition of high waters discloses a deep vegetable mould in their vicinity, favorable to the growth of grain or other produce.

A small bottom of rich sandy loam upon the opposite side lay at the base of a high ridge of table lands, which presented its rugged sides of red-sandstone, almost vertical in their position, and ornamented with an occasional stunted pine, or cedar, or shrub of the buffalo-berry, *(shepherdia argentea,)* while at their base reposed, in huge masses, a profuse medley of fallen fragments, strown around in all the wild confusion of savage scenery.

A few hundred yards to the left, the Platte forces its way through a barrier of table lands, forming one of those striking peculiarities incident to mountain streams, called a "cañon." [104]

Improving the opportunity afforded by a short stay, I ascended an eminence to enjoy a full view of the grand spectacle. The mountain through which the river finds passage, at this place, is from five to eight hundred feet high, opposing perpendicular walls upon each side, that at many points overhang the narrow stream which sweeps with its foaming waters among the rocks below.

This cañon is nearly two miles in length. About midway of the distance the whole stream is precipitated in an unbroken volume from a ledge of rocks, causing a cataract of some twenty or twenty-five feet descent.

Standing upon the dizzy verge of this frightful chasm, and gazing adown its dark abyss, the aspect is one of terrific sublimity, and such as one as will cause the beholder to shrink back with instinctive dread!

These walls are principally of red-sandstone, and ferruginous rock, the precise character of which I was unable to determine. Upon the summit I noticed an abundance of silex, with some elegant specimens of crystalline quartz, that, reflecting the sun's rays, shone like gems in the crown of a mountain-god; a number of singular ligneous petrifactions also met my observation, principally consisting of pine and cedar.

The surrounding country brought within the scope of vision an interesting and romantic scene. The lofty table land in front (with diversified surfaces of granite rock and vegetable earth, affording a scanty nourishment for herbage and foothold for dwarfish cedars and pines) spread far away to the snow-clad mountains of

[104] The Spanish word "cañon" implies a narrow, tunnel-like passage between high and precipitous banks, formed by mountains or table lands. It is pronounced KANYON, and is a familiar term in the vocabulary of a mountaineer. – [Sage]

the north,— while rearward at its base lay the broad valley through which passes the Oregon trail, shut in upon two sides by rugged hills; and farther on arise the snowy sides of the Laramie chain, with their cloud-capped summits. To the left, peak towering above peak, in gradual succession, point to the ridge dividing the waters of the Atlantic and Pacific; and, to the right, the lessening eminences, *vallons,* and plateaux, guide the eye to where the boundless prairie revels in wild beauty and owns itself the realm of eternal Solitude!

How magnificent must be the scene when spring arrays the surrounding landscape in her own loveliness, and bedecks the wilderness with gaudy verdure!

Bearing again to the left, we continued our course by a winding buffalo-path which soon brought us to a broad valley bordering upon the Platte.

Riding on, we soon came to a large sand creek; and, observing several bulls in the vicinity, we accepted the advantage offered by a small grove of cottonwoods and willows, with a clear spring, and struck camp.

During the day, the oddity of an old Franco-Canadian, who accompanied us, afforded me considerable amusement. Observing that he had carried his gun uncharged for several days past, a circumstance so singular in this country led me to enquire the cause. The old fellow, with the most laughable *sang froid,* answered as follows:

"Me carry fusee load? No, no! monsieur. No good, carry fusee load sur le printems. Certes, much bear come out — him dangereux. Me live long en le montagnes; oui, no remarque — duo, tree, great many year! Sacre dem bear,— vat you call him en la Americân?"

"Grizzly bear, I suppose you mean," said I.

"Oui, oui, monsieur; much gráces, monsieur! Oui, gizzle bear; me parler bon Americân, que no remarque gizzle bear! éntonner! Scare dem gizzle bear, him come out une day, kill me de prés."

"Well," continued I; "what has that to do with carrying your gun unloaded?"

"Oui, oui; pardonner, monsieur. Me parler tel une bon Americân! Me réciter, sacre dem bear,— vat you call him, monsieur? Oh, gizzle bear! Sacre dem gizzle bear, me see him une day, en le printems; big, grand felleu. Shoot him fusee; make him much blood; no kill him. Sacre dem bear, gizzle bear, him jump for me. 'Wa-r-r-h!' he say, (imitating the bear.) Bon Dieu! me no stay dare; me bein fast run; me abandonner la fusee; me climb une leetle pine. Sacre dem bear — vat you call him? Ah, oui, gizzle bear. Certes, monsieur, me parler bon Americân, tel une naturel! Sacre dem bear, him come to tree; no climb him, — he too leetil. Look him all round, den; sacre dem bear, gizzle bear did. See fusee lie; pick him up; cock him fusee, sacre dem bear, gizzle bear did. Take him aim at me; snap him fusee tree time. Oh, mon Dieu! mon Dieu! Suppose him fusee been load! Tonnerre de batême! Him shoot me; kill me dead! sacre dem bear, dem gizzle bear vould! Certes, monsieur; por le assuré, sacre dem gizzle bear, him kill me! en le vèrité, monsieur, him kill me dead!"

"So," resumed I, "your reason for not carrying your gun loaded is, you are fearful that a bear might chance to get hold of it and shoot you!"

"Certes, monsieur; en le vèrité! No carry gun load, sur le printems. Sacre dem bear get 'old of him, he shoot!"

Towards night, two of our party, who had gone in pursuit of buffalo, returned laden with meat, which, though poor, was far preferable to the lean venison we had fed upon for the last twenty-four hours.

The male buffalo, at this season of the year, is generally fatter than the female, unless it be one of the few barren cows that sometimes are found in large bands; but, neither is worth boasting of.

After our long fasting and indifferent fare for six entire days, it is not marvellous that we improved, with quickened zest, the present opportunity of feasting.

The day following, two parties started in quest of game,— one of which killed three bulls, at as many shots, within half an hour after leaving camp.

The other party also killed two, but, in securing one of them, they met with an exciting adventure.

Both animals were extended upon the ground, one entirely and the other apparently dead — the hunters, having butchered one of them, proceeded to the other, and were in the act of raising him to the right position for the commencement of operation. The old fellow, not relishing the like familiarity from new acquaintances, sprang to his feet, and made a plunge at the affrighted hunters, who only escaped the fatal charge by one of those admirable feats of quick dodging so often in requisition among mountaineers.

The bull, passing between them, fell head foremost against the ground, two or three feet beyond the spot they had occupied scarcely a second previous; — then rising, with glaring eyes and distended nostrils, and mouth foaming with blood and rage, he pursued one of them in hot chase, for a distance of several hundred yards. So close was the bull in a few leaps, that with a sweep of his horns he gored the hunter's back, tearing away his pantaloons and coat, and prostrating him upon all-fours at the edge of a deep ravine, down which he tumbled; — the enraged beast followed, but the force of an unbroken headway landed him, with a tremendous shock, against the opposite bank, far beyond the hunter. Improving the advantage thus gained, the latter escaped through the windings of the ravine, and ascended the bank, without the reach of his pursuer.

Having procured his rifle, after nine more shots had riddled the lights of the bull's carcase, the business of butchering was again commenced and terminated without further mishap.

Our stay at this camp was prolonged for three or four days.

The geological character of the vicinity corresponds very much with that previously remarked, and to describe it in full would seem too much like a repetition. I have, perhaps, said sufficient to give the reader a correct idea of the prominent characteristics of these parts, and hence, for the sake of brevity, shall hereafter forbear further notes upon this subject, unless some uniform change or striking peculiarity should call for a passing observation.

Prior to resuming our journey, a disagreement occurred between us relative to the proposed route.

Some were desirous of proceeding southward into the Plains of Laramie; thence, bearing eastward to Laramie river, following its valley to Fort Platte; — others were anxious to continue up the Platte to Sweet Water, or further, and from thence proceed as circumstances or inclination might suggest.

This difference finally resulted in a division of the party,— four in favor of the western, and three of the southern route,— myself being included with the former.

Selecting two pack-mules for the conveyance of provisions and camp equipage, the day following we mounted our horses and were under way. With the exception of myself, the present party consisted of old and experienced mountaineers, well acquainted with the country and the nature of Indians. Though, in regard to the latter, little danger was apprehended at this season of the year, as the Sioux had not yet left their winter quarters, and they rarely traverse the vicinity of Sweet Water before the middle of May. Other tribes we might look upon as friendly. We, therefore, anticipated a safe and pleasant excursion.

During the day our course led over a rough undulating prairie, bounded on the right mostly by the river, and on the left by the mountains.

In the heads of valleys and ravines I noticed numerous withered stalks of the bread-root, *(psoralea esculenta,)* indicating its great abundance, and also an increased quantity of *absinthe.*

At night we encamped at the forks of a small stream called La Bonte's creek.[105] Near the confluence of its waters with the Platte are the remains of a log cabin, occupied by a trading party several years since.

The creek is tolerably well timbered, and the valley, through which it winds its way, affords many beautiful bottoms of rich soil. The rock in the vicinity disclosed a furruginous character, especially the sandstone.

Among the usual fruit-bearing shrubs and bushes, I here noticed the "service berry."

This kind of fruit is very abundant in the mountainous parts of Oregon, where it attains a size but little inferior to the common plum, and is highly esteemed for its superior flavor.

Leaving La Bonte's creek, we travelled by easy stages, for three successive days, and struck camp at the mouth of Deer creek.[106]

Our course led over several beautiful streams, most of them well timbered with cottonwood and box-elder, and occasionally skirted by rich bottoms. Previous to reaching this point we followed along the Platte valley, for a distance of some twenty or thirty miles, which presented several fine bottoms of rich sandy soil upon either bank, together with numerous groves of cottonwood.

The face of the country is generally a succession of ridges and hollows, intersected by ravines and small streams of water.

---

[105] This stream still carries the same name. It enters the river near La Bonte station, about seven miles south of Douglas, Wyoming.

[106] Deer Creek flows into the North Platte at Glenrock, Wyoming. Sage has been following, generally, the route of the Oregon Trail.

At Deer creek, and for some distance before reaching it, the mountain chain to our left approaches within four or five miles of the river, rising abruptly to a height of from eight to fifteen hundred feet, with frowning brows and pine-clad summits.

Deer creek is one of the largest affluents of the Platte, from the south, between Sweet Water and Laramie. At this place it is about eight yards broad, with a smooth and transparent current that sweeps over a bed of rock and gravel. Its banks are well timbered with large cottonwoods, and present rich bottoms of alluvial soil, very luxuriant in grass.

Even this early in the season, the fresh grass of the vicinity affords tempting nourishment for our animals, and wishing to favor them as much as possible, we have concluded to remain a short time.

During the succeeding interval we were variously occupied in hunting, root-digging, and moccasin-making. The latter is a business in which every mountaineer is necessarily a proficient, and rarely will he venture upon a long journey without the appurtenances of his profession.

The process of *shoe-making* with him is reduced to its most simple form. He merely takes two pieces of buffalo (or any other suitable) skin, each being a little longer and wider than his foot, particularly towards the heel; these he folds separately, and lays them together parallel with the turned edges; then, rounding and trimming the sides, to render them foot-shaped, with an awl and the sinew of buffalo or other animal, or small strips of thin deer-skin, *("whang,")* he sews the vamps from end to end,— then after cutting a tongue-like appendage in the upper side, midway from heel to toe, and stitching together the posterior parts, his task is done.

Having obtained a quantity of sap from a grove of

box-elders near camp, we found it a sweet and pleasant liquid, and not inferior to that of maple. Sugar might be manufactured from it, with little trouble.

The leaves of this tree, as well as the general appearance of its wood, greatly assimilate those of maple, and, independent of its bushy tops and stunted, winding growth, it would be hard to tell the difference at a first glance.

Game was plenty on every side, both buffalo, deer, and elk, with some few bear.

The second day after our arrival, one of the latter, attracted by the scent of fresh buffalo meat, ventured within gun-shot of camp. Instantly the balls of four rifles were buried in his carcase. Aroused by this *feeling* salute, he rushed towards us at the top of his speed, when our horses, affrighted at the strange appearance, broke snorting away over the neighboring hills, and we ourselves took to trees as fast as possible.

In the midst of this general consternation a pistol ball, fired by one of the party, buried itself in the brains of our troublesome visitor and laid him prostrate.

He was one of a species common to the mountains, called the red bear, and must have weighed four or five hundred pounds. The fat upon his back was full three inches thick. His skin when stretched would have compared in size to that of a buffalo, and the claws of his feet were full three inches long.

At this season of the year, when these animals first leave their dens, they are much the fattest,— a singular circumstance, if we remember the fact of their remaining holed up for the entire winter, without eating!

After butchering the greasy victim, and bringing our erratic horses back to camp, we regaled ourselves with an ample feast of bear's liver, heart, and kidneys, basted with fat,— a dish that epicures might well covet. Then, filling a large camp-kettle with portions of the "fleece" and ribs, we allowed it to boil till the next morning, and thus prepared another delicious entertainment, such as is rarely met with in any country other than this.

Bear meat, to be tender and good, should be boiled at least ten hours. This is probably the most preferable mode of cooking it, though a roast of the article is far from bad.

There are four several varieties of bear found in the Rocky Mountains and countries adjacent, viz: The grizzly bear, the black, the red, and the white.

Of these, the grizzly bear stands pre-eminent in ferocity and strength. He will almost invariably flee at the sight or scent of a man, and seldom attacks any one unless wounded. When shot, he generally runs at full speed towards the sound, and woe to the unfortunate hunter who then comes in his way, unless fully prepared for a deadly encounter!

This animal reigns prince of the mountains, and every other beast within his wide realm acknowledges his supremacy.

Wolves and panthers dare not approach him, or disturb aught savoring of his ownership. Even the carcase of his prey, covered with the earth and rock his cautious instinct teaches him to heap upon it for preservation, is unmolested, though hundreds of wolves and panthers might be starving around.

Buffalo dread his presence far more than the dangerous approach of the hunter, and will sooner bring into requisition their swiftest powers of flight on such occasions. With great difficulty a horse can be persuaded to go within any near distance of one of them, even when led, and then he will quail and tremble in every joint, from extreme terror.

In short, the grizzly bear stalks forth at pleasure, in his majesty and strength, lord of the wild solitudes in which he dwells, and none dares oppose him.

Some writers assert that bears will not prey upon dead

THE GRIZZLY BEAR

carcases,— this is contrary to fact. I have often known them take possession of the carcases of animals, even when nearly putrid, and remain until they were devoured.

They frequently kill buffalo, horses, and cattle to gratify their taste for animal food, and, in such cases, always drag their prey to some convenient spot, and perform the task of burial by heaping upon it piles of rock or earth, to a depth of several feet, for protection against the voracity of other beasts of prey. It is not uncommon, even, that they drag the entire carcase of a full-grown bull a distance of several hundred yards, by the horns, for this purpose,— so great is their strength and so accute their sagacity.

CHAPTER XIV

THE adventure recorded in the preceding chapter called forth the rehearsal of many thrilling stories of frightful encounter with that proud monarch of the mountains, the grizzly bear. Two or three of these it may not be uninteresting to transcribe.

Several years since, an old trapper by the name of Glass, with his companion, while on an excursion, came upon a large grizzly bear.[107]

Bruin, having received the salute of two rifles, as usual, rushed towards his uncivil assailants, who broke from him with all possible despatch. But Glass, stumbling, fell prostrate in his flight, and before he could recover his feet the infuriated beast was upon him.

Now commenced a death-struggle. The pistols of the hunter were both discharged in quick succession,— the ball of one entering the breast of his antagonist, and that of the other grazing his back.

Smarting and maddened by the pain of additional wounds, the bleeding monster continued the conflict with the fury of desperation,— tearing from the limbs and body of the unfortunate man large pieces of trembling flesh, and lacerating him with the deep thrusts of his teeth and claws.

Meanwhile the sufferer maintained, with his butcher-knife, an obstinate defence, though with fast waning effort and strength. Finally, enfeebled by the loss of blood, and exhausted from the extraordinary exertions of a desperate and unequal contest, he was unable to

[107] The Hugh Glass story has been told many times. For an extended account *see* Charles Camp (ed.), "The Chronicles of George C. Yount," in the *California Historical Society Quarterly,* II, pp. 2-66.

oppose further resistance, and quietly resigned himself to his fate.

The bear, too, with the thick blood oozing from his numerous wounds, and faint from the many stabs among his veins and sinews, seemed equally in favor of a suspension of hostilities; and, extending himself across the hunter's back, he remained motionless for two hours or more.

But now another enemy commences an assault upon his vitals — that enemy is death. In vain is defensive effort. In vain are all his struggles. He falls by the hunter's side a lifeless corse.

The setting sun had cast his lurid glare upon the ensanguined spot, as the comrade of the miserable Glass ventured near to ascertain the result of the fierce encounter.

There lay the body of his deserted friend, stretched out, apparently lifeless and half-torn to pieces; and, by its side, lay the carcase of that enemy, which had waged with it such murderous war, cold and stiffened in death!

Now, doubly terrified at his loneliness, but still governed by sordid motives, he stripped the former of his arms and every other valuable, then no longer needed (as he supposed) by their owner, and, mounting his horse, started immediately for the nearest trading post.

On his arrival he recounted the particulars of the fatal occurrence,— carefully concealing, however, his own criminal conduct. The story was accredited, and the name of Glass found place upon the long catalogue of those who had fallen a prey to wild beasts and savage men.

Six weeks elapsed and no one thought of the subject of our sketch as among the living. The general surprise, therefore, may be readily imagined, on opening the fort-gates one morning, at finding before them the poor, emaciated form of a man, half-naked, and covered with wounds and running sores, and so torn the fleshless bones of his legs and thighs were exposed to view in places! and how this astonishment was heightened on recognizing the person of Glass in the illy defined lineaments of his countenance — the very man so long regarded as the inhabitant of another world! A veritable ghost suddenly appearing upon the spot could not have occasioned greater wonder!

But, sensations of pity and commiseration quickly succeeded those of surprise, and the unhappy sufferer was conveyed within doors and received from the hands of friends that careful attention his situation so much required.

The story of his misfortunes was thrillingly interesting. When left by his companion for dead, he was in a state of unconsciousness, with scarcely the breath of life retained in his mangled body. But, the soft night-wind stanched his wounds, and a slight sleep partially revived him from his death-like stupor.

With the morning, the slight sensations of hunger he began to experience were appeased from the raw flesh of the carcase at his side; and, thus strengthened, by a slow and tedious effort he was enabled to reach a near stream and quench his thirst. Still further revived, he again crawled to the carcase at the demands of appetite.

In this manner he continued for three days, when the putrescent corse compelled him to abandon it.

Then it was he commenced his tedious return to the fort, (some seventy miles distant,) which he performed during an interval of forty successive days! The whole of this long stretch he crawled upon his hand and knees, — subsisting, for the meanwhile, only upon insects, such as chance threw in his way, but passing most of the time without one morsel with which to appease the gnawings of hunger or renew his wasted strength.

Yet, great as were his sufferings and intolerable as

they may seem, he survived them all, and, by the kind attention of friends, soon recovered.

He still lives in the town of Taos, New Mexico, and frequently repeats to wondering listeners the particulars of this terrific and painful adventure.[108]

One of our party, whose right hand was much disabled from the effects of a wound, now told his story.

For several years succeeding his first arrival in the Rocky Mountains, he had permitted no opportunity of killing any one of the various species of bear, common to these regions, to pass unimproved. Never did he think of fearing them, and was always the last to retreat in case of a charge.

When a bear appeared within any reasonable shooting distance of our hunter, it almost invariably fell a victim to his unerring aim. But, ere long, this spirit of bold-daring proved the source of lasting regret to its possessor.

On the occasion alluded to, having shot at one of these animals, contrary to his usual good luck, he only wounded it.

The bear in turn now became the assailant, but received the contents of two pistols before it had time to advance far. Our hunter at this crisis sprang to a neighboring pine, which he commenced climbing. His pursuer, gaining the tree almost as soon, likewise began its ascent.

Here occurred a struggle between them — the man to force his way upwards, and the bear to prevent him. The former, drawing his butcher-knife, thrust it at the eyes and nose of his antagonist. Not fancying such *pointed* hints upon a delicate subject, Mr. Bruin caught hold of the hunter's hand, and, as an earnest of deep sensitiveness, crushed it between his teeth,— nor even

108 Most of the writers report Glass as being killed by the Arickaras in 1832-33; Yount recounts a subsequent career.

then relinquished the gripe. Transferred to the left hand, the knife continued its work, till the sickening beast commenced sliding downward – dragging the poor hunter also to the ground. Both struck at the same time; but, at that instant, the knife of the latter pierced the heart of his antagonist, and laid him dead at his feet.

The unfortunate man, however, lost two of his fingers in the affray, and his hand was otherwise so much injured he has never since recovered its use.

Another story related at the same time, though not possessing the deep and thrilling interest of the preceding ones, partakes a little of the ludicrous, and will doubtless amuse the reader.

The narrator a while since formed one of a trapping party, with which he proceeded to the Utah country. While there, on a certain occasion, having set his traps over night, he returned to examine them the next morning, in quest of beaver, and, to his surprise, one of them was missing. After cautiously examining the premises, under the impression that some lurking Indians had stolen his trap with its contents, he noticed the tracks of bears, near by, which served at once to unravel the whilom mystery of its disappearance.

He now began to muse upon his loss, as, without the missing trap, his set would be rendered incomplete, and, under present circumstances, the want of the thing was more than the worth of it. While thus ruminating, a slight noise, among neighboring cherry-bushes and cottonwood, caught his ear, which sounded like some one beating with two sticks.

This induced him to approach for the purpose of ascertaining the cause, when an opening revealed to view Mr. Bruin seated upon a log and holding to his face the missing trap, tightly clasped to his fore-paw.

The bear appeared to be regarding the strange instrument with close attention, as if to study into the principles of its construction; — now gazing at it endwise, then bringing its side in close proximity to his eyes; then turning it over to examine the opposite one; — now, he would essay its strength, and lightly taps it upon the log. But this is a painful operation,— he relinquishes it, and resumes his former grotesque movements.

Watching his curious performance, the trapper could scarcely retain his gravity, or master his fondness for the ludicrous sufficiently for the intended shot. He did, however, and the comedy was suddenly transformed to a tragedy, by leaving its actor struggling in death.

A light fall of snow during the last of our stay at Deer creek, rendered the ground quite muddy and soft; notwithstanding which we resumed our course early in the morning of the fourth day.

Continuing on, a ride of thirty miles brought us to the place where the Oregon trail crosses the Platte; and, after fording the river, we encamped upon the opposite side.

The stream, at this point, is about three hundred yards from bank to bank, and, at the time of our crossing it, swimming deep for a small portion of the way.

In ordinary stages, the water is but little over three feet deep, and the ford perfectly safe and practicable. The partial melting of the mountain snows had increased the size and velocity of its current, and rendered our passage slightly dangerous and difficult. The bed appeared to be rocky, and in some places rough,— requiring much caution in crossing waggons, to prevent them from overturning.

On the third day following, we arrived at another remarkable cañon, after travelling a distance of thirty-five or forty miles. Here, finding large numbers of mountain sheep, we were induced to remain a short time.

Our course for most of this distance was confined to the valley of the Platte, on account of the greater supply of wood found upon its banks.

Towards noon of the first day, we passed a point, called the "Red Buttes," [109] at which the river cuts its way through a lofty ridge of hills. This passage left a considerable bank upon both sides, shut in by abrupt walls of red argillaceous sandstone, towering to the height of several hundred feet.

The soil was generally a mixture of clay and sand, and, in some places, afforded a reddish loam which appeared to be very rich.

A short ride from the "Red Buttes" took us across a beautiful stream, with a broad bottom, well timbered with cottonwood.

Large herds of buffalo were continually in sight upon the whole route.

Several miles previous to reaching the cañon, my notice was first attracted to the extraordinary size attained by the wild sage; it having merged its shrub-like appearance into that of trees varying from five to ten feet in height and from twenty to twenty-five inches in circumference at the root.

The magnificent dimensions of this herb are retained for a large extent of territory to the south and west of this vicinity. It is frequently made use of for fire-wood, and the prairies, in many places, are covered with beautiful groves of it,— perfuming the atmosphere and revelling in perennial verdure.

The cañon before referred to, is caused by the river passing through a chain of hills, for a reach of nearly half a mile.

The current is here shut in by banks of perpendicular rock, four or five hundred feet high, which sometimes overhang it, and leave a narrow space of scarcely two hundred feet for its bed. These consist principally of white cretaceous sandstone, soft and friable, and fre-

---

[109] The Red Buttes are some ten miles up the river from Casper, Wyoming. *See* illustration in this *Series,* III, frontispiece.

quently present to view the appearance of regular mason-work.

During our stay we succeeded in killing five mountain sheep. Some of these were very large and quite fat.

The flesh of this animal is equal in flavor to that of buffalo. It is generally in good order, tender and sweet, and slightly assimilates our common mutton in taste.

The habits and appearance of mountain sheep resemble those of no other animal.

They select for their favorite habitation the rugged fastnesses of wild and inaccessible mountains. In the cold of winter, they descend to some of the numerous valleys that so beautifully diversify the scenery of these regions, where the verdure of spring so rarely fades; and, as the warm season advances, they commence their return towards the lofty snowpeaks, keeping even progress with spring and fresh flowers along the mountain-sides.

Theirs is a life of unbroken spring — beauty and grandeur are their dwelling place,— and, 'mid the awe-inspiring sublimity of nature's works, is their home. They gambol upon the fearful verge of the steep cliff, or climb its perpendicular sides, bidding defiance to all pursuers. There, secure from enemies, they rear their young, and teach them to leap from crag to crag in mirthful gaiety, or traverse the dizzy heights in quest of the varied sweets of changeful spring.

These animals are remarkably acute of sight, and quick of scent and hearing. The least noise or tainture of the air excites their attention and places them instantly upon the alert. Mounting upon some high rock, they will stand for hours in the same posture, gazing in the direction of the fancied danger. If fully satisfied of its reality, they abandon their position for another and a safer one, high among more rugged peaks, and often beyond the possibility of offensive approach. Their hue is so akin to that of the rocks which grace their range, they are with difficulty identified when standing motionless, and the hunter is constantly liable to mistake the one for the other.

In size the mountain sheep is larger than the domestic animal of that name, and its general appearance is in every respect dissimilar – excepting the head and horns. The latter appendage, however, alike belongs to the male and female. The horns of the female are about six inches long, small, pointed, and somewhat flat,— but those of the male grow to an enormous size. I have frequently killed them having horns that measured two feet and a half or three feet in length, and from eighteen to nineteen inches in circumference at the base.

These ponderous members are of great service to their owner in descending the abrupt precipices, which his habits so often render necessary. In leaping from an elevation he uniformly strikes upon the curve of his horns, and thus saves himself from the shock of a sudden and violent contussion.[110]

The color of these animals varies from a yellowish white, to a dark brown, or even black. A strip of snowy whiteness extends from ham to ham, including the tail, which is short and tipped with black.

Instead of wool, they are covered with hair, which is shed annually. Their cry is much like that of domestic sheep, and the same natural odor is common to both.

It is extremely difficult to capture any of them alive, even while young,— and it is next to impossible to make them live and thrive in any other climate than their own. Hence, the mountain sheep has never yet found a place in our most extensive zoological collections.

Remaining three days at this place, we were again *en route,* and, bearing to the right, passed over a ridge

110 These sheep often are called Bighorns. The report that they light on their horns is questioned.

of rough, rocky summits, and struck the valley of the Sweet Water. Continuing up the latter, a short ride brought us to the vicinity of a noted landmark of the country, known as Independence Rock, where we encamped.[111]

The soil of the river bottoms is good, but the adjoining prairies are sandy and somewhat sterile.

The distance from this to the cañon is not far from twenty-three miles.

Independence Rock is a solid and isolated mass of naked granite, situated about three hundred yards from the right bank of the Sweet Water. It covers an area of four or five acres, and rises to a height of nearly three hundred feet. The general shape is oval, with the exception of a slight depression in its summit where a scanty soil supports a few shrubs and a solitary dwarf-pine.

It derives its name from a party of Americans on their way to Oregon, under the lead of one Tharp, who celebrated the fourth of July at this place,— they being the first company of whites that ever made the journey from the States, *via* South Pass.[112]

The surface is covered with the names of travellers, traders, trappers, and emigrants, engraven upon it in almost every practicable part, for the distance of many feet above its base,— but most prominent among them all is the word "Independence,"[113] inscribed by the patriotic band who first christened this lonely monument of nature in honor of Liberty's birthday.

---

111 This famous landmark on the Oregon Trail we have visited on various occasions. Some of the names and dates pecked on this "Register of the Desert" in early years can still be deciphered.

112 Tharp and his party have not been identified. It is believed that the rock was named before any Oregon-bound travelers visited it. Its name probably dates from the sojourn of Thomas Fitzpatrick and companions at its base on July 4, 1824.

113 By whom and when this word was written on the rock has not been determined.

I went to the rock for the purpose of recording my name with the swollen catalogue of others traced upon its sides; but, having glanced over the strange medley, I became disgusted, and, turning away, resolved, "If *there remains no other mode of immortalizing myself,* I will be content to descend to the grave *'unhonored and unsung.'*"

The day following, a heavy fall of snow and sleet forced us to remain in camp, and the consequent muddiness of the route prolonged our stay still further.

The vicinity afforded an abundance of game and a sufficiency of dry fuel; it would, therefore, have been folly in us to care for wind or weather, detracting as did either so little from our comfort.

During this interval I rode into the prairie a short distance, in quest of game, and struck the river a few miles above camp, at a place where the stream cuts its way through a high ridge of hills, forming another cañon of three or four hundred yards in length, and about forty broad, called the Devil's Gate, as I afterwards ascertained.[114]

Its walls arose perpendicularly to a height of between four and five hundred feet, and consisted of trap rock, sandstone, and granite.

Dismounting, I ascended to the summit, where a grand and picturesque scenery burst upon the view.

Above, the broad valley of the Sweet Water stretched far away to the westward, bounded on either side by frowning mountains, that, towering to the height of fifteen hundred or two thousand feet, present their snowy summits in proud defiance of wind or storm, and laugh at the impotency of a summer's sun; — on the south, shaking their piny tops in scornful derision; and, on the north, with denuded crests of broken granite,

[114] One of the landmarks of the Oregon Trail and still bearing the same name. We have walked through this impressive gash through the mountain ridge.

challenging the lightnings of heaven and wooing its loudest thunders; — while further along, the clouds played in humble sportiveness around the base of the great chain dividing the waters of two oceans, nor dared ascend its dizzy heights to range amid eternal snow.

Below, in silent grandeur, arose to view the grantic mass that responds to the day-dawn of a nation's existence, surmounted by its lone pine, and bearing upon its broad register the sculptured names of the audacious disturbers of its solitude; and further yet, the parti-colored peaks of the Black Hills, now white with fresh-fallen snow, now darkened with clustering pines, seemed musing in modest retirement; while far around, in every spot accessible to discriminating vision, dense herds of grazing buffalo covered the prairie with their pall-like mantle of countlesss numbers.

It was indeed a magnificent prospect, and needed only the garnishing hand of spring to render it as enchanting in loveliness as it was impressive in wild sublimity.

CHAPTER XV.

PREVIOUSLY to leaving this place, considerable discussion arose relative to our future course.

The proposition was to continue up the Sweet Water valley to the dividing ridge at the head of Green river, and return by the same route; — *versus* the suggestion to cross the Sweet Water and proceed up the Platte to the confluence of a large tributary from the south; thence, keeping by the valley of the latter stream as far as the Medicine Bow Mountains, return to the Fort by the way of Laramie river.

The fast melting of the snow, and anticipated difficulties, not to say dangers, consequent upon high water in the passage of creeks and rivers, influenced us to adopt the latter as the most advisable course.

Such was the final decision, and, the men with me being familiarly acquainted with every nook and corner of the adjacent country, I improved the opportunity to elicit from them all possible information relative to the Oregon route from this onward; and, never having personally travelled from Independence Rock to the head of Green river, it may not be out of place to lay before the reader a succinct statement of some of the items thus gleaned.

The distance from this point to the famous South Pass is but little over one hundred miles. The trail follows the Sweet Water to its source, keeping the river valley for most of the distance. This valley consists of an undulating prairie, (at intervals rough,) varying in width from the narrow limits of a few yards to the more ample dimensions of four or five miles.

Sometimes, the adjoining hills close in upon the river

banks and force the trail among their rugged windings. In one place the road leads over a high stretch of table land for nearly a day's travel, when it again descends to the valley.

The stream, in places, is tolerably well timbered with cottonwood, oak, and aspen, and rolls over a rocky bed, with a clear and swift current.

The distance through the pass is about fifteen miles, and the ascent and descent are so gradual the traveller would scarcely notice the transition from the head of the Sweet Water to that of the Colorado. The hills at this point are low, and the face of the country rolling—but not rough, affording at all times a most excellent waggon road.

On the morning of the fourth day, we accordingly retraced our course, and, having traversed a rugged and hilly country for some ten or twelve miles, we camped in a small open prairie at the mouth of the Sweet Water.

During our ride we noticed several large bands of wild sheep, at intervals, gazing upon us from huge masses of granite that towered with isolated summits to a frequent altitude of sixty or one hundred feet.

The next morning, we crossed the Sweet Water a little above its mouth.

The ford was quite feasible, the stream being some ten yards wide and three or four feet deep, with a bed of sand and pebbles.

From this point, travelling up the Platte for about ten miles or more, we arrived opposite the creek previously alluded to, and, crossing at a shoal place a short distance above, camped in a grove of cottonwood and willows, at the delta formed by the confluence of the two streams.

There are several bottoms of very rich soil in this vicinity; but back from the river the country is rough and hilly.

Westward the Sweet Water mountains, distant some ten miles, showed their craggy peaks, and to the north and east the piny crests of the Black Hills burst upon the sight; while southward, a succession of high, rolling prairies opened to view a variety of romantic and beautiful scenery.

We remained at this place the two following days, for the purpose of hunting. Game of all kinds appeared in great abundance, particularly elk. At several points among the willows near the river were noticed fresh signs of beaver, and among the hills the recent marks of bear in digging for roots.

A large bird called the mountain fowl, quite common to these parts, was the occasion of some little curiosity, being the first of its species I ever saw. This bird is rather larger than our domestic hen, and of a grayish brown color. Little accustomed to the presence of man, it easily falls a prey to the hunter. Its flesh is tender and most excellent in flavor.[115]

Having obtained a fresh supply of meat, we resumed our course.

Continuing up the right bank of the creek (which I have named Medicine Bow, for lack of a better term)[116] and travelling by easy stages four successive days, we arrived at its head,—a distance of more than fifty miles above its junction with the Platte.

Many beautiful bottoms skirted the banks of this stream, which were well timbered with cottonwood, aspen, birch, willow, box-elder, and some few pines. The soil is generally of a reddish loam, and the luxuriant size of the dead grass, together with the rank ver-

[115] According to Dr. Vasco M. Tanner, Professor of Zoology at Brigham Young University, this bird was undoubtedly the Sage Grouse, *Centrocercus urophasianus Bonaparte.*

[116] This is still known as Medicine Bow Creek. Its entry into the North Platte is at a point considerably more than ten miles south of the mouth of the Sweetwater.

dure of the present season, gave evidence of its richness and fecundity.

I was pleased to observe not a few wild flowers, of rare beauty, in full bloom, lending their fragrance to the breath of spring, and blushing at the admiration challenged by their loveliness.

On the right lay a broad expanse of undulating prairie, covered with stately clusters of *absinthe,* and disclosing every variety of soil, from the rude sterility of an African desert to the rich productiveness of a garden; — on the left, the mountains, increasing in altitude, jutted their craggy sides in close proximity to the creek — now disclosing immense piles of granite, with red argillaceous, grayish micaceous, dark ferruginous, and white calcareous sandstone, limestone, and coarse-grained conglomerates, naked and variegated with almost every diversity of color,— and now, surmounted by stunted pines and cedars, or towering balsam, hemlock and pinion; and in front, the lofty peaks of Medicine Bow, rearing their snowy heads beyond the clouds, opposed an eternal barrier to further prospect.

As we passed along, I noticed three or four small branches that emptied into the creek from the opposite side, and, just before reaching our present encampment, we crossed three others from the right, all of them well timbered and graced by rich valleys and *prairillons.*

This section of country, being the great war-ground between the Sioux and Chyennes on the one side, and the Snakes and Crows on the other, is considered dangerous, particularly from May till November of each year. During that time it is extremely unsafe for a white man to venture within its confines, unless protected by a strong force.

A small creek at our right, became the scene of a bloody tragedy two months subsequent to our visit.

Three trappers, with whom I became acquainted upon my return to the Fort, tempted by the abundance

A CROW WARRIOR.

of fur-bearing game common to the vicinity, came here for the purpose of making a summer hunt. While successfully pursuing their occupation, unsuspicious of immediate danger, they were suddenly surrounded, early one morning, by a war-party of Sioux, whose first salute was a discharge of fire-arms, accompanied by a shower of arrows and the sharp thunder of deafening yells.

Two of them fell dead. The remaining one retreated to a hollow tree, close at hand, into which he crawled; and, though severely wounded, maintained from it an obstinate resistance till near sundown,— keeping at bay the whole host of savage assailants, and thinning their numbers, one by one, with the deadly discharge of his unerring rifle.

Six warriors lay stiffened in death, and as many more had felt the burning smart of wounds,—one of the latter having had his tongue shot out, close to its roots!—and still he continued the unequal contest.

His triumph would have been complete had not the remorseless crew, as a last resort, set fire to the woods and burned him from the shell-like fortress from which they could not drive him.

He fell with his companions, mingling his own blood with that of their murderers; and the scalps of the three were treasured among the horrid trophies of savage victory.

Of these unfortunate men, one, named Wheeler, was a Pennsylvanian; another, named Cross Eagle, was a Swede; and the third, name not remembered, was a native of France.[117] They were men of noble hearts and much esteemed by all who knew them.

In the neighborhood I noticed many indications of coal, of which there appeared to be extensive beds, as well as iron and mineral salts.

Continuing on, a short ride brought us to the pass-trail, following which, after travelling a few miles by a road intercepted by frequent ravines between a defile of mountains, we were finally ushered into the broad prairie, opening eastward, known as the Plains of Laramie.[118]

The mountains upon both sides were heavily coated with snow, which intruded to the trail, while groves

[117] The story of the deaths of Wheeler and Cross Eagle are recounted by G. F. Ruxton in his *Life in the Far West, op. cit.,* p. 107-08. Ruxton has doubtless borrowed the story from Sage, but he changes the locale to the Blackfoot country.

[118] The Laramie Plains generally are drained by the Laramie River. Sage has crossed from the Medicine Bow to the Laramie River basin.

of pine and aspen relieved the eye in scanning their rough escarpments.

The prevailing rock appeared to be a compact red granite, with occasional strata of sandstone.

While winding among the ravines and aspen groves, we obtained an indistinct view of a strange-looking, dark-colored animal, that my companions pronounced a *"carcague."*

Of the character, or even the existence of such a creature, I cannot speak from positive knowledge — this, if one, not being sufficiently near for a scrutinizing observation, and no other of its kind ever came in my way; but, in answer to inquiries, I am enabled to give the following description,— for the correctness of which, however, I will not vouch, though, for my own part, inclined to accredit it.

The "carcague" is a native of the Rocky Mountains, and of a family and species found in no other part of the world as yet known. He seems a distinct *genus,* partaking the mixed nature of the wolf and bear, but is far more ferocious than either.

His color is a jet black, hair long and coarse, and body trim and slender. His head and neck are like those of a wolf, but his tail and feet assimilate the bear, and his body presents the marked qualities and appearance of both.

In size, he is considerably larger than the common cur-dog, and is more agile in his movements. Unlike the bear, he will not run from the presence or scent of man, and regards the "lord of creation" with neither fear nor favor. Hence he is looked upon as a creature much to be dreaded by all who are anywise conversant with his character and existence.

The representatives of his family are seldom met with, which affords the principal reason why so little, comparatively, is known of his nature and habits.

If the information contained in the above description

is correct, (and that it is so, I have not the least doubt,) the "carcague" presents, either the extraordinary phenomenon of the creation of a new race of wild beasts, or, the living relics of an order now almost extinct; and, whether he be the one or the other, his existence is vested with deep interest to all lovers of the marvellous.[119]

An old trapper related the following story, soon after the incident above noticed, which will serve to give some idea of this ferocious animal:

A party of hunters, at their night camp, were seated around a large fire, at whose side were fixed several pieces of meat, *en appolas,* for the purpose of roasting. All were waiting patiently the kind office of the fire in the preparation of their longed-for suppers, when, attracted by the fumes of the cooking viands, a "carcague" came bounding from the mountain-side, directly over their heads, and made for the roasts, with which he disappeared before even a shot could be fired in their defence.

Thus bold and daring is their nature, and so little is their regard for the presence of man.

Bearing southward in the course of a few miles we came to a large creek,[120] and camped early in the afternoon, near the base of a lofty mountain of the Medicine Bow range.

In this vicinity were the relics of three Indian forts.[121] On the banks of the stream was an abundance of timber of various kinds; the bottoms were broad and of a rich

119 The wolverine, sometimes called the glutton. For a good description *see* Osborne Russell, *Journal of a Trapper* (Boise, Syms-York, 1921), p. 130.

120 This would be Rock Creek, which flows through the town of Rock River, Wyoming. Fremont mistakenly shows it as "Right Hand Fork" of the Laramie (on his large map accompanying the *Report* of his expeditions of 1842 and 1843).

121 Fremont in 1843 traveled, in this immediate area, the same trail that Sage did, but in the opposite direction. Fremont mentioned the three forts as being near the stream (Rock Creek) at his noon halt on August 2, 1843.

soil, shut in by abrupt acclivities that lead to the arid plains through which the creek traces its way.

Game appeared in great abundance in all directions, and seemed more than usually tame and accessible.

Soon after camping, three of us went in quest of a fresh supply of eatables, and, towards night, returned with the choice portions of a buffalo and a black-tailed deer.

The valley also afforded large quantities of wild onions,[122] which were shooting forth with singular luxuriance.

We passed the night in quiet slumber, neither of us dreaming of the possible existence of human beings, other than ourselves, within a less distance than one hundred miles.

In the morning, however, we were awakened by the wild yell of savages, and, on looking to ascertain the cause, saw a dense throng of painted monsters surrounding us, who were whooping, screeching, and dancing in a most terrific and fantastic manner. Seizing our guns, we levelled at the foremost of them, who immediately sheathed their bows and made the sign of friendship and their nation.

They were Crows, and, having discovered us the afternoon before, now came for a morning call.

The chief of the band bore the name of Little Robber, and was a large, portly, well-made man, as, in fact, were all his party. He was recognized by one of us as an old acquaintance, and was greeted as such, when several of his people came forward to shake hands, and we were soon on most friendly terms.

They informed us, by means of signs, that they were advancing against the Sioux, and their village was encamped upon a neighboring creek, a little to the

122 Fremont, in the vicinity of the three forts, first noted the yampah (*anethum graveolens*), a root much used by the Indians for food; and during the afternoon noticed that a "species of onion was very abundant" (p. 125).

right,— after which they insisted upon our accompanying them to it.

Not waiting for further ceremony, they drove up our horses and commenced saddling them. Supposing it useless to resist, we yielded compliance to their wishes, and, in about an hour's ride, came to the village. Here we were inducted to the chief's lodge, where commenced a series of feastings peculiar to Indians on occasions like this.

The Crows are a nation living upon the waters of the Yellow-stone, at a distance of about four hundred miles west-northwest of Fort Platte. Their number embraces not far from four hundred and fifty or five hundred lodges, being something near four thousand men, women, and children.

Ten or twelve years since they were enemies to the whites, but, more recently, have been on friendly terms.[123]

They never kill or injure the white man who comes within their power, and rarely take from him anything without returning for it an equivalent. For instance,— they may take his robe, horse, or gun; but, in that case, they will return another robe, horse, or gun; acting upon the principle that "exchange is no robbery," even though it be compulsory.

Less contaminated by intercourse with the whites than most mountain tribes, they will tolerate the importation of liquor among them upon no consideration, not even by traders for their own individual use. Whenever it is ascertained that any one in their vicinity, whether white man or Indian, is in possession of that article, they take it from him, if necessary, by force, and pour it upon the ground.

Their bitter hatred of this vile stuff, is said to have resulted in the following strange manner:

123 In the early 1830s the white trappers had difficulties with the Crows. Thomas Fitzpatrick and William D. Stewart, among others, experienced rough treatment at their hands.

The whites, as usual, came first among them bringing alcohol; and, at a feast given to the chiefs, soon after, several of the latter became intoxicated from too lavish potations of the new and curious drink.

In common with inebriates of civilized society, they acted very foolishly, and, on appearing before their people, the drunken chiefs became the subject of ridicule. This so shamed them, that, upon the return of sobriety, they could not be persuaded to taste another drop, and thereafter made use of their united influence to prevent its introduction and sale.

Ever since the above occurrence, alcohol has received, from the Crows, the appellation of *"Fool's Water,"* a term at once attesting their nice moral discernment and good sense.

Several years since, a missionary, on visiting them, began through an interpreter to rehearse the story how sin first came into the world, and how all men had become bad — whether white or red.

Thus premised, he proceeded to explain the great truths of Christianity, and averred that he had come to do them good, and to tell them how to be happy; asserting that, unless they listened to him and worshipped the Good Spirit in the manner he pointed out, they could never, at death, reach that happy country into which good people alone find admittance.

One of the chiefs upon this arose and made the following reply:

"My white brother is a stranger to us. He talks bad of us, and he talks bad of his own people.

"He does this because he is ignorant. He thinks my people, like his, are wicked. Thus far he is wrong!

"Who were they that killed the very good man of whom he tells us? None of them were red men!

"The red man will die for good men, who are his friends! — he will not kill them!

"Let my pale-face brother talk to the white man —

THE CROW CHIEF MAKING A SPEECH.

his own people — they are very bad. He says, he would do us good! He does no good to chide us and say we are very bad.

"True we are bad; and were we bad as the pale-faces it would become us to listen to him!

"Would my brother do us good? Then, let him tell us how to make powder and we will believe in the sincerity of his professions; — but let him not belie us by saying we are bad like the pale-faces!"

These Indians rarely kill the women and children of an enemy when in their power, and, in this particular, they show themselves unlike most of the wild tribes found on the American continent.

They are a brave and noble people, prosecuting their endless hostilities against the Sioux and Blackfeet, (the only nations with whom they are at variance,) not so much to gratify an innate love for war, as from a just hatred of the meanness of those they war against.

In the summer of 1842, a war-party of some two hundred Crows invaded the Sioux country by way of Laramie pass, and penetrated as far as Fort Platte, and beyond, in pursuit of their enemy.

A few miles above the Fort, having met with a lone French engagé, who was rather *green* in all that pertains to Indians as well as some other things, they began by signs to enquire of him the whereabouts of the Lacotas, (the sign for them being a transverse pass of the right front-finger across the throat).

The poor Frenchman, mistaking this for the avowed intention of *cutting his throat,* commenced bellowing *a la* calf, accompanying the music by an industrious appliance of crosses in double-quick time — not forgetting to make use of sundry most earnest invocations of the blessed Virgin to graciously vouchsafe to him deliverance from impending danger.

The Indians, perceiving his strange conduct to be

the result of fear, felt disposed to have a little fun at his expense; so, mounting him upon a horse, they bound his hands and feet and guarded him to a post of the American Fur Company as a prisoner.

The Fort gates being closed against them, they demanded admittance on the plea of wishing to trade.

"What would you buy?" asked the commandant.

"Tobacco."

"What have you brought to pay for it?"

"A white man."

"A white man?" exclaimed the former; "at what pricc?"

"Oh, he is not worth much. A plug of tobacco is his full value!" continued the warriors.

The commandant now began to understand the joke; and, on recognizing the prisoner as an employee of the other Fort, he told them they might possibly find a market for him at the next post, but for his own part he was not disposed to purchase.

The Indians then paraded around the Fort, and, after saluting its inmates with three deafening whoops, proceeded at full charge towards Fort Platte.

When arrived, having prostrated two scaffolds of dead Sioux by the way, they informed the person in charge, that they had brought back one of his men, and claimed from him a plug of tobacco for their trouble. The circumstances attending this request were of so comical a nature, the commandant felt disposed to humor the joke, and gave the tobacco, upon which they immediately left in pursuit of their enemies.

Having remained prisoners to the hospitality of these Indians for two days and a half, we were at length permitted again to resume our journey.

Following the creek downwards for the two days next succeeding, and then bearing to the left [right], after a ride of some twelve miles, we struck Laramie river at a point which presented broad bottoms upon each side with an abundance of timber; here we remained encamped till the subsequent day.

In journeying thus far, we passed over a sufficient extent of this broad expanse to give a general description of it, from personal observation coupled with information derived from others more experienced.

The Plains of Laramie are bounded north and east by the Black Hills, south by a ridge of naked elevations, (composed of soft, arenaceous rock and terrene limestone, embedded in marl and white clay, sterile and almost entirely destitute of vegetation,) and west by the Medicine Bow Mountains.

This section includes an area one hundred and sixty miles long by seventy broad.

The northern portion of it is a high plateau, almost destitute of springs or streams of water, having a mixed soil of clay and sand, producing the grass and other peculiarities incident to the grand prairies. Westerly, it is composed of red sand and gravel, tolerably fertile and abundant in rocky fragments. The southern portion is watered by a number of streams that rise in the Medicine Bow Mountains and flow eastward; some of them pouring their waters into Laramie river, and others losing themselves in the sand.

Towards the southwestern extremity, at the base of a lofty, isolated mountain, is a salt lake of considerable dimensions. Several other lakes are also found adjacent to the Medicine Bow Mountains, whose waters are strongly impregnated with mineral salts.

In numerous places the surface, for small distances, is entirely naked and whitened with saline efflorescences, that vie in their appearance with the unspotted purity of fresh-fallen snow.

The Laramie river [124] traces its way through the whole

[124] This river received its present name from one Joseph Laramie, a French trapper, who was killed near its mouth, several years since, by the Indians. – [Sage]. Jacques La Ramie, as the name is usually given, was

extent, — rising in the southern extremity of the Medicine Bow Mountains and in the desolate highlands that form the dividing ridge between its own and the waters of Cache a la Poudre, and, after flowing a distance of some three hundred miles, discharges itself into the Platte.

Upon this river and its branches are many beautiful bottoms of rich alluvial soil, well adapted to cultivation, varying from five to ten miles in length, and from two to five in breadth. These bottoms are to some extent well supplied with timber, consisting of ash, elm, cottonwood, box-elder, and willow, while the adjacent mountains and hills afford pine, cedar, and balsam.

Of the various kinds of wild fruits and berries are found cherries, plums, currants, gooseberries, service-berries, buffalo-berries, and some few grapes; among its vegetables and roots are the bread-root, pomme blanc, onions, and commote.

Its prevailing rock is sandstone, (gray micaceous, brown argillaceous, red granitic, and ferruginous,) limestone, (siliceous, testaceous, fossiliferous, and terrene,) and red granite, with various conglomerates and heavy boulders of fragmentary and transition rock.

Among the mineral productions incident to this region are salt, sulphur, soda, magnesia, nitre, alum, coal, iron, copper, and gold, (the latter only in small quantities.) Among its game is embraced nearly every variety found in countries adjacent to the mountains.

The high prairies skirting the tributaries of the Laramie, though favored with many valleys of fertile soil, are fit only for grazing purposes, on account of their general aridity and scarcity of water; a fault, by the way, too common with a large proportion of that vast extent of territory from the neighborhood of our western frontiers almost to the very shores of the Pacific.

---

killed by the Arapahoes in 1821. – Hafen and Young, *Fort Laramie, op. cit.,* p. 20.

CHAPTER XVI.

On resuming our course, we soon after struck into a lodge-trail leading to the Platte by way of Sibille's creek; — following this we travelled over an undulating and sandy prairie for about ten miles, and came to a chain of rugged mountains, bearing from north to south, through which we passed, by a tedious and circuitous route, for a considerable distance, winding among rocks and narrow defiles of naked hills, till we were finally ushered into a beautiful opening facing the east, known as Sibille's-hole.[125]

This valley is situated at the confluence of two small streams, heading in the adjoining mountains, that unite to form Sibille's creek.

It is shut in upon three sides by lofty ridges, many hundred feet high, consisting of immense piles of earthy limestone and marl, whose rough, naked sides, ornamented with occasional dwarf-pines, cedars, or fruit-bearing shrubs, present a wild and romantic scenery.

The valley is four or five miles in length and of variable width, with a strong, black soil, affording a goodly supply of timber .

The season was further advanced in this than in any other place we had yet visited. Several specimens of wild flowers were in full bloom, belading the soft air with their sweetest odors. The grass too had attained a height of some three inches, and furnished a most sumptuous entertainment for our jaded animals, which they were nowise backward to accept.

---

[125] At the head of Sibille Creek, branch of the Laramie River. Apparently it was named for Mr. Sybille, of Sybille, Adams, & Company, who came into possession of Fort Platte in 1842. *See* Fremont's *Report, op. cit.*, p. 35.

Wishing to afford them an opportunity to recruit their strength, we remained encamped the two following days.

During the interval we were successful in killing two very fat bulls, and were thus enabled to renew the series of feasting which had graced the greater part of our journey.

I here became for the first time acquainted with a kind of beverage very common among mountaineers. The article alluded to may with much propriety be termed "bitters," as the reader will readily acknowledge on learning the nature of its principal ingredient.

It is prepared by the following simple process, viz: with one pint of water mix one-fourth gill of buffalo-gall, and you will then have before you a wholesome and exhilarating drink.

To a stomach unaccustomed to its use it may at first create a slightly noisome sensation, like the inceptive effects of an emetic; and, to one strongly billious, it might cause vomiting; — but, on the second or third trial, the stomach attains a taste for it, and receives it with no inconsiderable relish.

Upon the whole system its effects are beneficial. As a stimulent, it braces the nerves without producing a corresponding relaxation on the cessation of its influence; it also tends to restore an impaired appetite and invigorate the digestive powers.

As a sanative, it tends to make sound an irritated and ulcerated stomach, reclaiming it to a healthful and lively tone, and thus striking an effective blow at that most prolific source of so large a majority of the diseases common to civilized life.

From what I have seen of its results, I consider it one of the most innocent and useful medicines in cases of dyspepsy, and will hazard the further opinion, that, were those laboring under the wasting influences of this disease to drink *gall-bitters* and confine themselves exclusively to the use of some *one* kind of diet, (animal food always preferable,) thousands who are now pining away by piecemeal, would be *restored to perfect soundness,* and *snatched from the very threshold of a certain grave* which yawns to receive them!

Resuming our course, we continued down Sibillis creek to its junction with the Laramie; then, following the course of that river, in the afternoon of the third day we arrived at Fort Platte, after an absence of nearly two months,— having travelled, in the interval, a distance of more than five hundred miles.

To give a general description of the country passed over during the concluding part of our journey, would seem too much like a recapitulation of previous remarks.

Our observations in reference to the river and creek bottoms, may be again correctly applied; as may, also, those relative to the timber, and the geological character of the adjoining prairies.

Several miles above the Fort we crossed the Chugwater,[126] a large affluent of the Laramie, from the right. This creek takes its rise in a wild and desolate section of the Black Hills, near the head of Horse creek.

Thirty miles or more of its way is traced through a dreary wilderness of rock, sand, and clay, almost entirely devoid of vegetation.

This region, it is said, affords gold; [127] and, indeed, I have received frequent assurances that the valuable metal has been procured, in small particles, from among the sand of the creek-bed.

This region also claims many natural curiosities, of which I may take occasion to speak more particularly hereafter; — one, however, situated upon Chugwater, here seems more appropriately to demand a passing notice.

---

126 Still known by the same name.

127 No gold in paying quantities has been found in the region. The Colorado gold seekers of 1859 prospected the area.

It consists of a columnar elevation of sandstone and marl, towering aloft to the height of several hundred feet, like the lone chimney of some razed mansion,—standing as the melancholy monument of the ruins that surround it.

This singular pile of rock and earth is nearly of a quadrangular form, quite regular in its structure, and compares very nearly with the "Chimney" below Scot's Bluff, in its general outlines. It stands within a short distance of the east bank of the Chugwater, and gives the creek its present name.[128]

Our arrival at the Fort dated the 26th of April. The boat being completed, all things, save the spring rise, were in readiness for the intended voyage.

This craft was put together in regular ship-shape, and finished in a workman-like manner. She measured fifty feet keel by thirteen beam, and, without her lading, drew but an inch and a half of water. Her intended burthen was between two and three tons. While admiring her beauty and symetry, little did I think of the sufferings in store for me with her hardy crew.

Several important changes had taken place during our absence. The Fort with its fixtures now claimed different owners, and was occupied by the men of two companies besides our own.[129] This swelled the present number to some forty or fifty, and afforded quite a lively scene.

Now was an interval of leisure to all hands, and the time, unemployed in eating and sleeping, was passed

128 The word "Chug" implies chimney; of the derivation of the term, however, I am ignorant. – [Sage]

129 Lupton must have sold out to "Sybille, Adams & Company," whom Fremont found as owners of Fort Platte in July, 1842. – His *Report, op. cit.*, p. 35. In August, 1843, Theodore Talbot was at the fort and spoke of it as "Sybille & Adams' post," and also as "Bissonette's Fort" (Talbot's *Journal, op. cit.*, p. 34).

in story-telling, ball-playing, foot-racing, target-shooting, or other like amusements.

Several, forming themselves into a club for forensic debate, secured a prolific source of entertainment, for the time being. A partner in one of the trading firms, whose men were now stationed at the Fort, made himself quite conspicuous as a participator in these discussions.

He was very self-important and conceited, and not a little ignorant withal, and with regard to temperance, being uniformly about "three sheets in the wind," and the other *fluttering,* his spoutings were an exhaustless fund of laughter.

At his request, in order to render the exercises more *spirited,* the merits of the arguments presented were decided upon by a committee of three, and the speakers decided against, sentenced to *liquorize* the club.

The treating, however, was always on one side; for as the whole business was an affair of sport, the committee of arbitration generally had this primary object in view while pronouncing their decisions. When these were averse to our orator, he of course paid the forfeit as an affair of debt; and when favorable to him, he was equally prompt in proferring a common treat, exultatory upon his fancied success.

My own part in this performance was that of a mere looker-on, but it required of one more than my usual self-mastery, to retain his gravity under the potent influences of so ludicrous an exhibition.

Other matters of interest, however, occurred at this time, and, as they tend to throw some light upon Indian habits and customs, perhaps the reader will not look upon it as altogether out of place for me to notice them.

At the two Forts in this neighborhood were some ten or twelve squaws, married to the traders and engagés of the different fur companies. These ladies were in the habit of meeting, occasionally, for gambling purposes. In this they acted as systematically as the most experienced black legs of a Mississippi steamboat; if they failed to play as high, it was only for the lack of means.

Ball-playing was one of the games upon which heavy bets were made. The instrument used in this amusement consisted of two globular forms, about two inches each in diameter, which were attached by a short string. The play-ground was the open prairie in front of the Fort, and embraced an area of nearly a mile in extent.

As the initiatory step, each party, composed of equal numbers, selected an equal amount of valuables, consisting of beads, scarlet, vermilion, rings, awls, shells, &c., which were placed in two piles about half a mile apart, and equi-distant between them was placed the ball. Each gamestress, armed with her club, then repaired to the spot, and the opposing parties arrayed themselves, the one facing the other with the ball between them. At a given signal they all strike — the one party striving to propel it towards its own valuables, and the other to force it in a contrary directon. The party propelling it to its own pile, wins, and becomes entitled to both.

As success in this game depends more upon fleetness of foot than skill in striking, a large party of squaws, thus engaged, opens to the beholder a rich scene of amusement.

Another game is still more extensively practised among them. This is somewhat upon the principle of dice, though different in its details.

Six plum-stones, smoothly polished, and marked with various parallel, triangular, and transverse lines, are thrown loosely into a small, plate-like basket, around which the players are seated with their stores of trinkets. The leader then receives the basket in one hand, and, briskly moving it to change the position of the dice, suddenly strikes it upon the ground, tossing the plum-stones from their places and catching them in their descent.

The amount won depends upon the number of triangular and transverse lines left uppermost.

The loser, having paid the forfeit, next takes the basket and describes the same movements, receives her winnings in like manner, and returns it to her opponent, — and so on alternately.

Much cheating and trickery are practised in this game.

The game of hand, for a description of which the reader is referred to a previous marginal note, is also a favorite play with squaws as well as men. Large parties of both sexes not unfrequently engage in this amusement, and many a poor Indian loses his all by the operation.

Speaking of squaws reminds me of not having previously described their dress and appearance.

The dress of a squaw is scarcely less simple than that of an Indian. Two pieces of skin, sewed together in a bag-like form, (of sufficient size to envelope the body from neck to knee, leaving an aperture for the former with the arms,) constitute her gown, which is completed by two other pieces of skin sewed from neck to waist so as to fall loosely upon the arms as far as the elbow; then, with leggins of thin deer or antelope skin, garnished moccasins, and a painted robe, you have before you the full rig of a mountain squaw.

Some of the younger ones, however, flaunt dresses quite tastefully ornamented, with full capes and fringe-works, garnished with beads and porcupine-quills, that present a wild, fantastic appearance, not altogether estranged to beauty.

A squaw prides herself much upon the number of rings in her ears and upon her fingers, as well as the taste displayed in plaiting her hair and beautifying her face.

Women, in savage alike with civilized life, are vested with a good supply of pride and vanity in their composition,— all, fond of show and gaudy equipage. But the mountain squaw, next to ornaments, displays the most vanity in the gay caparison of her riding horse, and the splendid trappings of his saddle. Both of them are fancifully garnished with beads and paint, and bestrung with various trinkets, that impart a tinkling sound, as they strike each other at every movement, and fill the rider's ears with that wild and simple music so consonant to her feelings and thoughts.

Men and women practise the same mode of riding, (astride,) and a squaw is as much at home on horseback as the most experienced cavalier.

This fashion is properly considered unbecoming for ladies of civilized countries, yet improper as it may seem, it is quite common with the ladies of New Mexico.

As my subsequent travels in the countries bordering upon the Rocky Mountains preclude the opportunity of speaking connectedly of the Sioux nation, I cannot forego the present occasion for presenting to the curious, some few items relative to the language of these Indians, that tend to shed no small amount of light upon the ancient history of the American continent.

There are several remarkable peculiarities in the Sioux language, that cannot fail to prove interesting and satisfactory, so far as they go, to all lovers of antiquarian research.

The first of these consists in the striking similarity observable in its general structure to that of the ancient Romans, when the two are carefully compared with each other.

In regard to the arrangement of words and the construction of sentences, they are both governed by the same fixed laws of euphony, irrespective of the relative position otherwise maintained by the different parts of speech. It will be observed that the leading purpose of the speaker of either language is, to avoid a harsh and inharmonious intermingling of words, such as would grate upon the ear when pronounced in an abrupt connection; and, by so doing, to give a smooth and musical turn to the expression of his ideas.

The few brief sentences, hereto subjoined in the same order as they occur in the original, accompanied by the translation of each word as it appears, will serve to illustrate this matter more fully:

LATIN	SIOUX
Invictum animi robur ostensit. Invincible of mind strength he displayed.	Tepe nea-tour toocta? Lodge your own where is it?
Omnia delicarum instrumenta e All of delicacies the instruments	Mea warchee muzarka nea-tour. I want gun your own.
castris ejecit. from camp he cast.	Kokepa warneche wecharcha ha. Afraid nothing the man is.
Non amo nimium diligentes. Not I love overmuch the careful.	Minewarka appello warktashne ha. Medicine-water I say not good is.

A mere glance at the foregoing will at once show the constructional similarity between the two; and, to illustrate the proposition still farther, I here subjoin yet other proofs of a more important relationship:

LATIN	SIOUX
Appello, (pres. ind., 1st per. sing.; inf. appellâre,) *I declare, I proclaim.*	Appello, *I declare, I proclaim, I tell, I make known.*
Bestia, *a wild beast.*	Beta, *a buffalo.*
Cæca, *uncertain ambiguous, confused, rash.*	Ceicha, *bad, disorderly, unsound.*
Cogor, *one who collects, brings together, compels, forces, or heaps up.*	Cogor, *a maker of anything, a manufacturer, one who produces a thing by an ingenious arrangement of materials.*
Mea, (meus, a, um,) *of or belonging to me.*	Mea, *I, myself, me.*
Mena, *a narrow sharp fish.*	Mena, *a knife.*

LATIN	SIOUX
Ne, (this when affixed to a word or a sentence gives it a negative signification,) *no, not.*	Ne, (this word is used precisely the same as in Latin, and has a similar meaning,) *not.*
Papæ, *rare, excellent, wonderful.*	Papa, *meat, flesh used for food.*
Pater, *father.*	Pater, *fire.*
Pes, *the foot.*	Pea, *the foot.*
Taurus, *a bull.*	Tau, (or tah,) *a bull.*
Tepor, *Warmth.*	Tepe, *a lodge.*
Tuor, (tui, tutus sum,) *to look, to see.*	Tula, (astonishment,) *look! see there!*

I might pursue this comparison to a yet greater extent, were my knowledge of Sioux sufficiently full and critical for the task, (for I have a firm confidence that many other similarities might be pointed out, quite as glaring in their character as any of the above;) but, enough, I trust, has already been said to fortify the position so largely warranted by the premise, to wit: that in former ages the Romans maintained a foothold upon the American continent and held *intercourse* with this nation, either by arms or by commerce.

The argument drawn from the foregoing is still further strengthened, when we take into consideration the fact, that language is constantly varying in its form, and changing the meaning and pronunciation of its words, as time progresses. To exemplify this more clearly and forcibly, let the reader compare the works of standard English authors of the present day with those of the like not more than five hundred years since, and he will readily acknowledge the palpable indications of progressive change.

If so short an interval has produced a transformation so bold in a written language, what might we look for in one spoken only?

But, an interval of three times five hundred years has passed since the Romans and the Sioux held intercourse with each other, and we yet find the general structure of the two languages strikingly similar, and several of their words identical in meaning and pronunciation! And, though the latter observation fails in some cases, even this, so far from proving anything averse to the position before assumed, serves to strengthen it.

The word *pater,* for instance, pronounced alike in both languages, differs in signification; being used in the one to imply *father,* in the other *fire.* This apparent discrepancy of meaning may be explained in a few words. The Sioux are accustomed to venerate the *sun* as one of the more especial manifestations of the Divine Essence, who is regarded as the FATHER or creator of all things; and it, being the great source of light and heat, is naturally looked upon as an immense body of fire. Thus, in the course of ages, the term became perverted in its meaning and application, and, instead of being used to express the sun, or Great Spirit, the father of all, it now only implies the simple element of fire, an emanation from the sun.

So in relation to the Latin word tepor, *warmth,* and the Sioux word tepe, *a lodge.* The lodge is employed in winter to retain the heat within itself, and exclude the cold air; nor is it wonderful that, in the progress of years, the term *tepor,* or *tepe,* should become the only one by which a lodge is known.

The word *mena,* is also pronounced the same in both, though different in its signification; meaning, in Latin, a narrow sharp fish, and, in Sioux, a knife. In explanation of this, I would barely refer to the similarity of shape between a knife and a narrow sharp fish.

The relationship disclosed between these two languages is seemingly too close and significant to be attributed to mere chance or accident, and can be in no other way satisfactorily accounted for, than by admitting the correctness of the premises before quoted.

But this position, curious as it may seem to some readers, and impregnable as it must doubtless prove, has other weapons to protect it at command; and, ere dismissing the subject, I will briefly notice some of them.

It is by no means a conjecture of recent origin, that the ancient Romans did actually colonize portions of the American continent. The industrious researches of antiquarians have long since brought to light many items which prove and strengthen it, though none of them so tangible and obvious as those previously noticed.

Several obscure hints of the existence of extensive Roman colonies planted westward of the Pillars of Hercules, (doubtless alluding to the American continent,) have been detected in the writings of ancient authors yet extant; but still further proof is afforded in the relics of temples, cities, roads, and fortified camps, long since discovered in Peru, Mexico, and the United States, which strongly savor of Roman origin.

The ancient works at Marietta, Ohio, have been regarded, by not a few, as the offspring of Roman industry and military science,— and various other remains, that signalize the Mississippi valley, point quite plainly to this nation for a parentage. But a proof, still more conclusive than any yet adduced, is afforded by the discovery of a genuine Roman coin, in the State of Missouri, several years since.

Taking all these corroborative circumstances in connection, the fact that Roman colonies *did* exist, to some extent, upon this continent in past ages, must be regarded as placed beyond successful controversy.

The Sage Map

The Rufus B. Sage Map owes much to the Fremont map which accompanied the Report of the Fremont expeditions of 1842 and 1843-44, published in 1845. See letters 3, 6 and 7 in the Appendix to the present volumes (volume 5, pages 333-335).

But Sage includes geographical features not on Fremont's big folding map of 1845. Sage and his map maker fill out the Oregon country, Missouri River area, Texas, etc. They probably used data from David H. Burr's map of 1839, Charles Wilkes' maps of Oregon and California of 1841, Josiah Gregg's map accompanying his *Commerce of the Prairies* (1844), and possibly others.

Sage does not show the Humboldt River, nor does he have the accurate data exhibited in the Preuss-Fremont map prepared in 1847 and printed in connection with Fremont's *Geographical Memoir,* etc., 1848. For a discussion of maps of the period see Carl I. Wheat, *Mapping the American West, 1540-1857* (Worcester, Mass., 1954).